CAMPUS DESIGN

CAMPUS DESIGN

RICHARD P. DOBER

JOHN WILEY & SONS, INC.

New York • Chichester • Brisbane • Toronto • Singapore

Library of Congress Cataloging in Publication Data:

Dober, Richard P.
  Campus design / Richard P. Dober.

      p.   cm.
  Includes bibliographical references.
  ISBN 0-471-54258-X
  1. Universities and colleges—United States—Buildings.
2. Building materials—United States.   I. Title.

LB3223.3.D63   1992
727'.3'0973—dc20   91-32385
                                                      CIP

Printed in the United States of America

10 9 8 7 6 5 4 3 2 1

For Patrick and Claire

CONTENTS

CAMPUS DESIGN

University of New Mexico. A strong image campus design with landmark buildings, referential and reverential regional architecture, visual continuity in building materials, and an evocative landscape. (RPD)

Prospectus

Campus design is the art of campus planning, the culminating act of those processes and procedures that give form, content, meaning, and delight to the physical environment serving higher education. Designs thus created can define and celebrate a sense of place; communicate an institution's purpose, presence, and domain; and generate an image charged with symbolism, graced by history. As a professional activity, there are few tasks more challenging than campus design, and none more satisfying. Colleges and universities cover a broad range of human activity and habitation. Whether new campus or old, each institution deserves to be shaped by a plan that is responsive to its own realities, marked with its own distinctions, and guided by concepts that are as workable as they are attractive.

Undergirding this view is the thought that higher education has become the common ground for acculturation in the late 20th century. There are 3,587 accredited colleges and universities in the United States. In recent years they have enrolled about 12 million people annually; a population served by approximately 2 million faculty and staff. An estimated 40 percent of the American population has been involved with these institutions directly at one time or another as students enrolled in degree programs. Rightfully or wrongly, higher education seems to be the only dependable route for the underclass to scale the ladders of opportunity. For many others, some credible higher education experience is equally important. Where there has been no direct contact, colleges and universities are nonetheless familiar to other Americans as a crucible for science and technology, or as a provider of health care, or for their participation in seasonal athletic events watched by a national audience. Being instruments for diverse social, economic, and cultural activities affecting so many lives, the physical forms of colleges and universities obviously earn attention.

The 3,587 institutions vary in purpose, prospects, organizational structure, mission, history, sources of funding, size, location, environs, and combinations of teaching, research, and community service. Self-evidently, these factors and related circumstances help determine the physical forms that shelter, serve, sanc-

3

tion, and signify higher education. The articulation and understanding of such determinants is thus essential in generating useful campus designs. The plea here is for a physical environment that combines the visionary and the pragmatic, with ideas verifiable and pertinent, expressed in designs vigorous and persuasive. Designs thus conceived will resonate with reality, without compromising ingenuity or idealism, art or function.

What is evident in the United States is increasingly so overseas, where the percentage of population involved in higher education has also grown impressively in the number of people enrolled and the number of institutions. For developing countries, the founding of a new campus is a rite of passage, a three-dimensional indicator of aspiration, status, and achievement. Among older nations, the physical extension and enhancement of existing institutions is seen as a vital undertaking, drawing the best talent available to guide development, both from inside and outside the institution. Representing as it does the discovery, interpretation, and dissemination of knowledge, the league of higher education has no geographic boundaries. History gleaned reveals commendable examples of the supremacy of good ideas which, freely exchanged, find their way from one country or state to another as educational models and architectural paradigms worth emulating. With the understanding that each situation must be dealt with independently—with sensitivity to local conditions and influences—the principles, methods, and procedures outlined in this book are intended to have universal application.

Having indicated the complexity of higher education, and having argued for diversity, how does one proceed to describe campus design methods in general so they may be adapted to current problems and opportunities? The approach chosen combines aspects of traditional town planning and urban design techniques, contemporary participatory planning, and the ecological and visual heritage of landscape architecture. In this method, the chief components of campus design are buildings, landscapes, and circulation systems. The activity called campus design utilizes these components in placemaking and placemarking.

Placemaking is the structuring of the overall design, the broader skeleton, the articulated pattern, that is, the campus plan. At minimum, placemaking entails the positioning and arrangement of campus land uses and pedestrian and vehicular routes, the location of buildings and functional open spaces, such as playfields and parking lots, the definition of edges, and the interface between campus and environs. A plan thus created serves as the framework for specific designs, enabling them to be integrated into a unified scheme to meet overall objectives, programmatic, functional, and visual.

At the least, such integration ensures orderly and economic growth. A well-formulated campus plan will also define the institution's place within the larger community, justify land ownership, adjudicate site location decisions, mediate conflicts in land uses and circulation systems, and rationalize the construction and extension of infrastructure. On the visual side, the arrangement of the campus plan components can be accomplished to achieve aesthetic satisfaction from the site, by responding to variations in topography and tree cover, for example; or by ordering the sequence of views and vistas experienced as one approaches, enters, and passes through the campus; or, by promoting development policies that preserve and enhance existing buildings and landscapes. In some instances, through the articulation of a unitary architectural style (modern or traditional), the overall design, or a mosaic of styles, can serve as an institutional metaphor.

In times past, placemaking considerations and objectives, of the kind described, were either carried in the minds of the institutional leaders as quotidian matters requiring no documentation, or implicit in grandiose architectural schemes that were drawn to encourage sponsorship and support. As higher education blossomed, the pace of physical development quickened. Casual planning had to give way to more disciplined efforts. Beginning in the mid-19th century, the impulses to guide the development of towns, cities, parks, and neighborhoods had their counterpart on campus. The extraordinary growth of colleges and universities in the decades 1945 through 1975—unparalleled in recorded civilization— was sufficient in scale and magnitude to give campus planning a visible, central, and productive role in determining the physical forms of institutional life. That activity and those products—campus planning and campus plans—were pertinent and timely to the extent that they intermeshed with other institutional planning activities, academic, financial, and strategic. The master plan (fixed and static) gave way to the campus plan (flexible and dynamic). Process and plan became interdependent.

Professionalization of campus planning in recent years has eased the way for these kinds of efforts. This is exemplified by the incorporation of the Society for College and University Planning (1965), and the attention campus planning receives in workshops and annual meetings sponsored by educators, fundraisers, governing boards, physical plant directors, and administrative officers. Campus planning is not an arcane art. Paul Venable Turner's *Campus/An American Planning Tradition* (MIT Press 1984) splendidly traces its beginnings, flowering, and current status. The professional literature today is substantial and kept up to date through newsletters, journals, articles, and reports readily and generously shared by those engaged in the work.

Placemarking, in contrast to placemaking, involves the definition, conceptualization, and orchestration of certain physical attributes which give a campus a visual uniqueness appropriately its own. Placemarking elements include landmarks, style, materials, and landscapes. In varying combinations, these imprinting devices will be found in abundance on strong image campuses.

Landmarks are cultural currency. Building, monument, garden—fragments of a larger scene, these are the medium of exchange through which one generation honors another, contributors to a sense of place. The subject of style as a placemarker is charged with allegorical significance and perceptual connotations and meaning. In some instances, stylistic placemarkers reflect an evolution of campus design concepts deep-rooted in regional, national, and international traditions, for example, the utilization of sovereign styles such as Collegiate Georgian and Collegiate Gothic. Their mantles have cloaked or choked several centuries of campus architecture, memorably or meanly, but vividly, as one would interpret that legacy. Other styles, equally powerful as placemarkers, may be idiosyncratic. These are physical embodiments of campus leadership striking out in new directions, abetted by professionals who serve that cause with notable and singular designs that defy convention. The selection of building materials can be a placemarking action equally loaded with cultural import as well as visual consequences. As art, symbol, and function, landscapes can also be potent and eloquent placemarkers.

The manner in which these kinds of placemarking elements may serve campus design has been fallow ground in recent years. A synoptic view of the subject is missing, a void which this book may begin to fill. With campus planning methods now universally accepted as a modus operandi for guiding physical development, the time has come to further the placemarking aspects of campus design without subordinating the importance of the broader plan as a matrix that co-ordinates the individual design actions into a unified scheme. Why?

First, in a world dulled by dismal duplication, where the ersatz so easily replaces the genuine, each college and university should have the opportunity to be an authentic place. Authenticity comes from a close reading of site and situation, as well as the history, traditions, and aspirations which bestow on each campus its own persona. The reading has to fathom the forces of continuity and change, and trace their consequences for physical development. Change is the essence of institutional life; continuity, the stabilizer. Campus designs can bring into balance both aspects of institutional vitality. The abstraction becomes real when one notes that not many campus buildings continue through historic time to serve their original functions. The landscape evolves in pace with the natural rhythms of propagation, maturation, and death. If a sense of place requires the firm and the fixed, as well as that in flux, what kind of campus design serves these ends?

In the methods described below, vital campus designs combine the new and old with respect for both. As the source and expediter of knowledge, each individual campus can serve as a model of beauty wrapped around function, without compromise to either. The comely can be enlisted again to symbolize institutional attitudes and values worth displaying to all campus constituencies and publics. Where better to demonstrate ecological ethics than a campus, where intrinsically the environment works best with appropriate greenery and evocative landscapes? Models do not have to be invented. There are many campuses with a recognizable and attractive sense of place which possess these characteristics. As indicated throughout this book, these places can be examined, deciphered, apreciated, and mined for ideas applicable elsewhere, or reaffirmed in their own locale.

Secondly, because of inter-institutional competition, an uplifting and extensive round of campus design improvements are necessary for survival. No existing institution will be able to ignore this factor, for several reasons.

A knowledgeable interpretation of demographics indicates that in mature countries, few new campuses will be developed. At existing campuses, capacity will exceed demand through the turn of the century, certainly in North America. While government support and intervention may have some effect on the distribution of students, most institutions will be competing for students, within whatever niche the institution occupies in higher education. Some institutions will not gain their share of the higher education population unless their campuses are physically attractive and distinctive.

There is precedent worth noting in these seemingly dire circumstances. As they often are, the chronicles of older institutions are informative. Christ's College (Cambridge) was built expediently with clunch (chalk) and brick at the start of the 16th century. Toward the end of the following century "its walls had acquired so repellent an aspect that . . . people were deterred from entering their sons at this college." To survive, the fellows had to rebuild the outer fabric. In Japan "dozens of the country's 465 four-year colleges and universities, many esteemed, are deciding to change" to deter closing or mergers during the predicted sharp decline in enrollments in the '90s. "The most practical approach is cosmetic, through new names and stylish buildings," notes one observer. Trend-conscious Japanese want to "attend a pretty ivy-covered campus." In England, comparable undertakings have been announced for a clutch of older institutions, including Oxford, where the rate of decay and the need for renewal outpaces existing funding. An appeal for philanthropic assistance has been broadcast internationally to help stabilize the University's reputation. The underlying mood—the search for pleasant not intimidating places for higher education, workable not wornout—is evident world-wide. Many campus design efforts in the coming decades will thus focus on the restoration, renewal, and enhancement of existing facilities.

The strategy of designing a campus to attract patrons, students, and support is as venerable as higher education itself; and of itself will promote campus design initiatives. At the important junctures in every campus history, one will find architecture and landscape embraced as an indicator of institutional change. The arrival of a new president, the adoption of new modes of teaching and research, alterations in institutional size, and changes in outlook and philosophy give cause for campus design. Those tides will continue to flow, perhaps faster than before because of institutional competition, not just in America, but also abroad.

Finally, and conclusively, campus design now merits renewed attention because of the deplorable physical condition of many campuses today. In the interests of balancing budgets at a time of rapid growth and inflation, colleges and universities deferred facility maintenance, often constructed cheap and low quality buildings, and failed to allocate sufficient funds for campus landscape and infrastructure. Plant renewal costs in the United States have been estimated to require $4 billion a year (1989 dollars) for the foreseeable future. Expenditures have been averaging about $1.2 billion. Significant efforts are being launched to close the gap. Dollar estimates for replacement and rejuvenation have not been estimated, but informed opinion and surveys would indicate that most American campuses expect to enhance their physical situation through building restoration, renewal, and replacement in the coming decade.

Given this context, one senses that the years of maturation have arrived for all American colleges and universities, as they have for many overseas. Despite pervasive physical neglect during the past decade and uncertainty about their future, there are too many reasons not to expect their continued importance, existence, and strength. Unless civilization collapses, colleges and universities should be able to command the financial resources to improve themselves physically. Whether small actions or grand plans, each improvement should contribute to some larger and longer view of the campus as a designed environment, with each campus having its own image, shaped by its self-selected destiny.

For all the reasons stated, a renewed interest in campus design seems timely, pertinent, and productive. To advance those objectives, this book begins with descriptions of placemarking at campuses that have a strong image. The selection represents the author's experience with campuses visited and studied during the past forty years. Equally good examples could be cited from other sources, but to discuss a place unseen might erode critical judgements already vulnerable because of the desire to address a complex topic comprehensively. Even within the narrow subset of a larger universe, thus defined, not everything worth exploring and evaluating can be usefully compressed within the confines of a professional reference work that was written to help those participating in campus design. A review of several hundred college and university histories and campus plans reveals an extraordinary architectural and landscape legacy, animated by the lives of the people who prompted and produced the built environment. As much as possible, the citations draw on documents that catch the spirit and enthusiasm of those who roiled the waters of campus design, the accomplished, as well as those whose intentions and achievements may be shadowed today by passing fashions.

The book ends with an outline and discussion of placemaking—the articulation of the unifying campus design concepts. "To be rational in anything is great praise," said Jane Austen. In a procedural work, form has precedent over content. Placemaking binds the individual campus design actions into a coherent entity or, at least, makes known the context into which individual actions can be best fitted for optimum effect. Campus plans conceived in this manner can also have aesthetic and symbolic merit as an expression of aspiration and image. This section of the book categorizes and describes the current range of campus plans, as well as placemaking processes and routines which will generate such plans, and the steps that can be taken to implement them.

As to sources, the combining of contemporary and historic examples is intended to yield lessons worth learning. Recent plans, works-in-progress, and the opinions of those now engaged in campus designs and their clients have been appraised. Where applicable, outlines of useful methods are accompanied by reasons, and both are translated into insights and procedures that can be adapted by those seeking assistance with or knowledge about campus design, and whose experiences, however dated, offer enlightenment to those engaged in similar tasks. In several instances pivotal ideas are examined in depth, using the words and images of those whose efforts have made a fundamental contribution to campus design. Taken as a whole, the selection of accounts and processes are also intended to be a record of how some charged with campus design opportunities considered this specialized subject at the approach of the 21st century.

The acknowledgments and bibliography later express the author's thanks for those who encouraged this effort and assisted in the undertaking. One source in particular should be mentioned up front. The categorization of the campus design elements that constitute the image of a campus—landmarks, style, materials, and landscape—benefits from Kevin Lynch's pioneering efforts in urban design, conducted at the Massachusetts Institute of Technology (1954). Lynch explored the ways people see, remember, and interpret the built environment. As a young member of Lynch's research staff, the author became convinced then, and remains so now, that planners and designers, working with clients and their constituencies, can articulate a strong and meaningful image of a particular place; and that such images help foster pride and participation in community life. A campus is a community. Campus design in this respect is the collective stewardship of a communal art form.

In summary and to reiterate the book's themes, each college and university should have an appropriate image of its own making, an amalgam of buildings and landscapes that communicates a distinctive sense of place, functionally suitable for the institution's particular purposes. The image and reality should promote community, allegiance, and civility, while at the same time encouraging diversity in discourse and vision which gives our colleges and universities a special status in a humane and civilizing world. Singular master plans that launch and guide extensive new development and establish a powerful institutional image have a legitimate role in campus development. There are and will be opportunities to establish such schemes in the coming decades. The experiences, examples, and insights offered in this book will help those given that responsibility. In the main, however, the coming decade will be a time when the regeneration of the physical environment is the primary objective at most colleges and universities, not wholesale expansion. Campus design methods and concepts will have to be flexible and responsive to balancing continuity and change in the physical environment, and the orchestration of improvements, which most likely will occur in small increments stretched over time. Accordingly, it is useful to know how campus designs—image and reality—have been created in the past so as to draw on those methods in creating the future. Within the context thus defined, campus design essentially involves placemaking and placemarking, hence this book's structure and content.

Bucknell University. Rites and rituals on the mythic lawn against the background of Collegiate Georgian. (RPD)

Carleton College. A landmark building using Collegiate Gothic as a campus design accent. (RPD)

Arizona State University. A visually prominent architectural complex united by a single building material. (RPD)

Radcliffe College Quadrangle. The classic landscape pattern of buildings and lawns and trees. (RPD)

University of Minnesota. Placemarking with contemporary architecture. (University of Minnesota Planning Office)

Pomona College. Continuity in building materials and shapes, evoking a sense of place. (RPD)

University of Pennsylvania. The campus walkway made memorable with placemarking artwork. (RPD)

University of Houston. A significant interior open space designed as an imagable campus crossroad. (RPD)

Conceptual Diagram
Campus Design Factors

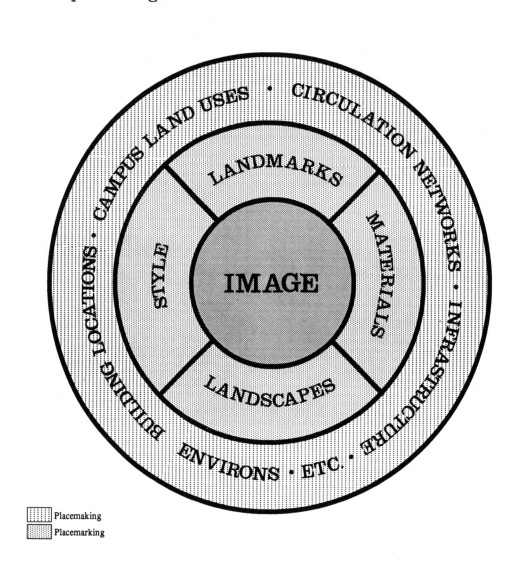

Placemaking

Placemarking

Bates College Campus Planning Studies 1990
Dober, Lidsky, Craig and Associates, Inc.

Conceptual diagram, campus design factors. (Dober, Lidsky, Craig and Associates, Inc.)

Placemarking

The campus designer's challenge: to determine a physical concept in which image and reality are not far apart. But, which reality, especially when examining an existing campus? Both physically dismal and attractive campuses will convey strong images to their publics, but for different reasons and through different means. Admittedly, decay and decline can inspire noteworthy artistic scenes as demonstrated by 16th century draftsmen capturing on paper the picturesque ruins of an ancient monastic, educational foundation in southern Italy. Nathaniel Hawthorne was enchanted by Oxford's scaling stone, as was Henry James, who saw crumbling "battlements of silver-gray, outshouldering the matted leafage of disseverable plants . . . a kind of dim and scarred ideal of the Western intellect." Few campuses with visible deterioration would wish these days to have their deficiencies lauded in this or similar manner. Rot and rust should activate repair and renovation, not a romantic's rumination over fading antiquity. Campus design methods, obviously, should aim to promote a sense of place that will be favorably remembered because the campus works well functionally, is attractive aesthetically, and helps symbolize the institution's history and existence. Thus articulated, the results of a visually engaging campus design concept will locate us in space and time, as do many skillful art works. In creating such campus designs, in most instances, the desired sense of place will be first described through maps and drawings. But because college and university landscapes and buildings change once they are built and used—waxing and waning cyclically—the long-term dimensions and dynamic characteristics of such concepts are not so easily depicted. Arguably, the damning criticism applied to traditional campus master plans is their inelasticity. That deficiency, where it exists, can be moderated through placemaking and placemarking campus design methods which bring image and reality into congruence for positive reasons. A placemaking plan creates the armature for the campus design, and placemarking techniques flesh out the concept. As time passes, the clarity of the designer's original intention may be occasionally obscure. But if well conceived, pentimento, the underlying vital con-

13

cept (the sense of place) will emerge referentially or reverentially—lending itself to regeneration, enhancement, or amendment, or even rejection in favor of a new concept, when there is cause, cash, and conviction to do so.

Of many placemarking devices, four seem especially applicable in devising or strengthening campus designs: style, materials, landscapes, and landmarks. These methods have weight and meaning, precedent and results. Recall a campus worth remembering as a design, and one or more of these features will be present in the memory bank.

SCUP SEATTLE STATEMENT

1. A campus is a work of art whose stewardship should command the attention and respect of successive generations.

2. The art is expressed through the melding of buildings and landscapes into a physical environment called the campus design.

3. Appropriate campus designs define and celebrate an institution's purpose, territory, accomplishments and aspirations.

4. Appropriateness is achieved by addressing and resolving the issues of continuity and change in the physical elements and forms which generate the campus design.

5. To deny or demean the campus design legacy is to diminish an institution's vitality — symbolically or actually.

6. In support of this statement of principle, each institution should undertake an assessment of its campus design heritage — identifying those buildings and landscapes which are or could be essential components in creating or sustaining the campus image and the sense of place.

7. Incorporated in the overall campus plan, the assessment should be used to seek and encumber funds to conserve, enhance and enlarge the campus design legacy — a legacy that legitimizes, facilitates and proclaims the institution's existence.

A statement of principle on campus design adopted by the Society for College and University Planning, 1991.

Cutler Hall, Ohio University. Focal point of the College Green Historic District containing 30 buildings and 23 acres. Cutler Hall was completed in 1818, renovated in 1947, and restored in 1974 as a central administration building. (Office of Public Information, Ohio University)

Landmarks

By dictionary definition, landmarks are prominent features that identify a locale. Five landmarking techniques are illustrated in the examples and notes below: buildings, architectural elements, monuments, color, and special spaces. Some campus landmarks, from their beginning, were conceived to play a landmark role. As worthy works, they would ennoble and equip the institution with an architectural statement that demonstrated institutional advancement. Typically assertive, not timid, the landmarks were cast as, and continue to be, the leading players in that long-running drama called campus design. Other landmarks may have been launched with fanfare, but then faded, only to be revived as landmarks in tribute to their history or antiquity. Some landmarks capture the eye and are readily recalled because of size, grandeur, and position; others are attention-getting eccentric designs, whose quirky character make it difficult to ignore them when visually scanning the campus. Some designs are the folklore of higher education, etched in memory as a landmark because of their association with a particular institution.

Landmark also has a legal definition—an historic, cultural, and natural resource recognized by government as possessing exceptional value or quality in illustrating or interpreting the local, regional, or national heritage. Designation as a landmark creates an obligation to protect and preserve. Enforcement varies in accordance with the laws that created the landmark designations. The National Register (1990) contains about 2,000 entries. About 630 are associated with higher education, a modest number given 3,500 campuses. Under-representation may reflect a reluctance to identify campus landmarks legally because the designation might constrain physical redevelopment. A fresh look at the subject is warranted. The contributions landmarks can make to campus design and institutional morale are substantial, as they have been for Ohio University (Cutler Hall) and Fisk University (Academic Building).

LANDMARK BUILDINGS

Cathedral, palace, capitol building, opera house, boulevard, park—in the culture in which they appear, these objects usually are understandable images as they mark a venue, serve as points of geographic orientation, and celebrate and symbolize the values and purposes that engendered their construction. Thus central Vienna, a strong image city, could be described as a collage of landmarks, stretched over time and locale: St. Stephen's, the Hofburg, Parliament, Staatsoper, Heldenplatz, the Ringstrasse, and so on. Each epitomizes a glorious moment in civic development. Together they provide a richer design experience than they would singly. Chapel, library, administration building, sports arena, and the quad are examples of campus equivalencies. A sense of place can be induced by one of these buildings individually, but the collective imagery of landmark buildings is stronger, such as the impression given by the group of buildings that define the Green at Brown University, each having a distinctive style.

Many campuses will have about 100 buildings. Not all are landmarks, but strong image campuses have a greater than average share. Often, the heritage reflects the institution's age. These colleges and universities have been in existence long enough to construct stately buildings that dignify and document era and locale.

Three landmark structures at the University of Vermont exemplify this kind of placemarking. The buildings demonstrate the permanency of architecture and the impermanency of interior function, vivid metaphors of the tides of institutional continuity and change. Billings (1885) was designed by H.H. Richardson as the university library. The rounded arches, recessed front door, and elaborately carved stonework are his signature pieces. When a new library was constructed in 1962, Billings was converted into a student center. Williams Hall (1896) is externally a copy of the University of Oxford Museum. The Vermont Gothic-style version was erected as a science building and was recently converted to house the art and anthropology departments. Ira Allen Chapel, designed by McKim, Mead, and White, was originally intended for religious services, but has been adapted into a concert hall and lecture hall. A subterranean connector to Billings was built so both could work in tandem as a campus center without changing the traditional view and image of the University of Vermont Green.

All of Fisk University has been designated as a National Historic Site, and most of the older buildings are officially designated landmarks. "That older–historic–buildings are much more expensive to preserve and maintain, is an undisputable fact," says Dr. Henry Ponder, president of Fisk. "Nonetheless, the importance of these structures to Fisk, the black community and to black higher education and intellectual achievement requires that every effort be expended to preserve these symbols for future generations." Fisk's Academic Building (1908), for example, was also originally a library, a Carnegie gift-funded structure, the first at a black college. Designed by two of America's earliest black architects, Moses and Calvin McKissick, the two-story red brick building currently houses a potpourri of university functions, awaiting a third generation of renewal. It is Fisk's hope that landmarking will sustain an image, and generate interest and funds in renewing and reviving a sense of place.

Parenthetically, the Vermont trio and the Fisk endeavor bring to mind a recurrent campus design issue. Recognizing that change is inevitable, might not archi-

Ira Allen Chapel. Placemarking chapel architecture (1927) by McKim, Mead and White, now used for lectures and concerts. A subterranean connection joins the structure to Billings to form a campus center. (Office of Vermont Relations, University of Vermont)

Billings. Designed by H. H. Richardson as the university library (1885). Space reallocated for campus center activities in 1962. The traditional green has been preserved as a landscape front piece. The placemarking view marred by intrusive parking. (Office of Vermont Relations, University of Vermont)

Williams. Constructed in 1896 as a science hall, reminiscent of the Oxford Museum. Now used for the art and anthropology departments. (Office of Vermont Relations, University of Vermont)

19

Massachusetts Institute of Technology. Air view of Charles River side. Bosworth design and subsequent construction. (RPD)

Fisk University. Academic Building, 1908. (Fisk University)

MIT. A sense of place ingrained by masonry architecture—classical and modern. (RPD)

tects devise a prototype building which would be easily adaptable to meet new needs? What kind of universal space, over time, could eventually serve the chapel, library, art and music, classrooms and laboratories, dining, office, and social activities? Could it be a landmark building? And would such architecture be susceptible to stylistic imprints which declare the age and aesthetic attitudes of those who sponsored and designed the buildings? The questions as posed would suggest no easy answer, yet two such buildings grace the pages of campus design histories: the William Welles Bosworth complex at the Massachusetts Institute of Technology and Charles Z. Klauder's skyscraper structure for the University of Pittsburgh. Both are large, image-making, landmark buildings, superbly sited, dominant features on their skylines, adroit functional architecture, overlaid with references to classical styles, and possess recognizable symbols associated with the history of their respective institutions.

The MIT complex has the edge over Pittsburgh for long-term flexibility. Bosworth coupled ten building segments, double-loaded corridors, into a series of courtyards, the largest of which was open at one end to the Charles River. Two major intersections in the corridor system are domed and colonnaded. The exterior masonary and detailing suggest a Roman influence. The overall site plan was a classic Beaux Arts scheme as suitable for a government ministry as an institute devoted to science, engineering, and technology. Inside the buildings, function and flexibility were given precedence over stylistic allusions. The corridor walls were load-bearing, the lateral easily moved for new room configurations. High ceilings made it easy to thread various and changeable utility systems throughout the structure. Room finishes, interior detailing, and furnishing would vary as needs and purposes dictated. The outside of the original MIT buildings remains constant. The interiors have been reconstructed several times. Later additions mark their time and place with exterior materials sympathetic to, but different from, the Bosworth palette.

The University of Pittsburgh was the Cathedral for Learning as the Woolworth Building was the Cathedral of Commerce. Cathedrals are acts of faith, audacious architecture, serving well-defined purposes, with new architectural forms and styles, and are often controversial when first conceived. The Pittsburgh enterprise fits this template. The idea came into being with the help of a sometimes reluctant, though talented architect, (Charles Z. Klauder), who was spurred relentlessly by the University's chancellor (John Gabbert Bowman). The project was funded and constructed during a decade of economic uncertainty.

What Bowman visualized was a university architecture that would "express power, nobility, courage, daring, achievement and spiritual reverence." Only this would overcome the poor image, physical deprivation, and overcrowding that was dooming (he judged) the University of Pittsburgh to mediocrity if not extinction. Emphasizing the university's association with the city's industrial successes, Bowman persuaded Andrew and Richard Mellon to pay off the university's debt, to purchase 14 choice acres for a new campus, and to encourage the university trustees to proceed with plans for a skyscraper building that would dramatize and "project the image of the university to all within sight."

He found in John Ruskin's *The Seven Lamps of Architecture* a rationale for his architectural style and the tower; for "ornament could be sacrificed in favor of increased scale." With a simplified version of the Gothic Revival, Bowman expected he could build his layered cake and pay for it, too. The first tower version is incorporated in a sketch plan prepared by Edward Purcell Mellon, a Pittsburgh architect and nephew of the university's patrons. Young Mellon spent two years on his plans, visiting Cambridge and Oxford to spark his design concept. The result was an extraordinary pastiche in which medieval precincts are linked like sausages, with no apparent rationale other than leading the eye to the 35-story centerpiece. For Bowman, the building was not tall enough; a second Mellon version, 50 stories, was also dismissed. Apparently, Mellon could not draw the dynamic forms that Bowman sought, and so Klauder was engaged to prepare a set of presentation plans for fund-raising.

This effort, too, almost foundered as Bowman rejected Klauder's first proposal. One of America's greatest architectural draftsmen, Klauder was determined to get on paper the chancellor's vision. Bowman was invited to Klauder's home for dinner, with the evening set aside for a sketching session. "After about three hours the floor was pretty well covered with (drawings). We were both getting cross," Bowman recalled. Klauder decided to ease the tension by playing a phonograph record of Wagner's Magic Fire theme from *The Valkyrie*. As the music rose in crescendo, Bowman said, "That music is the building. And it did not get its height, its meaning, its awful power by one leap. It took many. And isn't each leap a buttress, a buttress on a tower?" With vigor and vision renewed by Bowman's enthusiasm, Klauder began sketching again. By dawn an acceptable parti was completed.

"The audience sat in stunned silence when they saw the lantern slides of the proposed $10 million building," writes Mark M. Brown, recounting the reaction to Klauder's presentation drawings at their first public viewing. The thumbnail sketches had been translated into polished drawings of a 52-story gothic tower, soaring from a base larger than a football field, the single building serviced by 16 elevators, enclosing 11 million cubic feet of space, suitable for 12,000 students. But the money was not available to proceed as planned and modifications had to be made in the design, which was eventually down-scaled to 42 stories, but no less impressive as a skyscraper. Excavations begin in September 1928. The building was opened for the public in June 1937. Bowman's ability to convince others of the logic of his concept prevailed: "a visable symbol of an emerging University in a burgeoning, vital city . . . (carrying) the message that education is both the means and results of aspiring to great heights."

As inflections in the campus design, built or adapted for that purpose, buildings do not have to impress by size to mark and celebrate a sense of place. Honored then is Manasseh Cutler Hall (1819), Ohio University. Named for the New England minister who wrote the university's charter, it is the oldest college building in the Old Northwest, a fine piece of craftsmanship,, a responsible example of landmark preservation and continuing use, a building whose appearance on a large, public campus is welcomed for its scale and human dimensions as well as its historic connotations.

Sometimes, a single landmark structure can serve as symbol of institutional presence. More often than not, a single structure can effectively serve as the campus landmark building. Page 30 is a collection of such images, abstracted profiles of architecture and landscapes associated with the particular colleges and universities. The buildings are too important historically and architecturally to alter their exteriors or demolish. The lives of such landmark buildings and the institutional memories they embody can be extended through new purposes as in the Indiana University Student Building and the Haas Library, Muhlenberg College; and re-captured in new buildings that evoke through their designs some of the memory-making features of the older structures.

OLD BUILDINGS/CONTINUING LIFE

Constructed in 1928, Haas announced Muhlenberg's coming of age as a mature institution. The building was a linchpin in a campus design that lined up a group of academic buildings on a topographically commanding site, along the edge of the campus green, with the library tower reminiscent of medieval Oxford or Cambridge. Too solid to demolish, a public symbol of the college's achievements, a paradigm placemarker, the building was scheduled for renovation into administrative offices and reception areas, when a new library was opened in 1988, and Haas was vacated. The project is a typical example of how older buildings designed for one function can be reused for another.

The Indiana University Student Building began as a proposal (1901) for private funding of a building for women "to contain a gymnasium, a small auditorium, parlors, rest-rooms, kitchen, etc." The project was shelved because alumni and friends were reluctant to pay for that which they thought the state legislature should appropriate, and the legislature questioned whether this was "a legitimate University expense." The university president Joseph Swain then argued that:

> To desire this building for its own sake, for the comforts and appliances it will afford, is commendable. But far more important than the building itself is that we should have here on campus a memorial gift that will be a constant expression of the faith, love, and unfailing good will of the children and guardians of the University. Our devotion is so much increased by our gifts.

With a successful appeal for help from John D. Rockefeller, Jr., Swain and his successor, William L. Bryan, were encouraged to proceed. In the interval, the university enrollments grew, as did the estimate of facility requirements. A $60,000.00 project trebled. To the nucleus of space set aside for women, rooms were added "for social and religious purposes for men, offices for various student organizations, etc." A tower was added for a clock and chimes. University professor Arthur L. Foley's study indicated a price range of $1,200 to $3,600. "The difference in price depended mainly on the weight of the bells. The tone in general increased with the weight. The President urged purchase of the chimes even if it made incomplete furnishing necessary." The building was dedicated in 1906, de-signed with a west wing for women, and east wing for men, joined by a central auditorium; an immediate university landmark architecturally, as a model of public-private participation in fund-raising, and a landmark in the history of campus unions. A swimming pool was added in 1937, with state and W.P.A. funds. When the new Indiana Memorial Union was opened in the late 1950s, the Student Building was reused pro tem for a museum, administrative offices, classrooms, and as a temporary home for the School of Law, during the renovation and reconstruction of the school's building. A third life has now been ascertained. Beginning in

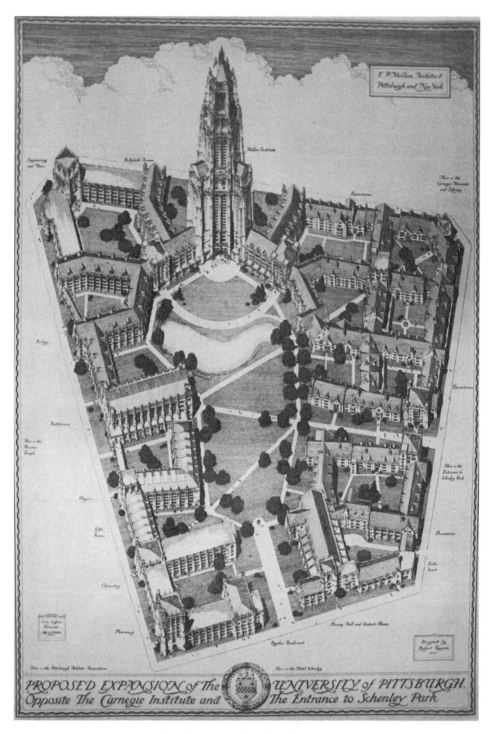

E. P. Mellon's 1927 concept plan for the University of Pittsburgh. An image of Collegiate Gothic unfettered by the realities of site, program, or budget. (University of Pittsburgh)

The University of Pittsburgh, Tower of Learning. Charles Z. Klauder's placemarking masterwork. The structure holds about ten percent of the university's 1990 space inventory. (University of Pittsburgh)

University of Moscow. Pittsburgh recalled.
(RPD)

1990, the entire building will be reconstructed for departments of anthropology and geography, the geography library, a four-room computer cluster, and general classrooms.

Carleton College's 1910 Sayles-Hill Gymnasium, an architecturally simple building, in sound structural condition and free of stylistic pretensions, was recycled as a campus center. Yearbooks, campus and town newspapers, and personal reminisces from older alumni indicated the building touched many lives. It seemed fitting and proper that the building be restored to serve again as a landmark. Throughout these interior transformations, the basic profile of the exteriors of the buildings cited remained intact, a discourse in stone on institutional change and continuity, as well as a placemarker beloved and entrenched in the campus design.

DESIGNATING LANDMARK BUILDINGS

How, why, and when do buildings such as the Haas Library and the Indiana University Student Building earn status as landmarks? In a broad view of truly distinguished architecture, neither would rank high on critical lists. How is the genuine and the authentic separated from the dross? The answers loop back to justifying landmark preservation for any of several reasons. The landmark could be an outstanding example of a style or period design, or notable for its craftsmanship or technology, or for its association with people, events, and geographic area.

Whatever the rationale, the end results are worthwhile today, advocates believe, because on many campuses the preservation record is so appalling. The cycle of indifference leading to landmark destruction seems to have followed this track: new construction eventually becomes honored for its antiquity, then reluctantly admired for its durability. Without sponsors and interpreters, a constant watch, even these certitudes fade away. Diminished, not sufficiently understood, the old designs become vulnerable to new views about appropriateness, or worse, temporizing enthusiasm for fads and fashions. Under the guise of necessity, real or supposed, landmark buildings are removed, sites altered, and three-dimensional treasures lost.

Fortunately, a maturing culture now recognizes the value of landmarks. The waxing, waning, disappearing cycle seems to be stemmed. Generally, it is now understood that identifiable landmarks have substantial reason to be considered as special elements in the campus design. As cultural institutions, colleges and universities have affirmed society's mandate to conserve and interpret history, among other responsibilities. Landmarks are accepted as history's architectural artifacts. Each case, of course, should be judged on its own merits. In some instances, the technical differences between preservation, restoration, and conservation may be significant in determining what action to take. Recent experience indicates that restoration of older buildings may cost more than comparable new construction. To make those determinations, the National Historic Trust routines, or equivalent methods, can be applied. Using those, or similar reckonings, the possible role the landmark might play in campus design should be given special weight. To save and savor is better than to destroy or diminish, not because the

Haas Library (1928), Muhlenberg College. The flagship building now been adapted for an administration building. The tower evokes Oxford, a symbolic campus design gesture and binder to the traditions of higher education. (RPD)

Student Building (1901). Indiana University's contribution to the fine art of historic conservation. (Indiana University)

Sayles-Hill Campus Center. A landmark gymnasium recycled. Carleton College. (RPD)

Interior, Sayles-Hill Campus Center. (RPD)

old is better than the new, but because blending the two communicates best, physically, the essential character of viable institutions; which, reiterated, is the signification of continuity and change. This philosophic view of campus design is particularly challenging as one deals with complexities of architectural style.

If nothing else, campus architecture in the 1980s was energized with forms, materials, colors, and textures that gave almost every new building the chance to be a landmark, whether intentional or otherwise. The carnival of wit and guile, seen in facades and massing, offered a collage of visual impressions which might resonate with local references. Michael Graves Alumni Center (University of West Virginia, 1987) captures that spirit with a hybrid structure that is a banquet hall for the university graduates and friends. An instant landmark, the Alumni Center gains its strength and vitality from its visual references to other landmarks on the Morgantown campus. The interpretation of landmark symbolism and metaphor can be appreciated here as an echoic gesture, less than literal but substantial in spirit.

SITE AND LANDSCAPE AS SIGNIFIER

For landscape architect Garrett Eckbo the physical landscape is a "four-dimensional sequential pattern of earth, rock, water, plants, man-made structures, air, weather, light and energy." In this short sentence, the constants and variables in the site designer's quiver are readily identifiable—which arrow for what effect, in assessing, conserving or creating a campus landmark? The mundane is separated from the special by understanding that all nine factors can be manipulated in site design; subtly, consciously, intuitively. The play of sun and shade patterns, microclimate influences as in prevailing winds, differences in topography, terrain, and the arrangement of greenery and structures—these are differentials that afford the opportunity for each campus to obtain a design accent intrinsically its own.

The perceptibility of the design image may lie in the demarcation of the authentic from the artificial. One is not better than the other; for, in fact, many memorable landscapes are artifices, invented design concepts, nature synthesized and recalled, not captured. The gardens of the Ming Dynasty in Suzhou and Capability Brown's Georgian Sussex landscapes were creative inventions, masterworks that rank with the porcelain, painting, and architecture of their respective eras. The rules that govern each of these contrasting aesthetics have been codified. Thus, some degree of replication is possible by following those rules. Campuses are artificial landscapes whose differing designs can also be codified. Coding is placemarking. Codes will differ over time. The history of campus design can be written as a sequence of code changes in buildings—outside on the facades, inside with differences in spatial sequence, amplitude, function, and technology. A parallel history can be written about changes in the campus landscape. When such changes are evidently different and survive, the resulting image produces a sense of place, a landmark. Oxford's charm is not just buildings, but also a unique group of differing landscapes; instructive laminations of taste, talent, and institutional temper.

Site arrangements can be a campus design signifier, a landmarking device. Landmarks (buildings or landscape) can be positioned as dominant or subordinate elements in the campus design composition. Background and foreground buildings

University of West Virginia. The Michael Graves' facade, Alumni Center. (UWV Alumni Association, Inc.)

College of Law, University of Iowa. Gunnar Birkerts recalls the farm country silos and dome of the Old Capitol. (Iowa Law School Foundation)

Washington and Lee University. The topography used to good advantage in composing a landmark building setting. (A.J. Lidsky)

Building forms and landscape elements; images as campus symbols. (RPD)

can be orchestrated for visual reasons as well as symbolic effects, especially when giving prominence to referential buildings.

A referential building has physical forms, colors, and materials that are immediately associated with the surrounding physical context. Referential landmark buildings can be categorized as design concepts invented, or design concepts revived and reinterpreted. when a dramatic site and a referential building are combined, landmark status usually follows, unequivocally, like a force of gravity. The College of Law Building (University of Iowa, 1987) is an image-evoking case example by Gunnar Birkerts. The law school structure was inserted into a hilltop, overlooking the Iowa River, with thick woods on one side and a curving highway on two others. A bridge connects the circular building to the woods and campus paths. The ramparts at the building base suggest the medieval, monastic beginnings of the law profession. The cylindrical shapes and dome recall the grain silos that can be found throughout the state, as well as the dome of the Old Capitol Building across the Iowa River, a building preserved that once housed the College of Law.

The engagement of land and building, accented by topography, dramatizes mundane and magnificent campus designs. The fabled 19th century hill-top colleges that populated the once rural mid-America are fine examples of simple architecture made prominent by a commanding site. Thomas Jefferson's University of Virginia lawn, bricked-in gardens, and buildings (considered by many as an epitome of campus planning and design) is informed by the gentle sloping of the Charlottesville terrain. The range of buildings at Washington and Lee University, following the ridge line in orderly fashion, generates a distinctive sense of place, as the architectural composition is adapted to the natural contours, and, in turn, the contours are subtly adjusted to achieve the desired landmark effect. Scraping and sculpturing landforms for building sites is a well-documented art; Greek temples overlooking the Ionian Sea, Mont St. Michel, Rhine River castles—their counterparts can be found among the 3,500 colleges and universities in the United States.

LANDMARKS OTHER THAN BUILDINGS

Landmark building elevations and skyline profiles command attention close up and at a distance. Chapels, libraries, refectories, gymnasia, and auditoria are designed to achieve this prominence. The structures serve the special functions, rites, and rituals which institutions wish to emphasize as part of their purpose and heritage. Graphic descriptions of early American campuses are arranged and drawn to highlight these landmark elements, thus suggesting their importance. Then, and later, these forms were carefully scaled and detailed for their visual and emotional effect. As such, they were (and are) appealing to donors and benefactors. The buildings usually are the best architecture of their time, epics in ashlar and brick, metal and wood, testimonies to aspiration and achievement, constructed to endure. But the weaning of the willing and wealthy to pay for something more than a "mason's concept of efficient and economical building" should not be taken lightly or for granted. To gain support for his project financially, Bowman had engineers estimate that the University of Pittsburgh tower would "resist natural disintegration for at least 500 years."

University of Manitoba. The evolution of a university symbol. (University of Manitoba)

Saint Joseph College. Landmark building, college image. (Saint Joseph College)

Landmark buildings and fragments of buildings with these seemingly immutable qualities become institutional emblems, appearing in logos, stationary, flags, and other symbolic manifestations. These are graphic codes that bond successive generations as members of the campus community. Towers, spires, domes, and facades abstracted from landmark buildings are popular symbols. The one invests the other with sentiment, solemnity, and stature. Old Centre (1819), Centre College of Kentucky, is a fine example of this kind of abstraction, Northwest Missouri State University's Administration Building another. Sixty percent of the Missouri Tudoresque structure was destroyed by fire in 1979. Its significance as a campus landmark helped justify reconstruction. The building's four turrets have been adopted as the school's main logo, celebrating the structure's restoration.

The Renaissance lantern and the Corinthian porticoes on the University of Manitoba's Administration Building (1912) were translated into a simple symbol in 1960. The drawing was modified in 1980. The rectilinear lines are intended to recall the building elements in the earlier logo. The curving lines "represent the meandering Red River which dominates the main campus and/or tilled fields," writes the university's Director of Building Services. "The lines are truncated at an angle. The advertising agency had no good explanation for this design element. We have laughed that it represents 'cutting corners' such as in budget readjustments during the last decade of financial restraint."

At Saint Joseph College (Connecticut), the Collegiate Georgian spire of McDonough Hall (1936) helps locate the college geographically in its neighborhood, and educationally as one of many institutions that found that style and form a suitable symbolic expression of presence and purpose, architecturally and graphically. As shown in the collection of images on page 36, landscapes can also serve as institutional symbols. In reality, many are distinguishable landmarks such as trees, and views of mountains, hills, and other geographic features. These are representational symbols, descendents of cave paintings, or the pictoglyphs carved on rocks telling the clan this is a special place.

Conceptually, it is difficult to imagine a campus without an imageable landscape of some kind. As indicated earlier, the campus greenery is artform taken for granted, and not usually appreciated as an invented concept. Like some buildings, legendary spaces such as Harvard Yard, the Lowe Library steps at Columbia University, and the Plaines at West Point, the greensward over which the Long Gray Lines march, are campus design elements invested with landmark status. Once identified and incorporated in the campus design, such landscapes can charge the campus plan with a comely, visual coherence that also has symbolic import. As discussed later, unlike buildings, the greening of the campus is not dependent on changes in enrollments, program, or institutional mission. Further, the concept of greenery as a campus landmark would seem to have universal appeal in an age concerned about ecology and environment.

Certain statues, carillons, monuments, and gateways are also placemarking, physical elements which may be identified as landmarks connected with a particular institution. The Thomas M. Storke Student Publications Building, University of California, Santa Barbara (1969) is a dramatic example. The base houses student publications and media. The 175-foot tower is the tallest steel and concrete structure in Santa Barbara County. The upper level has an observation platform, accessible by elevator or stairs, and a 61-bell carillon, which at the time of construction was the only five-octave chromatic bell system in existence. The bells

Harvard Yard. (RPD)   Library steps. Columbia University (RPD)

are inscribed with words that reflect institutional values and pay tribute to Storke, a publisher who was instrumental in relocating the campus from an inadequate site to its current magnificent ocean-side setting. Clark Kerr is also quoted: "The University is not engaged in making ideas safe for students. It is engaged in making students safe for ideas." The Storke monument neatly typifies the essential characteristics of a singular campus design landmark: physical presence, functional purpose, and symbolic power.

At the other end of the physical scale, a splash of color may be a landmark for those who recognize its meaning. Ancient China regulated the use of color in architecture. At a distance, the educated and the illiterate could read the importance of site and structure through these devices. In the Lutheran code, red signifies hospitality. Using that tradition where architecturally possible, Muhlenberg College paints its doors a bright crimson, a sign and symbol signifying a special place. Embedded in the dense development surrounding Manhattan's Washington Square, New York University marks its places with purple colors. The hue is used in building panels, signs, canopies, outdoor furniture, and in flower arrangements displayed in windows that can be viewed from the sidewalk. Particular colors, of course, have long been connected with particular colleges and universities as emblems proudly worn or carried. On ties, hats, banners, and the seemingly bizarre body paint some adults wear at athletic events, color has been used to link people and their institutions. Given these manifestations, the judicious use of symbolic color as a landmark device in campus design merits attention.

At Dickinson College, a local stone that clothed its first architecture (selected by Benjamin Latrobe, 1803) is extensively used throughout central campus, producing a distinctive landmark effect. To provide visual continuity, a prominent brownstone structure was refaced with the grey, textured material, and the quarry that supplied the stone was recently purchased (1989) to ensure a future supply for repairs and new buildings. The consistent use of a single building material, as discussed later, is a proven approach to placemarking.

Occasionally, all the landmark elements discussed blend into a transcendental, iconographic metaphor of institutional presence and purpose. Image and reality

West Point, the Plain. A landscape land-mark, unique, commanding, memorable. (RPD)

Storke Tower, University of California, Santa Barbara. (UCSB LRC)

Old West (1804), Dickinson College. The Benjamin Latrobe materials are extensively used throughout central campus—effective placemarking. (RPD)

Bosler Hall. When converted into a class-room and faculty office building, the 1884 brownstone library was refaced with the Latrobe materials to help unify central cam-pus. (RPD)

Hamilton College. A splendid example of the historic American residential college. Lawns and trees, landmark building, place-marking building materials consistently used. (Hamilton College)

Illinois Institute of Technology, air view. A landmark building grouping, a model of modern architecture. (IIT News Office)

then overlap and reinforce each other to convey a sense of place that is higher education's equivalent of a Roman forum, a medieval cathedral precinct, a town square. Two such examples are depicted on page 36: Hamilton College and the Illinois Institute of Technology; the former, a traditional aesthetic, the latter a modern idiom.

The Hamilton image pays homage to the Collegiate Georgian chapel that dominates the central campus. The design laminations that reinforce the landmark's presence include the adjacent masonry architecture, and the arrangement of buildings into an open quadrangle, with trees and paths that lead the eye to the chapel portico. The ambience is pastoral, informal, multi-textured; the site composition unassertive. Here the elements of style that radiate from the landmark are subordinated. Placemarking is achieved with multiple design inflections.

In contrast to Hamilton College, the Illinois Institute of Technology setting and site is hard-edge, urban, formal. The sense of place is reinforced by Mies Van Der Rohe's buildings. His landmark architecture pays tribute to and exemplifies an historically important three-dimensional interpretation of modernism, as such was defined sixty years ago. Here an invented architectural style is utilized as the grand placemarking action. The buildings are arranged in a geometric site pattern that echoes the linearity of the architecture. Facades are arranged to emphasize the structural elements. The enclosing fabric joined metal and glass through meticulous detailing. At its inception Mies's style was symbolically neutral, stripped of any decoration. With subsequent changes in taste and fashion, the Mies buildings are now positioned by many critics as a specific aesthetic phenomenon, associated with a definable era and personality, appreciated as a past occurence, but not an art to be emulated in contemporary buildings.

The above comparisons illuminate the utilization of style as a subordinate or dominant element in campus design. Further discussion of style as a placemarking gesture now follows, especially the determination of an aesthetic consistent with institutional aspirations, and the desire to balance continuity and change as expressed architecturally.

Oxford University. The historic quads and environs. (City of Oxford)

Style as placemarker. Everyone knows what a college should look like. (*U. S. News and World Report*)

Navajo Community College. The hogan-shaped central academic building. (RPD)

Concordia College, detail. Eero Saarinen's expression of regional architecture and cultural continuum. (RPD)

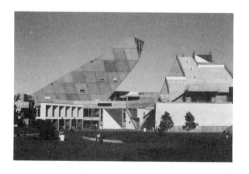

San Francisco State University. Eccentric but dramatic placemarking architecture. (A. J. Lidsky)

Style

Purpose, size, location, style and cost are the primary architectural issues which, addressed, and resolved, produce feasible college and university buildings.

Of these five intertwining factors, style is the least tangible to rationalize, though the most visible part of the architectural undertaking. Stylistic questions involve status, taste, emotion, symbol, philosophy, and perception—a full range of cognitive, scientific, and aesthetic matters.

As a word, the earliest citation published in the English language dates to 1777. From this and subsequent usage, the *Oxford Dictionary* defines styles as "a definite type of architecture distinguished by special characteristics of structure or ornamentation." The definition is exact enough for a crossword puzzle, but lacks depth when explaining the relationship between style and campus design.

How does the idea of style inform traditional and emerging modes of creating, seeing, and appreciating college and university architecture? How does style contribute to a sense of place, especially ensemble groupings of buildings and landscapes? How does style reinforce the image of a place?

In response to those questions, this definition is offered as a beginning: Style is the recognizable, special, and definitive way in which building parts are shaped into a vocabulary of forms; the forms assembled into distinctive and repeatable patterns; an outer fabric selected with materials that become associated with those forms and patterns; and the whole organized and sited to serve function, to appeal visually, and to signify client attitudes and values.

Style is a signal, an indicator of institutional presence to those who know the language of cultural artifacts, as in the abstracted building that announces a cover story on higher education in a weekly news magazine, or the air view of Oxford, or comparable, if esoteric, shapes and forms.

Style is a powerful placemarker, charged with visual energy and symbolic import. The concept itself—style—thus deserves further comment as an introduction to its application in campus design.

American College and University Architectural Styles

Colonial
Early Georgian
Late Georgian
Federal
Jeffersonian Classicism
Greek Revival
Early Gothic Revival
Romanesque Revival
Victorian Gothic
Italianate
Richardsonian Romanesque
Georgian Revival
Industrial
Beaux Arts Classicism
Regionalism
Chicago School
Ornamental Modern
Art Deco
International
Miesian
Fashioned Materials
High-Tech
New Brutalism
Contextural
Post-Modern
Neo-Modern
Deconstruction

Compilation based on 18 guides and stylebooks describing American architecture and published between 1975 and 1990.

Oxford/Cambridge Styles

Saxon
Norman
Domestic Norman
Gothic
Early Perpendicular
Domestic Perpendicular
Tudor
Elizabethan
Jacobean
Early Renaissance
Wren
Palladian
Georgian
Baroque
Picturesque
Neo-Classicism
Gothic Restoration
High Victorian
Arts and Crafts
Jacobean Revival
Neo-Traditional
Modern

Mercia Mason, *Blue Guide/Oxford and Cambridge*, A & C Black, London, 1987.

STYLE AS CONCEPT AND CHOICE

Describing buildings, or a place, by style is a relatively recent intellectual conceptualization, about which there are many theories. G. H. Gombrich's definitive bibliography on the subject lists over 50 standard works. His gloss ranges from ancient authors to modern linguists; on one side, morphologists proposing theories based on scientific evidence, on the other, dogma supported by intuitive connoisseurship. In his overview, Gombrich indicates that the word *style* came into use as a way of dating choices in "performance or procedure . . . only against the background of alternative choices can the distinctive way also be seen as expressive."

How such choices are made for college and university buildings, and the implications this has on placemarking designs will be seen shortly, as we examine the derivation and endurance of two sovereign styles long associated with American campuses: Collegiate Georgian and Collegiate Gothic. The first is an obeisance to the colonial heritage, the beginnings of higher education. The second is memory's import, homage to a medieval concept of scholastic life. Their holding power defies architectural logic, if logic is defined as structure and space serving purpose and function. Modern styles are not immune to this criticism, when fad and fashion hold temporal reign on campus designs.

AVAILABLE STYLES

As to available styles, a standard guide to architecture for two of the oldest universities (Oxford and Cambridge) lists 23 distinctive styles. A recent compilation for the United States has 25 entries. As itemized in the sidebar, the subject is complex, the definitions, at best, approximate.

The closer the style is in time to the generation describing its manifestations, the more diverse the interpretations and descriptions. Thus, the style called modern, in some lists, would embrace such diverse work as Robert Stern's patterned designs and Norman Foster's articulated building technologies. In other lists they would be categorized as respectively representative of High Classicism and High Tech, with little common ground except being alive in the same century.

Hoping to divest style of certain historical connotations, which seemed vague and unconvincing after the dawn of the skyscraper and his own novel work for the University of Colorado, America's leading college architect in the first half of the 20th century, claimed: "The choice of a style will be influenced primarily by the nature of the the the terrain, the nature of the boundaries, the traditional identity of a style with the locality in question." Charles Z. Klauder then categorized styles as The Formal (regular, symmetrical, rectilinear) or Informal (picturesque, irregular, unsymmetrical). Style was linked with site planing concepts. Klauder thought the terrain would inform the building compositions. Thus, the formal styles would be arranged in symmetrical compositions, with "an emphasis of horizontal lines and the level bases or terraces upon which in most cases buildings in this style are set . . . An informal style is more flexible. Its masses can be molded to fit a rolling ground without the necessity of extensive grading."

Style: Whose and why? The prestige attached to experimentation, the middle-ground between the poetic and the pragmatic, or some social instinct requiring

Old West, Tufts University. (RPD)

Olin Center. Construction photo, fall 1990. Elements of the Old West facade are re- called in new construction. Architectural Resources of Cambridge, Inc. (RPD)

Art and Architecture Building, Yale Univer- sity. Paul Rudolph's pioneering essay in bush-hammered concrete. (RPD)

College of Architecture and Environmental Design, Arizona State University. Left side, the 1965 structure, concrete evocative of Rudolph's Yale building. Right side, the critically acclaimed new addition 1989 by Hillier Group. (RPD)

architectural encapsulation? The master designer Eero Saarinen searched out an architectural idiom (Scandinavian rooflines) which he believed reflected Concordia College's history; the Navajo Indians did likewise in adopting hogan-like forms to establish their sense of place in higher education.

Style: Word games or helpful descriptions in describing campus designs? The dividing line between pastiche and paradigm is not easily settled. From the lists, one can observe the sequence of design preferences and their cyclical nature: styles ascending, dominating, fading away, distaste, rejection, and sometimes revival.

Style: Fashion or something else that endures because it pleases and signifies? Style does differ from fashion. The latter term connotes "fluctuating preferences which carry social prestige." On this point, a definitional detour could be instructive.

STYLE AND FASHION

Style as one would like to use the word in campus design is not fashion, but an architecture that seemingly remains constant "as long as it meets the needs of the social group." In this regard, the choice of a style is not as easily determined now, nor was it a century ago.

Needs will vary in time, an early lesson in the catechism of campus design. The changes may be stimulated by advances in building technologies, or by an infusion of new aesthetic ideals, or by moral precepts that seek to balance the "eternal tension between form and function." The latter can be appreciated as the dilemma of style, the sorting out of allegiances to architecture as reason, or alliances with architecture as sentiment.

Art historian Heinrich Wolfflin writes: ". . . style then can mean nothing other than to place it (architecture) it its general historical context and to verify that it speaks in harmony with the other organs of its age." Caught up with the enthusiasms of their time, the manner in which institutions, will signify to their peers and patrons acknowledgment of what they consider to be appropriate architecture enlivens critical debate, if not institutional archives. More recently, older styles have been examined as sources for new buildings, suggesting continuity in institutional values. For example, the facade of Old West (Tufts University's early 19th century landmark historic building) has a distinctive set of architectural features that mark time, place, and aesthetic values. To replicate these features would be unfair to the old and the new. The aspects of the older style can be carried forward to inflect the new construction as in the arrangement of the exterior of the new Olin Center at Tufts, Fall 1990. As another example, Paul Rudolph's designs for the Yale School of Art and Architecture (1958), has its counterpart at the College of Architecture and Environmental Design, Arizona State University (1965). They are linked by surface mannerisms, which cognescenti quickly recognize and appreciate. Here an invented style (Rudolph's) gained praise and publicity, and emulation at ASU. In retrospect, however, the fashion was not continued in the college's expansion. ASU's latest building (1989) is enclosed by a clearly different exterior, which arguably may be the fashion of a decade.

As with landmark architecture, the excitement of being at the edge of progressive design movements can be contrasted with the comfort of being in the middle of the continuum. A style that binds institutions to a time is comforting in principle, but may gravitate toward fashion, when that style provides no continuity. In these instances, the architecture may say more about the tenacity of prevailing tastes than their contributions to enduring campus designs. After scanning the chronicles of American campus architecture, there are many reasons to believe the creation of new styles and the adaptation of old will continue. Critics and historians will decipher this work, organize it into canons of taste and certitude, and the list of recognizable styles will be extended. On these matters, what is a reasonable stance? Rolling the drums for a new architecture (1947), the prescient Joseph Hudnut said: "We need a new tradition which shall at long last deliver our universities from the vagaries of architectural succession." The question is germane a half century later, and the answers are not yet clarified.

How then to address the issue of style in the broader framework of campus design? Are there ways to determine appropriate styles? Since the focus is place-marking, the subject of style is treated here as it pertains to the overall image of the campus—the appearance of the place expressed generally, not a particular building.

Selecting an appropriate style for campus architecture is no easy task when the menu of choices these days seems so diverse, exotic, perplexing, and idiosyncratic. The advent of the "decorated shed" in which one architect does the exterior design and another handles interior functions and utilitarian spaces, adds spice to the selection of the design team, and further unbraiding of conventional architectural practice. Perhaps, what Hudnut saw as "vagaries" in style could be recognized as a necessary expression of institutional vitality, dictated not by fashion (though such influences may be present), but, as Wolfflin would suggest, a statement of principles and values at the time the style was determined. In some instances, colleges and universities will choose to continue the beginning style through emulation or reinterpretation. In other instances, the campus will be marked by examples of successive styles. These may be beacons announcing carefully determined institutional advancement; or they may be an accommodation to the wishes of patrons, the privilege of leadership, or the balancing of private interests. Whatever the causes, campus designers must deal with the effects.

CATEGORIZING STYLE FOR CAMPUS DESIGNS

The aphorism prevails: "Buildings are the books that everyone unconsciously reads." In terms of style, campus designs can be categorized as monoforms, metamorphorics and mosaics. The reference here is the overall visual impression; the architectural ensemble seen in a quick scan, or as it unfolds in deliberate examination. Sometimes the surrounding landscape will inform and reinforce such images and sometimes be part of the design vocabulary.

A *monoform* is a singular style applied to a campus or a sector of a campus. A sense of finite unity is accomplished in one surge of construction, such as the Graduate College, Princeton University (Collegiate Gothic) or the Scarborough College (Contemporary). Each was lauded as an architecture that communicated important values, one celebrating the past, the other presenting hope for the future. For Woodrow Wilson, the Gothic style "added a thousand years to the history of Princeton . . . (pointing) every man's imagination to the historic traditions of learning in the English-speaking race." The Scarborough complex was seen as the designer's "instruments to express their aspirations and faith in high-density urban environments," a counterstroke to the "laissez-faire planning policies that disemboweled our cities," The complexes seemed so complete at birth, both philosophically and physically, that further addition in a style other than their own would seem unlikely.

Metamorphics are campus designs where the beginning style is acknowledged, respected, and reinterpreted as an architecture suitable for its own time. Aspects of the carapace, such as building materials, can be abstracted to serve as an institutional metaphor in new designs. As will be demonstrated, this method can provide visual and symbolic continuity, creating memorable placemarking effects that transcend historicism.

Metamorphosis is a change in form, structure, or substance induced by external pressures or effects. In medicine, the process is degenerative. In mythology, witchcraft, and magic, mystical and arcane influences, known only to the initiated, may be at work. In zoology, a higher form emerges; the tadpole becomes a frog. How tempting it is to apply those definitions to recent architecture. A clutch of buildings from the 1970s and 1980s could thus be examined in terms of sick buildings; or one could track the manner in which certain autoreferential statements from design gurus were translated into architectural icons; or follow the track of buildings whose style gained instant publicity, but which were eventually deadends in everyday practice.

On campus, the metamorphic process may come about because new functions demand new forms; a convincing version of an earlier style may no longer be fundable; or the skills needed to create an accomplished work are no longer available. A string of buildings that interpret with cause, rather than imitate through caprice, are thus metamorphic, and will yield a strong image. As noted below, the Duke University West Campus is an illuminating example of this approach to campus design, as is Stanford University.

Mosaics are campuses that have no singular style. Each generation contributes an example of the architecture of its own time. The buildings differ in shape, form, color, size, and detailing. Visual vitality comes from variety. Typically, memorable ensembles, such as the central campus at Bowdoin College, are arranged around a greensward, usually an open-plan campus, in contrast to formal Beaux Arts compositions, or simulations of the closed medieval Oxford and Cambridge quadrangles.

CAMPUS DESIGNS EXTENDED

When adding new space, all three categories of campus design styles pose challenges, whose eventual resolution may have dramatic effect on the overall campus image. Typical undertakings may involve building expansion or siting a totally new building. Should the new building or addition be subordinated to the existing ensemble, or should it be designed without reference to the existing context? Without this judgement, the project's potential contribution to campus design can be likened to a boat with a sail undone—noisy, power lost, direction unstabilized.

The word *subordinate* here is used in terms of desired functional relationships among buildings, the symbolic implications of continuity versus contrast, and the

Graduate Center, Princeton University. In site composition and detailing, an exemplary edition of monoform placemarking in the Collegiate Gothic style. (RPD)

Scarborough College, John Andrews' stripped-down concrete. A monoform style that celebrates an era, an aesthetic, a locale, and a campus design paradigm. The latter, like the MIT East campus, being a set of connected buildings facing a unique site feature, at MIT, the Charles River, at Scarborough, a steep, wooded ravine. (RPD)

Bowdoin College. Placemarking exhalted through a mosaic of styles bound by green lawns and New England trees. (RPD)

Cornell University. I.M. Pei's audacious, free-standing, assertive landmark structure. Complete in its own terms, the building has no apparent visual or symbolic connection to the context within which it is situated. (RPD)

orchestration of visual effects; that is, the play of foreground and background buildings. These fundamental campus design issues should not be subject to hasty resolution. The older the campus, the more productive these deliberations will be in determining and fitting in appropriate architecture, whether seminal, sentient, or sensational. As a facility program will inform the interior building functions and space arrangements, a campus design program can guide these stylistic discussions and outcomes. Placemaking analytical studies can be helpful, such as the identification of existing campus design features, views and vistas, landscapes, building heights and materials, and other visual items that generate a sense of place.

Some campus designers would impose a simple principle on all plans at their inception: anticipate and provide for expansion. The idea percolates through sovereign styles and the paradigms of contemporary campus design. The former may be expressed in an airview rendering of an expandable campus, such as the Johns Hopkins scheme, page 50. The latter might be a communicative sketch that could be called, in deference to the medium upon which it may have been first drawn informally, napkin design.

Adding to buildings with traditional styles seems easier than expanding buildings with modern styles. The former usually are arranged in comely and beguiling site compositions. The accretions often give the first buildings a picturesque scale and visual eccentricity that supplements and enhances the original construction.

A justifiable criticism of some contemporary architecture is its assertive, if not arrogant, siting; particularly those monumental conceits which, however powerfully expressed in their own terms, stand alone in the campus landscape, and contribute very little to defining or accenting a sense of place, except as a possible landmark. The simplicity of the modern idioms is deceiving, as extraordinary care must be given to construct a visually unifying addition.

Adding new space to old obviously has costs and visual consequences not to be taken lightly. Some recent examples are the architectural equivalent of an indictable offense, so poorly are they contrived. Matching and melding is an art unto itself. Here the lessons to be gained from contextual architecture are most useful—designs that emerge from a systematic examination of the visual surrounds. The easiest solution is to continue the general appearance of the older structure. More often than not, program requirements and budgets will not permit a faithful reproduction. The resolution then involves interpretations of massing, rooflines, exterior fabric, windows, and door patterns. For architectural ensembles having recognizable merit, the Brown University experience (page 247) may be a harbinger of what many American colleges could accomplish in their future as they too identify a group of buildings deserving conservation, preservation, renewal, and additions.

Additional comments on the sovereign styles now follow, with an accounting of the implications that choosing a style has had for placemarking in campus design; and the connotations such choices may have in promoting contemporary architecture.

Nassau Hall, Princeton University. (RPD)

Old State House, Boston. (RPD)

Reflecting the values and aesthetics of the mother country, England, Georgian was the preferred style for America's earliest civic and college architecture. Several times succeeded by other styles, Georgian emerged time and again on campuses in the United States as a favorite manifestation of time and place. In part, this may be due to the xenophobic nostalgia, or the certitude the style possesses for those not wanting to risk adventuresome essays in contemporary design. In part, the style's longevity may be due to simplicity and economy of construction, the human scale apparent in articulated facades, and the appeal the building forms have as recognizable landmarks when viewed close-up, or terminating a vista.

Collegiate Georgian

How simple those options once seemed: Collegiate Georgian and Collegiate Gothic. In American higher education, these sovereign styles are mortmains on values and nostalgia; visually enticing, seemingly enduring, ripe with readily understandable historic associations.

Collegiate Georgian has had many supporters because it implied connections to the country's first colleges. The legacy embraces the nine degree-giving institutions which were developed shortly after the first English settlement of the Atlantic seaboard. For their time and place, the resulting architecture was impressive in size and scale. Princeton's Nassau Hall, for example, was said to be the largest building in North America the year it was constructed (1753).

In those beginning years, government, church, and college buildings not only served a common heritage, but displayed a common architecture. In pictures they all have a family resemblance. Spire, roof, pedimented portico capture the eye at first glance; then the brick fabric and white detailing on windows and doors. The source is Georgian London, often some version of James Gibb's churches, by way of pattern books, construction manuals, and craftsmen's memories.

Brick was the favored material because it was relatively inexpensive, resisted rot and fire, had reasonable structural strength, was readily transportable, and easily handled on the job site. Red and pink colors predominate in Harvard and William and Mary's first brick architecture. An affection for the red spectrum seems to be a hallowed tradition, continuing as it did in the Harvard Yard buildings through the 20th century. By the time Hollis Hall was opened (1762), the fashion in brick colors in England had moved to gravy browns, yellows, and greys, but not significantly so in the Colonies.

Definitionally, the word Georgian covers a broad range of shapes, exterior cladding, colors, and detailing. Expert John Summerson brackets its history in England as that architecture built during the reign of the Hanoverian monarchs. Christopher Wren and Inigo Jones are influences at one end of the time span, James Gandon and John Soane at the other. The manner in which this work inflected

Johns Hopkins University Campus Plan (1915). The empowering majesty and conviction of a noble diagram for guiding university development. What we ask to be drawn, and approve with enthusiasm and certitude, is not necessarily what we get. The Parker, Thomas and Rice scheme was abandoned early, but the idea of Collegiate Georgian as a sovereign style informing and marking the campus as a special place was respected for several generations. (Johns Hopkins University, Ferdinand Hamburger, Jr. Archives)

some American interpretations of Georgian, and the way in which the prerevolutionary Atlantic seaboard college architecture maintained itself in later revivals, deserves more discussion than space here permits. Suffice to say that around 1750, elemental American Georgian buildings became more complex. The heritage is impressive. Several thousand versions of Collegiate Georgian, old and recent, can be found country-wide; meretricious placards in some eyes; an ennobling architecture in others.

Collegiate Georgian appears time and again in panoramic surveys of historic American campus development. Like Josephine Tey's moor fire, critics will whip the style to a cinder; but it will not be extinguished. It seems to run on under the surface to break out ahead, yielding three centuries of dutiful institutional architecture. Episodic revivals may reflect a surge of patriotism at a time of celebration, such as that promoted by Philadelphia's 1876 centennial exhibition; or be a symbolic response to cultural fears engendered by heavy immigration, at the end of the 19th century; or serve as a testimony to older values at a time of social unrest, such as the Depression. Collegiate Georgian is then a triumphant affirmation of nationalism; thus, the selection of Collegiate Georgian at the start of the modern American University, (Johns Hopkins, 1915); its utilization at a citadel of modern commerce (Harvard Business School); its application at a secular, urban institution in the early 1930s (Brooklyn College); and its persistence as symbolic architecture at Southern Methodist University.

JOHNS HOPKINS UNIVERSITY

On Dedication Day, 21 May 1915, the faculty assembled on the new campus of Johns Hopkins University, and "Each man took his guest this morning to lecture room, clinic or laboratory." The facilities were designed as the culmination of Daniel Gilman's aspiration to bring "new ideas and aspirations into the academic life of America." His educational model was the late 19th century German university, where "undergraduate and post-graduate work, drill and instruction, preparation for the sciences and opportunity for scientific achievement, are closely woven into a compact whole, so mutually depending upon and supporting each other." The architectural concept was Collegiate Georgian. The two opening day buildings were the first paragraphs of a never completed but eloquent essay in campus design by Parker, Thomas, & Rice, in a style and with a plan that exudes confidence and certitude.

The concept came into being through the generosity of a trustee, R. Brent Keyser, who gave (1902) the university $10,000.00 to cover costs "for a general scheme determining what style of architecture should be used and what arrangement of the property can best be made looking to its gradual development . . . so that in years to come the groups of buildings, campus, athletic grounds, dormitories, etc., will form a symmetrical whole." The interval between idea and opening day, 13 years, was used to brief an advisory committee of architects on the university's educational objectives, consolidate land holdings, conduct an architectural competition, salve the bruised egos of the losers, raise construction money, revise the winning concept to fit "present needs" and "future needs," orchestrate the faculty's involvement in the first building plans, and complete construction. Faculty and alumni "are all certain that the cash will come. Theirs is a faith that, if it does not move mountains, will erect university buildings." And so it did.

The Advisory Committee, which included landscape architect F. L. Olmstead, was appointed because the university president believed "the best assurance of unbroken harmony of design during the life of an institution could be had from a permanent board of advisory architects, rather than a single expert." Their first task was "to plan a complete group, each structure harmonizing with the others, the whole forming a picture without a single discordant element."

To achieve that end, five architectural firms, differing in their reputations for handling various styles, were invited and paid to produce concept plans. The winner was a grandiose scheme of 30 buildings, organized into quadrangles, approached by an oval-shaped driveway and a gateway building, through whose aperture could be seen the theme building, Gilman Hall. Initially, there "had been talk of reserving this large building for later construction, perhaps with the hope that some benefactor might choose to immortalize himself by presenting it." But the pressure to accommodate the academic programs early in a landmark structure could not be defrayed. Faculty and designer than "spared no pains . . . to secure a building efficient and to its occupants satisfactory"; a fitting memorial to the university's first president through "its primacy in size, position and architectural distinction."

When announced, the overall plan was declared to be "finest exhibition of Colonial architecture in America, and probably will have a distinct influence upon the architecture of the country." The style was championed for two reasons. It was "distinctively a Maryland type, for the old Homewood mansion (an historic building on the site) forms the keynote." Homewood was mined and mimed for its symbolism and design features. Secondly, it is "inexpensive." The university has "always felt the obligation of investing more largely in brains than in brick and stone and mortar. And that is what has made it famous."

The idea that Georgian was economic and at the same time symbolically appropriate was restated in numerous building projects across the country. The convergence of attitudes about how much architecture should cost and the desire to achieve a recognizable design solution that communicated institutional values gave Georgian a staying power unparallel among many styles promoted as suitable containers for higher education. At Johns Hopkins the grand plan failed. The style remained alive for decades.

HARVARD BUSINESS SCHOOL

The development of the Harvard Business School on the south bank of the Charles River is instructive in many respects: the choice of style for the design competition, the winning solution, the first construction, and subsequent buildings which departed from or interpreted the seminal Georgian architecture. Of equal interest is the preliminary work and decision making that carried the ideas from inception to successful conclusion, an effort that delivered Harvard's first realized overall campus plan after three centuries of aborted schemes for building groupings. Earlier plans were denied by land constraints, changing circumstances, a brighter vision, or the lack of money and will to see good ideas through to their ultimate ending.

The B School design was part of a larger endeavor that Harvard launched in 1924, which itself was an outcome of negotiations over what new facilities should be represented in a national fund-raising appeal. The effort was encouraged by the Associated Harvard Clubs who wanted a memorial for alumni who served in World War I, but not one of "a primarily utilitarian nature." The alumni urged a solution based on:

> A landscape study . . . made of the area now occupied by the University and that needed during the next fifty years, with the view of securing unity by planting; the closing of certain streets to vehicular traffic . . . and cutting new streets where necessary or desirable . . . Once such a plan has been adopted, it should be strictly adhered to, and no building should be permitted which does not conform to the plan, and which is not first approved by a standing committee of experts. Princeton shows what can be accomplished in beauty and consistency by a strict observance of such a procedure. Harvard with its traditions and aspirations, can certainly do no less.
>
> (N.Y. *Times* 28 May 1921).

The objective of having a 50-year plan was not accomplished. The drawing that described building locations and relationships in the supporting documents for the 1924 capital appeal was crude and vague. On the other hand the selection of new facilities and their rationalization was a masterpiece of educational statesmanship; the locations chosen uncompromised; and the preliminary planning for the B School exemplary.

Retired President Charles A. Eliot summarized Harvard's capital needs succinctly in a letter to Bishop William Lawrence, the campaign chairman. Eliot believed "a handsome building was one that was soundly constructed and effectively planned to serve a useful occupation." As Harvard's greatest builder, his views were respected, his language direct. Parenthetically, Eliot's commentary could be applied to many American campuses today, not in specifics, but generally as an accounting of current facility trends.

For the scientists, there would be a new chemistry building, fulfilling a departmental request made 30 years earlier to replace a building "dark, inconvenient and not fireproof . . . The ventilation cannot be made adequate . . . a defect which involves discomfort and even danger to all who work there." Relocation from the Harvard Yard to a site near the biological sciences and engineering would benefit all.

For the aesthetic side of the university, the new money would be used for a new Fogg Museum—a workplace for the "strongest group of Fine Arts teachers in the country, and the best University Museum." The existing building was "crippled in its lack of room for its growing collections . . . its library . . . space for drawing and painting classes, and for advanced students engaged in research." A site opposite the Harvard Yard was identified to keep the fine arts within the inner university orbit.

As for the Business School: "hopelessly inadequate . . . It has no building of its own except a small wooden building lately erected as temporary quarters for its offices. It borrows all its lecture rooms, drafting rooms, and reading rooms from other departments . . . accommodations are scattered all over the University grounds and are detached from each other in a very inconvenient manner." To

The southeast bank of the Charles River circa 1920. Scarce acreage that was intelligently and thoughtfully planned. (Baker Library, Harvard Business School)

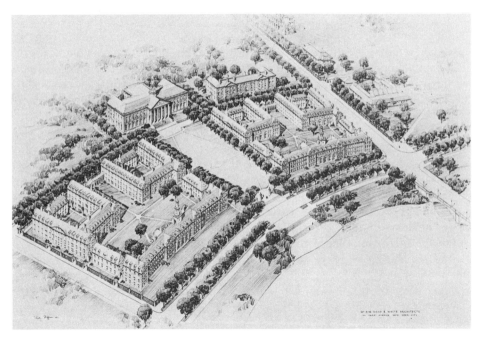

McKim, Mead and White's landmark scheme. The Collegiate Georgian features continue to inform a sense of place, despite later tastemakers who may have found the style stale and sentimental. (Baker Library, Harvard Business School)

Opening day, Harvard Business School. The raw site is now well landscaped. In recent years various interpretations of Collegiate Georgian have ranged from respectful and skilled renditions to those which ignore site and context. (Baker Library, Harvard Business School)

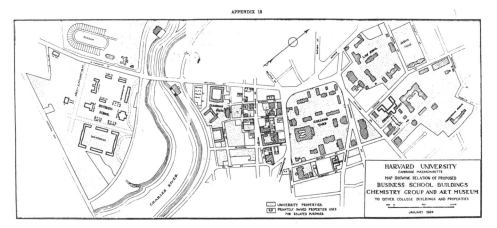

APPENDIX 18

The 1924 location diagram that guided Harvard's leap forward in science, the fine arts and a professional school for business. (Baker Library, Harvard Business School)

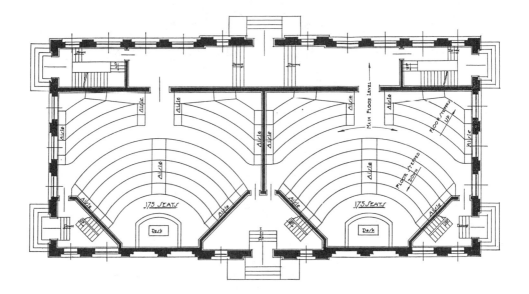

FIR/T FLOOR PLAN

CLA// ROOM BUILDING

HARVARD /CHOOL OF BU/INE// ADMINI/TRATION

BUILDING OF /IMILAR TYPE WITH PROVI/ION/ FOR
4 ROOM/ OF 125 /TUDENT/ EACH

Charles Killam's facility program diagram. The scaled drawings established the spatial and functional criteria for the architectural competition and the buildings that followed; a campus design technique that continues to guide responsible solutions for college and university development. (Baker Library, Harvard Business School)

meet the projected needs for 1,000 students, the B School required 38 buildings, a large site, and $5 million for construction.

The money was given by George F. Baker, adroitly secured by Bishop William Lawrence. His memo of his meetings with Baker should be recommended reading for all fund-raisers. Page 13 of Lawrence's typescript includes Baker's words on how he wanted to honor his family by erecting a bridge spanning Manhattan and the Palisades, but was deterred by the War Department, which would allow only a single span structure bridge crossing the Hudson. The costs would then be more than Baker would pay, and so he endowed the Business School and paid for its first buildings; and the public built what is now the George Washington Bridge.

As to the B School site, an earlier benefaction from Henry Lee Higginson and friends yielded 1.3 million square feet of choice land in Brighton, across the Charles River from Cambridge. Higginson had hoped that the acreage would entice the Massachusetts Institute of Technology to relocate from Back Bay, Boston, and merge with Harvard. The bold scheme was not achieved, but the university was given title to the marshland. When the decision was made to use the site for the Business School, arrangements were made with the local government to adjust the boundaries so as to give the site better frontage on the river. The seemingly haphazard arrangement of earlier Harvard buildings, exacted by limited land, was thus avoided. A unitary scheme could go forward.

Anticipating that his cause could not be denied, the B School dean, Wallace B. Donham, had started planing the new facilities four years earlier. With the assistance of Boston architect Harold Field Kellogg, he circulated a sketch plan (1921) for faculty perusal and donor enticement. The former would feel more secure with their physical plight recognized. The latter would appreciate that the designs were necessarily conjectural, to be tailored to the funds available.

The question of cost was never isolated from the issue of style. Kellogg's concept envisioned "several colonial buildings with simple red brick walls and stone or wood trim." It was believed that this approach would give the most space for the money, avoiding the ostentatious and expensive detailing of other styles then in vogue. With the Baker gift in sight, Donham proceeded with studies that would further define the buildings functionally. The information would also serve as a check on projected costs, and enable the university to undertake a competition for final designs, with objective assurance they could be built with funds available.

Under the direction of Harvard's architectural professor, Charles W. Killam, a working group spent the summer of 1924 in Donham's Cape Cod garage organizing functional floor plans and elevations which would express the client's requirements.

As to the floor plans, Donham had nurtured the B School's curriculum and mode of teaching, and was firm in describing room size and configuration for the case study methods which he espoused. As to the residential halls, these too were seen as opportunities for students in residence to participate in educational exchanges beyond the classroom, and thus were laid out with specific dimensions and arrangements. The didactic drawings became mandatory requirements in the "Program For Architectural Competition," but elevations were not.

The pros and cons of a competition were themselves thoroughly debated. On one hand, there was the pressure to get on with the tasks; on the other, a wish to motivate the chosen designer to view the B School as an important commission. "A collegiate grouping in Brighton, economically built in brick, is not as inspiring

Harvard Business School (1928), Baker Library. McKim, Mead and White. (RPD)

Harvard Business School (1967), Cotting Hall. Robert S. Sturgis. (RPD)

Harvard Business School (1953), Aldrich Hall. Perry, Shaw, Hepburn and Dean. (RPD)

Harvard Business School (1969), Teele Hall. Kubitz and Pepi. (RPD)

Harvard Business School (1970), Baker Hall. SBRA (RPD)

Harvard Business School (1990), Shad Hall. Kallmann, McKinnell and Wood. (RPD)

Aldrich Hall picks up a Williamsburg design theme, presumably faithful to Collegiate Georgian. Cotting Hall is an accomplished replica of the early McKim, Mead, and White designs, late in the sequence, but completing the range. Teele pays homage to concrete, and not much else. The Baker Hall brick continues the placemarking themes evident in the adjacent Baker Library. Shad loops back to beginning style with materials and forms suggesting continuity. Several other recent buildings, not shown, evoke a sense of place through contemporary versions of the 1928 HBS brick architecture.

a chance or as good an advertisement as a single large monumental building of fine materials, richly decorated, and located in New York, Washington, or Chicago," noted the keeper of the minutes authorizing the competition. The ground rules included this caution: "Harvard does not owe its graduates a chance for a job—it should get the best service possible regardless of personalities."

The concerns Harvard had for getting the best are as relevant now as they were then, not just for Harvard, but all institutions. A choice paragraph from a steering committee memo is thus worth quoting fully as to insights to be remembered and a process worth following, whether for a competition or quotidian architectural selection.

> An architect may design beautiful buildings, but may be slow or unbusinesslike, he may plan and construct uneconomically, he may lack force or tact, may be in different ways unsatisfactory. This project demands of course an architect fitted to visualize a relatively new type of education like this, to understand the intellectual and social atmosphere which is desired, whose training and experience have taught him how to arrange a number of large buildings of diverse uses in an harmonious ensemble and to clothe them in refined detail appropriate to the Harvard environment. But the project also demands buildings economically planned and constructed, well lighted, with low maintenance cost, and the University authorities want to deal with an architect who can produce such a group with reasonable promptness and in a businesslike and harmonious cooperation with them. Correspondence with owners will furnish information as to these qualities of the applicants.

The fears were unfounded; Donham and cohorts were prepared to seek and demand excellence. A two-stage competition drew several hundred proposals. Qualifications and references were checked. From this group, Harvard selected six finalists, and added six firms, who were thought to be reliable because of their size and reputation, and by being located within reasonable traveling distance to Cambridge. All met the standards that Harvard had set in determining how best to conduct the competition. They had "acquaintance with Harvard traditions . . . done good work in Georgian or Colonial . . . shown business ability, practical sense, and energy."

Killam meticulously vetted the final submissions against the program requirements, including a measurement of every building and space as to square footage defined in the program, and an assessment of manner in which the designs would "conserve as much as possible the area of land which must be provided for the future growth of the University." Having been rated as to program compliance, the schemes were then reviewed anonymously for their design merit. McKim, Mead and White was the unanimous choice. Their air-view rendering, in all significant regards, was the scheme built. Within a year of the Cotuit conference, ground was broken, June 1925, and the completed ensemble dedicated two years later. Secure that designs and construction costs were compatible, Hegeman-Harris were engaged as contractors on a cost-plus basis. Foundations were laid as working drawings proceeded. Donham was said to have been on the telephone with the builders "250 times a month." Harvard's President Lowell inspected the site often, once scrawling his suggestions on a paint color on a yet unfinished wall. A venerable Boston Brahmin, he knew Georgian architecture, and what he saw needed immediate remedy.

The competition program segued into the selection of style by implication.

Where the functional floor plans were precise, the outer fabric was implied. The program stated the designs should be "compactly planned . . . consist of more or less enclosed and secluded courts and quadrangles rather than buildings separated by large open space. Buildings designed in consonance with Harvard tradition, with appreciative use of materials and careful detail, with variations enough to avoid monotony, and with as much domestic feeling as reasonable, is desired." The 1924–1926 ensemble met the criteria. Later buildings, stylistically, drifted back and forth, for a long time uncertain as to how to pay homage and respect to the beginning.

BROOKLYN COLLEGE

"It is the realization of a dream. The style of architecture is typically American and the materials incorporated into its structure have come from all parts of the United States." Thus began the dedication pamphlet for Brooklyn College of the City of New York, October 1937.

The college started in rented quarters in downtown Brooklyn, serving freshmen and sophomores in branches of two other city colleges. If successful, the students would then transfer to the "mother institutions . . . to finish their college training and receive their degrees." As Brooklyn was the most populous borough, and without a free college, a new institution was formed in 1930 to overcome the "unconscionable distances students had to travel."

The site selected was the geographical center of the borough, accessible by subway and bus lines. The development that followed was the result of a "combination of favorable circumstances, some of them supplied by adversity," wrote the college's first president, William A. Boylan. The adversity was the Depression, with widespread unemployment, and uncertainty about the national prospects. The spectre of hard times inflected the dedication speeches. America's future would depend on citizens educated to "dare to question, to doubt, and to think about politics and economics." The architecture that best reflected those values was believed to be that which "will conform to the traditional spirit of the American college," Collegiate Georgian. The buildings would "not have to borrow their atmosphere from the surrounding residential district. They will create their own through simplicity, grace, and unpretentiousness." The Brooklyn College complex was thus conceived as : "A new departure for New York City, it will resemble closely the buildings of the University of Virginia, the Yale Divinity School and the Dartmouth buildings."

The good side of the hard times was the availability of funds to construct public works, such as Brooklyn College. With President Franklin D. Roosevelt's blessing (he laid the cornerstone of the first building), Mayor Fiorello LaGuardia secured $5.5 million in federal funds for the first five structures, space enough to build a complete undergraduate college for 7,500 students. The chief conditions were that the project be built quickly and with designs employing the largest number of people.

Boyland organized faculty committees to define the type, number, and size of rooms and related facility requirements. The Board of Higher Education selected architect Randolph Evans, a fluent interpreter of the Georgian style, and paired him with Corbett, Harrison, and MacMurray to grind out working drawings and specifications for five buildings totaling 1.5 million square feet, thus assuring that the desired large work force could be mobilized.

The Georgian canon was stripped down to its essentials; brick and white trim, pediments, copings, dormers, and ventilation systems disguised as chimneys. "Gegaws have been vanished to spare the eye and save the pocketbook." The building interiors were simple and commodious. Classrooms, laboratories, studios, and offices were laid out on either side of double-loaded corridors. The gymnasium and library were large span spaces, configured and dimensioned for their interior functions. "While in the exterior architecture we have looked to the past for inspiration, the contemporary emphasis on functionality reigns within. The college is being built as it were around the requirements, equipment needed, and the special demands of the individual departments." Should the symbolic link to the past be overlooked, the 43-acre quadrangular site design, beautifully landscaped, was dominated by the 170-foot library spire, a carefully studied and crafted version of Independence Hall.

Brooklyn College, under construction in 1936. (Brooklyn College Library).

SOUTHERN METHODIST UNIVERSITY

The symbolic import of Collegiate Georgian for Southern Methodist University cannot be underestimated. Since the college's founding in 1911, the canon of red brick, pediments, and porticos has been used to clothe buildings in stylistic interpretations that are more evocative than faithful, more impressionistic then real, more an intention than replication. At times in its short history, when architecture was moving in contrary directions, SMU would remain faithful to its first convictions. If others sought publicity through avant garde architecture, SMU would not. For the university trustees leaders believed Georgian, as they would interpret it, was an unbreachable compact with the founders. Thus, in 1988 and 1989, two major buildings, the Hughes-Trigg Student Center and the expansion of the Cox School of Business, were constructed in Georgian. Building configurations, locations, and style fleshed out a central campus design concept, as imagined by SMU's first president, the polymath Robert Stewart Hyer, whose vision gave SMU its image and its campus planning traditions.

Those convictions were not without lapses, misjudgments, uncertainties, and contradictions. In 1961, SMU opened a new building which some thought might be "the first major indication that the university was considering the possibility of exchanging the nostalgia of the past for the architecture of the present." The Science Information Center (SIC) was boldly modern, a brick box sans-Georgian detailing. But the expectation that SIC might end the "embarrassing cultural lag," which left SMU well removed from architectural happenings at other colleges and universities, would not be consummated. Homage interdicted such hope. The hook of an ingrained appreciation for Georgian architecture was not to be uncoupled.

The buildings in the decade immediately preceding SIC ranged from "muted acknowledgments of architectural trends," where attempts were made to meld contemporary design concepts with the Georgian tradition through design features and forms, such as the portals to Moody Coliseum (1956) and the dormers on the Umphrey Lee Student Center (1955); to a cluster of wholesaled Georgian buildings for the School of Theology (1951); and the Fondren Science Building (1950), where an elephantine version of Georgian gives best evidence of the style's deficiencies. A wrap-around, three-sided cartoon facade disguises a building which deserved better.

The architecture that followed the Science Information Center has been equally uneven, including a dormitory grouping salted with Georgian details and a fine arts center which attempts to capture the grandeur of monumental Georgian with pillars and portico that are stripped of any classical reference, an allusion sans illusion; and a visually unfortunate addition to Fondren Library.

For all these criticisms, the SMU campus nonetheless conveys a strong sense of place. Hyer's hand remains at the helm, guiding development through four principles that override the architectural inadequacies of individual buildings. Hyer's were: a sovereign style, quadrangular development, a linear landscape which serves as an armature for the campus design, and a landmark building positioned on the highest elevation on campus.

Hyer's work came into being when American higher education was changing and adjusting to the industrial age. The westward expansion of colleges was being

Dallas Hall (1915), Southern Methodist University. A focal point in the campus design. The Shepley, Rutan and Coolidge rendition of Collegiate Georgian continues to dominate the campus visually, as the university's president Robert S. Hyer intended in his visionary scheme for the new campus. (SMU News and Information Office)

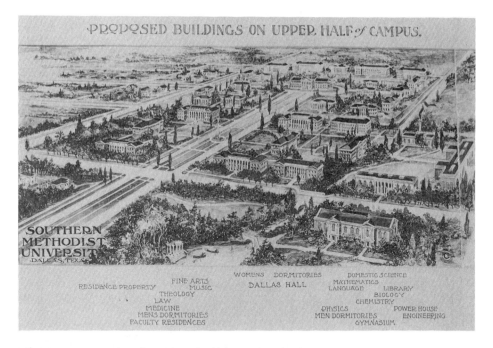

·PROPOSED BUILDINGS ON UPPER HALF *of* CAMPUS.

SOUTHERN
METHODIST
UNIVERSIT
·DALLAS, TEXAS·

	WOMENS DORMITORIES	DOMESTIC SCIENCE
FINE ARTS		MATHEMATICS
RESIDENCE PROPERTY	MUSIC	DALLAS HALL	LANGUAGE	LIBRARY
	THEOLOGY			BIOLOGY
	LAW			CHEMISTRY
	MEDICINE		PHYSICS	POWER HOUSE
	MENS DORMITORIES		MEN DORMITORIES	ENGINEERING
	FACULTY RESIDENCES		GYMNASIUM

The Hyer campus plan circa 1911. Ambition and aspiration wrapped in a style that honored America's oldest schools. (SMU News and Information Office)

The view toward Dallas Hall circa 1915, the landscape sparse, the Hyer vision still a paper plan, yet commanding. (SMU News and Information Office)

Central campus (1985). The grouping of Collegiate Georgian buildings and open space approximates the campus design ideal envisioned by Hyer. (RPD)

The brick box added to Fondren Library, a feeble gesture to architecture in context, one of the low points in SMU campus design. (RPD)

The contribution landscape can make to the imagery of Collegiate Georgian compositions is readily perceived from the Hillcrest Avenue side of the SMU campus, circa 1983, where its absence is visually devastating. (RPD)

followed by a wave of new universities. The public agricultural and mechanical schools were being transformed into multipurpose universities.

It was dawn for new privately supported campuses; Johns Hopkins, the University of Chicago, Vanderbilt, and Stanford, places Hyer visited and whose presidents gave him counsel.

Hyer's task was formidable. He started with nothing more than several hundred acres north of Dallas and instructions from the local Bishops to proceed with establishing "a real University for Methodism in the South." On reaching the site for the first time, Johnson grassland that seemed more suitable for a cattle ranch than a university, "Mrs. Hyer burst into tears."

Hyer saw promise, where others saw problems. He comforted Mrs. Hyer by saying the "surroundings are most inviting." The general view will not be obstructed or disfigured by high-towering skyscrapers, since the site is surrounded by a modern suburb with most beautiful and artistic residences." Hyer's certitude was contagious. There was no money, nor buildings, no faculty, no students; only pledges of goodwill and Hyer's faith in the enterprise. He rejected advice "to throw up some ordinary structures just to get the university off the ground." So SMU would not "resemble a freshwater college . . . I urged," said Hyer, that "here we do nothing until we had plans." It was a strategy Hyer pushed hard, using paper to excite where bricks and mortar could not yet demonstrate what he wanted, which was "the most comprehensive development of landscape gardening and magnificent architectural effects to be found in any educational institution, or perhaps of any institution of any other kind in the South."

Hyer worried that the initial capital would allow "the necessary buildings," but only "the cheapest construction, nonfire proof, and without any regard to architectural beauty." He asked the Bishops to pledge money for better architecture as an "object lesson" inspiring the Methodists of Texas "to do as much for their university as Dallas had done" in providing the site. The new university was thus conceived not only in educational terms, but also physically. Hyer believed a suitable architecture would draw qualified faculty and motivate students. The sense of place rendered architecturally would charge the enterprise with a three-dimensional vision that raised hopes, morale, and money.

Hyer's personality, beliefs, and accomplishments gave energy, wit, and creditability to the undertaking. A physicist, Hyer's scientific work in radio waves preceded Marconi's. Hyer built the first wireless transmitter station in Texas. He was equally versed in hypnotism and literature. He believed the new university's curriculum and faculty hiring should not be influenced by "the perpetuation of a narrow sectarian point of view." He taught a course in the New Testament; and admired Charles Darwin, whose *Origins of Species* he had memorized. Hyer sketched the university's first master plan and was the designer of record for one of its first buildings (Women's Gymnasium, 1919).

For architects, Hyer selected Shepley, Rutan and Coolidge, the Chicago firm whose work for the University of Chicago and Stanford would give prestige to a university then unknown. Hyer was proud to record that after their initial site studies, they changed the location of only two of the 30 buildings that Hyer had specified in his sketch plan. A close examination of the air-view rendering of Hyer's vision, as prepared by the architects, would suggest that the site coverage and the actual land were not quite congruent. Ambition was larger than actuality.

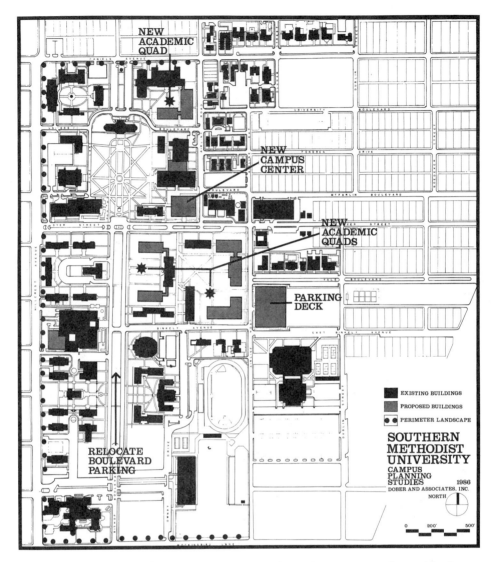

Detail 1986 campus planning studies showing locations of new construction and landscape so as to revive and extend the quadrangular development as a campus design principle. Left for later decisions are the specifics of style. (RPD)

As early site photos would indicate, Hyer's dream was for a long time an act of faith, whose realization is only recently coming into fruition.

Hyer was image-conscious, though the word image does not appear in reports from his hand. In picking the school colors, he choose red from Harvard and blue from Yale. Among several choices of style that the facile architects were ready to execute, Hyer chose Collegiate Georgian. It reminded him of the University of Virginia, a campus whose design had just been resuscitated with a renewed interest in revivalist buildings, and Thomas Jefferson whose "commitment to intellectual freedom" was philosophically appealing to Hyer.

"Things worth enduring require time for their accomplishment," said Hyer. By advocating a single style, he could "avoid the difficulty of so many of our older colleges and universities, which have no architectural interest and unity." The difficulty, as he saw it, was that "with every new building there was a change in style." SMU's buildings should not be "architectural incongruities, the one to the other . . . but will conform to the plan of individual attractiveness blending into a harmonious general effect."

Today, Dallas Hall recalls Jefferson's library at Charlottesville with its rotunda and dome. On a commanding site, it is a linchpin in the quadrangle concept and the exclamation point for SMU's Georgian buildings, 15 of which are on the National Register of Historic Places. Of these, Clements Hall (1915) is exemplary; "quite unrivaled by subsequent buildings," with a quality that exposes cheap imitations.

To acknowledge the plan's future dimensions, Hyer divided the central campus into four quadrants, each devoted to a special function. Buildings were grouped so that after the first construction, the ones that follow "will come to occupy their allotted stations . . . so as to be well seen . . . with the practical advantage of abundance of fresh air and light." Each quad would be grassed and edged with trees and hedges. The shadows cast would temper the climate and add the art of landscape to the architectural compositions, principles reaffirmed in SMU's 1984 campus plan. Old and new quadrangles visually relate to Bishop Boulevard, the campus design armature. The boulevard connects SMU's first front gate with Dallas Hall, the landmark building. Together the two are the dominant campus design

Expansion of the Edwin L. Cox School of Business using the traditional Collegiate Georgian palette, 1986. Harwood K. Smith and Associates. (SMU News and Information Office)

Hughes-Trigg Student Center (1989). Harwood K. Smith. The exterior arranged in the traditional SMU format. (SMU News and Information Office)

Library Building (1982), Fouts, Gomez, Moore. The 275,000 square foot structure continues the Bhutan style at the University of Texas at El Paso. (Office of the University Librarian, UTEP)

markers. A strong linear landscape, Bishop Boulevard was given new life by banning parking along the right of way—the last act of an embattled and departing president (1987).

STYLE AS ROMANCE

As it has in the past, SMU continues to debate its commitment to Georgian architecture. Discussions these days about the style's suitability focus more on appearance than symbol, function, and aesthetics. In reviewing plans for a new fine arts center (1989), the donor for a new fine arts center said the designs "were decorously in key with the rest of the campus, in beautiful Georgian architecture . . . This isn't nearly what I wanted. Romanticize it please." The facades were reworked and an outdoor fountain added to the site composition.

The idea that campus architecture might mark a place with an emotional style was not without precedent in Texas. About the same time Hyer was struggling to realize a Georgian campus in the grasslands of central Texas, what is now the University of Texas at El Paso (UTEP) was blasting its hillside to create a site for a local version of Bhutanese architecture. The connection between UTEP and a kingdom situated in the Himalayas may have been fortuitous; but the manner in which the fifth Dalai Lama's fortress-palace, the Potala, would be combed as a style for seven decades of university buildings was deliberate and purposeful.

UTEP was chartered as the Texas State School of Mines and Metallurgy (1914). A fire destroyed its first buildings and an emergency grant was authorized for replacements. Noting that the site resembled the rocky hills of Bhutan, whose photographs had been recently published in the National Geographic (April, 1914), the wife of the dean of the school, Kathleen L. Worrell, urged her husband to use the Bhutan images as a style. "The massive, gently sloping walls, high indented windows, projecting roof eaves, and dark bans of brick and stone at the high window levels," would seem to be a perfect fit for the stony El Paso hills. While MIT was looking to Rome for an appropriate style, UTEP was combing the romantic and remote Asia.

Worrell's instincts were persuasive. A contemporary recalled decades later:

> I once heard Cap Kidd, the Mines' legendary dean of engineering, say, referring to Dean Worrell, 'When the missus speaks up the Doc listens.' So if Dean Worrell had anything to do with designing the old Mines buildings, it is my guess that Mrs. Worrell made her influence felt. She was quite capable of designing those buildings herself!

In 1917 construction started on four new buildings reminiscent of the "world's last Shangri-La." Where the original Bhutan buildings were dramatically piled and linked, the El Paso structures were free-standing.

As the cost of thick walls and detailing became expensive, later versions were modified. When modern architecture arrived in El Paso in the 1960s, the distinctive style was denatured. Few were satisfied with the changes, particularly as the original campus architecture gained world attention. The Queen of Bhutan would write: "It is thrilling and moving to see a great new University built in far away America inspired by Bhutanese architecture." UTEP's first Bhutanese graduate (1978) expressed what many felt: "I am proud to see the tradition of Bhutanese architecture here at UTEP. It is beautiful, it is fitting, it is unique. I hope that it is never permitted to fade away."

The style was revived with the new Business Administration Building (1982) and given further life with the construction of a 275,000 square foot library (1984). Inside the $22 million structure, floor plans and furnishings fostered the art of library planning. Outside, sloping walls, turreted roofs, articulated windows recalled again an architecture redolent with romance, and as redoubtable for UTEP as the fortress city from which the style came.

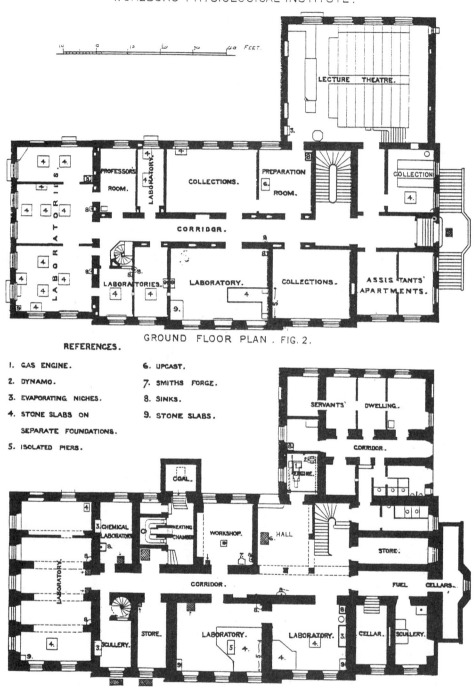

WURZBURG PHYSIOLOGICAL INSTITUTE.

PLATE 7.

LECTURE THEATRE.

PROFESSOR'S
ROOM.

LABORATORY.

COLLECTIONS.

PREPARATION
ROOM.

COLLECTION

LABORATORIES

CORRIDOR.

LABORATORIES.

LABORATORY.

COLLECTIONS.

ASSISTANTS'
APARTMENTS.

GROUND FLOOR PLAN . FIG. 2.

REFERENCES.

1. GAS ENGINE.
2. DYNAMO.
3. EVAPORATING NICHES.
4. STONE SLABS ON
   SEPARATE FOUNDATIONS.
5. ISOLATED PIERS.

6. UPCAST.
7. SMITHS FORGE.
8. SINKS.
9. STONE SLABS.

SERVANTS'   DWELLING.

CORRIDOR.

COAL.

CHEMICAL
LABORATORY

HEATING
CHAMBER

WORKSHOP.

HALL

STORE.

LABORATORY

CORRIDOR.

FUEL   CELLARS.

STORE.

SCULLERY.

LABORATORY.

LABORATORY.

CELLAR.   SCULLERY.

BASEMENT FLOOR PLAN . FIG. I.

Plate 7, Technical School and College Buildings. Edward Cookworthy Robins' pioneering effort (1887) to rationalize the planning and design of Victorian institutional architecture. (Avery Library, Columbia University)

Collegiate Gothic

Today's debates over style had their equivalent in the 19th century. "Omninium gatherum Victorianum," perceived Robert Kerr, King's College professor of architecture, circa 1885. Eclecticism was a style unto itself. This aesthetic would set no limits on a vocabulary of shapes and forms, he claimed, but judge the results in terms of harmony and proportions. Addressing the issue of appropriateness, the prescient critic Montgomery Schuyler summarized 19th century architecture as "the records and trophies of modern civilization," an architecture where historic precedents determined contemporary forms. Schuyler said the "main difference between our times and medieval times is that the scientific constructor and the artistic constructor was one person, now they are two. Accordingly, he thought, the "art of architecture is divided against itself." To overcome the burden of historicism, the joining of the two "sensibilities" was essential for development of a new architecture.

In higher education, however, few clients or designers gave much attention to function as a design determinant. A splendid exception, deserving notice as a precedent in the annals of the collegiate architecture, was Edward Cookworthy Robins' *Technical School and College Buildings,* London 1887. Robins stated that the "education of an architect is incomplete when he allows his mind to be so absorbed by the artistic side of his profession as to look with contempt on the practical." His reference book on the design and construction of applied science and art buildings raised the level of knowledge and appreciation of the technical side of the building arts. He gathered and reproduced examples of the floor plans and descriptions of model architecture, including many from Germany, where advances in science research and instruction were encased in designs established by function, mostly uncompromised by style. For Robins' good design would be "unfettered by symmetrical rules of sentimental proportion or balance of ornamental associations either of gothic or classic origin." Beauty, he pleaded, "is that which grows out of the fitness of things, the perfect adjustment of the means to the end desired, in the absence of which real beauty is nonexistent, and, like faith without works, dead." It would be nearly a century before his message reached the citadels of British higher education, Cambridge and Oxford, so that building functions would inform and affect exterior appearance and interior floor plans.

In America, A. D. F. Hamlin (1892) saw "the crystal of a new architecture, as perfect as any that has gone before." It would be an architecture "bound by no stiff canon of formulated rule and precedents . . . but strong enough . . . and flexible enough for all the boundless variety of climate, and habit, and materials and surroundings of this great land." In this paean to a virtuous architecture, Hamlin's "fingerposts" were "the Romanesque and Renaissance," whose synthesis would produce "a still more truly American architecture."

Most American college buildings through the mid-19th century could be categorized stylistically as:

Georgian, where memories of the early Colonial Colleges would be saluted with architecture derived from middle class England prior to the Revolution;

Federal, where Georgian would evolve into an American style, such as encouraged by Thomas Jefferson's interpretation of Palladian architecture for the University of Virginia;

Greek Revival, a style adapted at a time when Hellenic values and political struggles were sympathetically monitored and translated into architectural forms, chaste white, porticoed temples for learning;

Empire, "tutti Louis," the synthesis of Gothic and Classic that came from France with the restoration of the empire. The mansard roofs, center halls and connected wings, and big buildings, appealed to the Quakers who built Swarthmore College's landmark building, Parrish Hall; the founders of Vassar College for Women, whose James Renwick, Jr.'s masterwork dominates the campus image architecturally; and for brief moment, served as inspiration for English architects.

Against this background, a fifth prominent style, Collegiate Gothic, gained rapid ascendancy and prominence, presumably as a reminder of a more felicitous preindustrial age, and as an exemplar of virtues and scholarship stretching back to medieval ages. The style had the advantage of permitting large-scale site development, connecting buildings varying in function, but united through detailing defined by a single aesthetic.

When first seen on American campuses, circa 1830, Collegiate Gothic buildings were wrapped in the mantle of religiosity. The designs were imported from England, which had begun celebrating Catholic educational values in a style historically associated with Roman and Anglican rituals. Keynon College constructed the first such building (1827), the University of Chicago (1891) the largest single scheme, and Boston College the latest such interpretation (1987).

Pointed arches, narrow windows, gabled roofs, and traceries would not constrain a prudent combination of ancient forms, modern functions, and contemporary comforts. Initially, the Gothic was typically reserved for special buildings, a stylistic herald of new values and important events. Harvard departed from its Georgian traditions (though not for the first time) with Gore Hall (1838), itself a noteworthy event in the history of library architecture. Gabled and garbed in Gothic, the library is said to be the first college building with steam heat, a fire-resistant cast iron structure, and high density book stacks. Later demolished, Gore was important enough to be used in the City of Cambridge seal, when the town was incorporated (1846). Yale's version (the 1840 Gothic library) subsequently became a chapel. At Swarthmore, the Gothic-style chapel, among the last of its kind chronologically, was redesigned by Robert Venturi's firm into a student union (1988).

The Gothic style gained supporters because, in tandem with the symbolic associations, the buildings could be arranged into enclaves which could expand with small or large increments, as colleges and universities grew and prospered. Metaphorically, the humble Gothic pastoral church would become the larger Gothic monastic precinct, the precinct a desired symbolic venue for higher education. For their "size and elaboration" and especially their site compositions, American university architecture would merit ranking with the skyscrapers, wrote H. R. Hitchcock in his definitive survey of 19th century architecture. He was less pleased with the designer's concerns for "school-masterish respect for precedent in detail"; topics elaborately covered in architectural journals in those days.

UNIVERSITY OF CHICAGO

The larger schemes were enabled by clients and donors who saw in these undertakings an idealism worth fostering. For these institutions, Collegiate Gothic was preferable to an imperial architecture inspired by imperial cities, such as the Beaux Arts and City Beautiful architectural modes, or the equally popular Romanesque. With Collegiate Gothic, the site arrangements could be impressive without being monumental. The quadrangles could be enclosed to "carve out a bit of peaceful countryside within the city." The architecture would have the additional appeal of the picturesque, and convey a sense of ancient verities in a period rankled by uncertain economic and social change. For these effects a generous purse was essential, as well as time and skill to contrive reasoned and buildable designs.

All such conditions came into fruition for the University of Chicago's new campus (1891), where ridges and marshes on Chicago's southeast side were converted into "165 acres of gray stone and greenery . . . Gothic-style buildings . . . stunning reminders of a craftsmanship in stone, woodcarving, and sculptural effusion hardly attainable anymore."

For this considerable undertaking, the ambitious, 32 years old, Henry Ives Cobb initially wanted to use simplified Romanesque designs. Influential trustees thought otherwise, preferring something "mellow, memorable, majestic"—a design concept that would stand out in sharp contrast to the commercial architecture that was and is the city's architectural glory. Style was to signal a separation of the world of the mind from the world of real life. Arguably, the Gothic was also the reliable way to spend money for an architecture that would proclaim moral values in a city made great by mercenary industrial and financial practices, whose deficiencies were clouded by the magnate's contributions to exciting cultural enterprises: art, music, and higher education. As the century turned, the seeds were sown in Chicago for civic achievement and reknown in all three areas.

However reckoned, the flat surfaces, steel, and glass seen in downtown Chicago's pioneering architecture, modern in every critical sense, gave way to Indi-

Vassar College, the Upjohn scheme, Empire style, circa 1864. (Vassar College Library)

Parrish Hall (1865). Swarthmore College. (RPD)

Elevation Royal Holloway College (1879), England's first purpose-built college for women. W. H. Crossland's image-making design was intended by the donor to be "beating Vassar into fits." (RIBA Library)

Kenyon College, America's first Collegiate Gothic building.(Kenyon College News Office)

Boston College, Collegiate Gothic early 20th century. (RPD)

Boston College, Collegiate Gothic—a 1987 interpretation. Sasaki and Associates. (RPD)

Detail, New College, Oxford. The 14th century purpose built college in the Gothic style. Later versions in the United States were more literary in their interpretation than literal; functions, building technology, craftsmanship, and materials being different. (RPD)

University of Chicago. Henry Ives Cobb Collegiate Gothic (1891). (UC Planning Office)

University of Chicago air view circa 1985. (UC Planning Office)

ana limestone, piled up as if arranged by monkish masons. The "style of architecture selected," wrote Cobb, will "remove the mind of the student from the busy mercantile conditions of Chicago and surround him by a peculiar air of quiet dignity which is so noticeable in old university buildings."

Cobb's designs resonate with Ruskinian rhetoric and rationalization. Imagination and moral judgment are informed by training in history and fine arts. An architecture with historical precedents combines both. Sermons in stone: not a new idea in American higher education, for Thomas Jefferson, among others, would detail his University of Virginia architecture to achieve that objective. The Illinois Institute of Technology would publicize 20th century modernism on comparable grounds, as would the University of New Mexico in defending regionalism.

Of the several completed quads at the University of Chicago, the Hutchinson corner is considered the best; "a beautiful, harmonious, vivid picture," essayed the modernist Eero Saarinen in 1960. He encouraged the trustees to respect the design integrity of the Collegiate Gothic superblock and to place contemporary architecture needed for expansion outside the precinct. The good advice came at a time when revivalist masterworks such as the Chicago quads were targets for demolition; dismissed as out of fashion, too expensive, and with limited utility. In the mid-1940s, the style's suitability was not argued on philosophic grounds, though such issues were debated at other eminent institutions of higher education, but on economic. Interestingly, the financial constraints seemed to contradict the founder's wisdom. Early in the university planning, John D. Rockefeller stated: "Do not on account of scarcity of money fail to do the right things in constructing the new buildings. We must, in some way, secure sufficient funds to make it what it ought to be."

The gap between advice and actualization is not easily bridged, as many a college and university administrator will testify. The University of Chicago could not afford to emulate the first buildings, nor postpone solutions for pent-up facility needs. With the monies available, a new administration building "could only have the suggestions of the Gothic," a design course that angered many. The policy that then emerged was to maintain the main campus "as near to neo-Gothic as possible." Architecture in the expansion to the south "would be done in contemporary style with neo-Gothic recall in line and material." The west and north areas would be designed with brick and stone, with "lines to harmonize with the neo-Gothic." Critical opinion is divided as to the results. Architecture is not the good intentions that launch design, but the actual, built environment.

Fortunately, as the original quad buildings aged and interior functions changed, the university reinvested capital to give the structures new life and purpose. They stand today, a notable campus design, animated and admired as architectural history.

For some observers, the Chicago quads are sedated designs, as if they were constructed for a contemplative monastic order; not so at Yale. Professor William Lyon Phelps records his first impressions of the Harkness Quadrangle, Yale's version of Collegiate Gothic, which like the University of Chicago came into being through a generous benefaction intended to advance educational goals:

> . . . as one wanders around . . . viewing it from without and from within, one sees bits of humor, sardonic embellishments, queer platforms and recesses that (thank

Yale University, Harkness Quadrangle, Memorial Tower. Started in 1917, James Gamble Rogers' essay in Collegiate Gothic provided both the cause and the content for a visually rich interpretation of a sovereign style. (RPD)

Yale University, Pierson College. Gamble's Collegiate Georgian facade. (RPD)

Yale University, Davenport College. Gamble's Collegiate Gothic facade. (RPD)

heaven) are without any useful purpose and do not make for efficiency . . . The architect ought to be doubly happy—first in having dreamed such dreams, second, in having the marvelous art to make them come true.

Examining Yale's first Gothic, Ralph Waldo Emerson was said to have wondered if "there would ever be students worthy of living in such a magnificent building." Worry not, suggested William Clyde DeVane, "there lingers still about Yale some of that healthy, and a little touching, faith in the abilities of the common man." The architecture of the houses would help lift the uninitiated into a higher realm of responsibility and knowledge. The spaces were as comfortable and functional as an old tweed jacket. What truths were communicated, what lesson was learned? One critic complained that it is "impossible to appreciate how avidly many Americans viewed these (Gothic) buildings unless you understand how a history-starved and adaptive, but essentially unoriginal, people depend on imports from foreign lands."

Yale's ability to straddle any uncertainty as to the symbolic aspects of style can be seen in an adjacent residential quadrangle. Here, James Gamble Rogers succeeded in designing a residential complex that was Collegiate Georgian on the Park Street side and Collegiate Gothic along the York Street frontage. The seam that joins Davenport and Pierson architecturally is a masterpiece of campus design.

DUKE UNIVERSITY

With Collegiate Gothic, campus design edged toward the theatrical, which in contrast with stark modernism and stripped-down Georgian, may be its appeal today. Literary allusions, religiosity, or historic references are not tenable in explaining the pleasure it offers the casual viewer. The style's leading apologist was right. Ralph Adams Cram said it will produce "a romantic composition." For the moonstruck during daylight ". . . a building up of gables and towers, oriels and porches, dormers and pinnacles . . . an accenting of broad walls by vivid notes of traceried windows and unexpected ornament of crisp, rich carving" has few parallels in campus design. "Medieval sauce," was the judgement of Joseph Hudnut (1947), which can be spread over any building surface "without apparently the slightest impediment to its operations."

Cram and company would claim with certainty that time would not erode Collegiate Gothic designs because of their long-term philosophic suitability. The opinions barely outlasted the lives of the architects who voiced them. Collegiate Gothic buildings are lovely anachronisms—lovely for those who enjoy tactility and elaborate detailing, lovely with their orchestration of courtyards, views and vistas, especially when adjusted to varying configured sites and terrain. Though drawn by other hands, Cram's formula for Collegiate Gothic may have reached its apex at Duke University, where the West Campus's designs were so powerful as institutional symbols that modern buildings have been adapted in homage to this sovereign style.

Designed by Horace Trumbaucr's firm in the late 1920s, Duke University's West Campus is one of five development precincts that constitute the university's main campus in Durham, North Carolina. Considered a masterwork in campus design, the West Campus is shaped by a series of quadrangles and courtyards. The parts are hinged to the Chapel forecourt. The Chapel tower punctuates the vista from Chapel Drive, as well as marking Duke's presence on the Durham skyline. Surrounding all is a rolling topography, smoothed and planted with a native landscape that complements in color and texture the Collegiate Gothic masonry architecture.

Disaggregated, the West Campus design is a collage, whose pieces can be traced to English medieval churches, monasteries, and colleges. The Duke ensemble is the work of Trumbauer's chief designer, Julian Abele, an Afro-American, whose graphic skills Trumbauer admired early and whose professional opportunities he fostered.

The Gothic style was proposed by James B. Duke, in about 1924. A few years earlier his family foundation had transformed Trinity College (now Duke's East Campus) into a stately Georgian complex, in accordance with plans also produced by the Trumbauer team. Expecting that the architectural fulfillment of the Trinity site would require additional acreage, Duke was said to be angered "when the prices of adjacent land . . . climbed to levels which Mr. Duke declined to pay." Assisted by the University Treasurer, Duke "negotiated secretly enough to prevent another holdup," and assembled the dramatic property that became West Campus. The specific reasons Duke wanted Gothic for his westward move are problematic, but his ability to achieve that end are not. Unlike many other new campuses from the early 20th century, Duke's gifts permitted most of the original scheme to be built at one time. The Georgian East Campus was then utilized as a women's college; the Gothic West Campus was developed for men.

West Campus appeals to modernists and traditionalists because there is a sense of unity and completeness, variety and scale. The building style and designs were adaptable to university functions as they were defined in the 1920s: chapel, library, administrative, and faculty offices, classrooms, laboratories, student housing, social space, and dining. In truth, those functions could also have been enclosed by Georgian, Empire, or Bhutanese styled buildings without compromising their functions. What makes the West Campus work well visually was the skill the designer exercised in examining five centuries of English architecture and applying that vocabulary to the Duke situation. Towers, gateways, bay windows, arcades, pitched roofs, chimneys, and other features are not organized in true and faithful replication of some ancient monument, but brought together in a design driven by imagination, not formula.

At the time the outside appearance was being determined for Duke, Gothic was the heralded style, favored at Princeton and Yale. Coincidently, and coterminous with the Duke West Campus enterprise, the University of Bristol (England) also was developing its expansion in the Gothic style, and, like Duke, with money given by a family whose wealth came from the tobacco industry. The Bristol gateway building (1926) and the Duke Chapel (1928) play a similar role in their respective campus designs—skyline objects positioning and locating the university in a broader design context, and symbolizing what patron and university considered the institution's lineage.

Duke has a dilemma: once built, are there obligations to preserve intact a campus design considered an historic masterwork? How does expansion occur when the cost of comparable construction is no longer affordable? Is the Gothic style a tenable symbol for a University gaining recognition as a preeminent institution?

Vital institutions expand in two ways: space added and space adapted. The latter is expensive in Gothic-style buildings if there are significant changes in interior functions. The former is beyond reason, if replication is required; and, modern university uses, especially in science, engineering, and technology, are to be contained uncompromised in a sovereign style. And what about donors who may seek ennoblement through buildings with a style other than the existing traditional?

Duke had addressed this issues forthrightly because it recognizes the uniqueness of its West Campus design heritage. Lower-cost science and engineering buildings and a law school were located outside the West Campus perimeter in the 1960s. The business school complex (1983) was given a site in the adjacent woods for a free-standing, elegant, modern complex. The medical school and hospitals which anchored one end of the Trumbauer group have grown northward, with each increment gradually departing from the Gothic style, like family resemblances modified by a diluted gene pool. Close-in West Campus buildings have been experiments in architectural homage.

In the late 1960s, new student housing and a student center attempted to capture some of the Gothic's visual qualities through reductionist architecture. Elaborate detailing was simplified, as were building profiles. The housing was configured to fit a rugged site, which helped accent the verticality of the building compositions. Window treatments suggested the shadowed molding of the older architecture. Pedestrian bridges carry traffic through the complex, whose green landscape reflects the changes in topography and mediates the forceful masonry architecture.

The designs recognized that "Functional shortcomings of Gothic architecture and rising costs of duplicating it are bringing change to the Duke University campus . . . (the new halls) . . . represents an effort to retain the essence of the Gothic and yet provide more economical construction and a more functional plant."

The student center is less successful as homage, though otherwise impressive as to the manner in which diverse interior functions were contained under one roof. The edging of machicolated parapets are a clever obeisance to the nearby buildings. Where the thin edge of the stone was laid flat in the historic West Campus structures, the stone encased vertically in concrete surfaces of the new appears more like the peanut brittle of the confectioner's craft than the mason's art so evident in the older fabric.

The latest West Campus student housing (Schaefer House, 1989) signals its connection to the Gothic with exaggerated interpretations of windows, doors, rooflines, and loggia—a gesture more sentimental than studied. The building is awkwardly plunked on the site, the surroundings indeterminate as to graceful landscape connections to the older quads. However, like the first star twinkling after a stormy night, portions of the lower piers on Schaefer House catch the eye, as they are encased in the same type of stone that is used in the Duke's first Gothic buildings. As brick is associated with Collegiate Georgian, cut stone is Collegiate Gothic's partner.

The Duke stone is memorable for its color and tactility and its history. Mr. Duke admired Princeton's Gothic buildings and wanted that tone and texture for his Durham campus. Test panels were constructed so he could see for himself how the stone might appear on the Durham site. Some accounts say that he was appalled at the costs of importing the Princeton material and urged a search for a

Duke University, air view rendering. (Duke University Archives)

Gateway Building (1926), Bristol University. (RPD)

Princeton Graduate College (1914). (RPD)

Chapel (1928), Duke University. (RPD)

Duke University. View of the original West Campus Collegiate Gothic complex. (RPD)

Duke University, student housing. The 1989 complex incorporated forms reminiscent of the 1920–1930 buildings, and utilized as an architectural gesture the West Campus stone on piers and foundations. (RPD)

Tides of tastes flow in parallel directions as donors, patrons, designers and clients share common values.

Duke University. Lower budget, brick science buildings constructed at edge of the historic West Campus core after World War II. (A. J. Lidsky)

Duke University, Fuqua School of Business. Detail of a contemporary building grouping adjacent West Campus. (A. J. Lidsky)

Duke University, detail Bryan Center. The crenelated parapet and stone are intended to suggest a visual and symbolic connection with the historic Collegiate Gothic. (RPD)

Duke University, detail, student housing. Designs in thee 1960s used materials to suggest architectural continuity. (RPD)

Air view, Duke University, East Campus. An instructive essay in Collegiate Georgian, constructed in the 1920's, the buildings and site composition are comparable to similar efforts at Johns Hopkins University and Southern Methodist University. The site continues to serve the University though the West Campus Collegiate Gothic is Duke University's proclaimed campus design image. (Dober, Lidsky, Craig and Associates, Inc.)

local equivalent. Using information from a state geological survey, Duke's agent found and secured a possible supply on a farm about eight miles from campus. "It was the kind of find that delights a construction man's heart; and at heart Mr. Duke was a construction man." With Duke's approval, the University agent acquired rights to quarry the land. Other accounts suggest a "fortuitous discovery . . . not as a result of a conscious search." However secured, the stone was carried to the campus construction site on a short-spur track that was laid for that purpose. As noted, the same stone was later utilized as gross aggregates in the poured concrete panels that formed the exterior walls of the of the 1970 housing and student center, and as indicated, the stone shows up in the piers of the new housing. In this instance, the stone materials serve as an institutional metaphor, unbinding campus architecture from the strictures of style. When desired, the use of materials in this manner, to provide visual continuity and as a carrier of symbolic meaning for the institution, is a practical and powerful campus design concept and method, as illustrated and discussed more fully later.

20th Century Styles

As to 20th century styles, architecture invented in our age, general opinion sees the first rejection of traditional sovereign styles as the rationalization of industrialism. For many designers and their clients, it was an architecture that had to possess "the conspicuous look of technological efficiency." Advances in science, technology, engineering, and new ways of expressing the world of ideas and art, found their counterpart in campus architecture; as the polemics from those self-confident days would promise. Laminated wooden arches were promoted to span large spaces gracefully and inexpensively. Green, porcelain, paneled facades could be organized in value-free Euclidean symmetry.

The idea of a single modern style is, of course, itself misleading. The divisions and subdivisions of style by name, region, year, and motive may help in determining precedents and authorship, but throw little light on essential matters, such as building quality, symbolic intent, the choice of technologies, and materials. Of several thousand modern campus buildings, four examples evoke the reductive feeling that the modern style (defined here as typical works from the middle of the 20th century) was intended to communicate. Plan and structure, the play of light and space, not ornament, produced designs recognizable internationally. Decoration was stripped from buildings, a stylistic gesture itself symbolic. The act was heralded in Mies Van Der Rohe's (1938) proposals for Illinois Institute of Technology, and given widespread critical sanction through Harvard University's Graduate Center (1949). Those seeking strong placemarkers for new campuses in the 1960s championed the style enthusiastically. The University of Illinois, Chicago Circle was molded in poured concrete, sans ornament. In Bochum, West Germany, the forms, styles, and construction for the new university campus were rationalized and coordinated through computerized planning and design techniques and on-site factories that produced the industrialized building components. A comparable approach, less intimidating physically, was successfully devised for York University, one of Britain's ten post-World War II universities.

The Spartan works now seem dated. For all their presumed rationality, neither the Chicago nor Bochum campuses have gained critical acceptance as comely places. The Graduate Center is a landmark now because it expresses three-dimensionally the hopes of its designers, but not the realization of their objective to build a new architecture that would span the ages. Mies's buildings at IIT, extensively imitated in campus architecture elsewhere, no longer inspires emulation.

Unquestionably, the sovereign styles were set aside in the late 1940s. By one count, two-thirds of all college and university buildings have been constructed in the past 40 years, much of that in the mid-20th century styles. The dominion of brick and stone was superseded by extensive use of modern materials: concrete, glass, metal. On older campuses, the new buildings stood out as beacons of aesthetic enlightenment. More often than not, or so it seems in retrospect, each new commission offered the designer an opportunity to determine a fresh interpretation of a modern building. A sense of visual unity, that was the hallmark of sovereign styles, was traded in for a collage of disparate designs.

Stale as some such mid-20th century designs may now seem, their beginnings were charged with the excitement of pioneering ventures. Hope motivated creativity, as designers sought building solutions that were intended to be an art for our times. The results are not impressive. In the main, current critical opinion does not rate many campus buildings from the past four decades as exemplars of building technology, aesthetics, or site development. Despite a rhetoric that lauded the technological premises which should have engendered rationale designs, the building's mechanical systems were inadequate, costly to operate, and difficult to repair and maintain. Acoustics were poor. Experiments in roof shapes, cladding, and interior surfaces were economic and aesthetic disasters, though well received initially.

Late 20th Century Styles

The ornamentless styles that were promoted as being so appropriate in the mid-20th century now seem lifeless. Young critics would fault the movement—not for a lack of nerve in rejecting the picturesque, the eclectic, the pseudo-historic, "but a failure in eyesight." Less was a bore.

What then came forth were concepts of contextual architecture. The building environs would yield visual clues, fragments and images to be incorporated in the new construction; a cop-out, some would claim . . . "a consensus based on the aesthetics of conservation: old places, old buildings, old styles, old values . . . (calling) in the fading beauty of the old world to redress the squalor of the new."

In turn, Post-Modern and Post-Functional aesthetic concepts take their place on the architectural stage, with a script not yet finished. Some favor a rerun of early modernism, but done right. Others want an architecture that is sensual, sculptural, symbolic, highly imagistic, and sometimes culturally induced. This would not be a trans-global style, but regional in origin.

For a world where cultural differentiation is increasingly blurred, the possibilities of distinctiveness through invented styles, carefully deliberated, could be appealing to colleges and universities on philosophic and aesthetic grounds, when such styles are not fads and fashions. The idea resonates with an older truth, that architecture is a silent but persuasive teacher. What is called for is the architectural equivalent of *terrier,* the latter a gastronomy reflecting the products, techniques, traditions of a given region. Exploratory design studies for two new campuses, Saudi Arabia and Malaysia, suggest how such styles might be determined. In these examples, the searching eye seeks clues in ways of life, building forms, climate, and materials. Campus architecture does not then express a universal allegiance to recognizable worldwide aesthetic themes, such as those implicit in the International Style, but a sense of place responsive to local stimulus.

The dividing line between regional authenticity and the architectural gestures that entertain in Disneyland is not easily determined; but obviously worth pursuing. Whether trans-global or regional styles, the selection and utilization of building materials, a mark of authenticity, should get special attention in campus design. For in many instances, the dilemma of style, with the limitations of a codified vocabulary of shapes and forms, could be ignored in favor of the continuity that is offered by using a defined palette of building materials. Emulation does not have to be stylistic imitation. The beginning designs can be left intact to celebrate their time and proclaim their place. Building materials alone could provide the visual and symbolic linkages between generations and aesthetic attitudes.

The designers of the mid-20th century Trinity College academic grouping simulated the color and texture of the older masonry composition as concrete became the fashionable material for collegiate architecture. For some the simplified massing was a reasonable placemarker for its time and place; others would have preferred a modern interpretation of the small-grained detailing of the older buildings. (RPD)

Miesean style, Illinois Institute of Technology. (RPD)

TAC's Graduate Center (1949), Harvard University. (RPD)

Bochum, West Germany. (RPD)

York University, United Kingdom. Stylish essays in on-site mechanized concrete production. (RPD)

Trinity College, Hartford, 19th century. (RPD)

Trinity College, Hartford, 20th century. (RPD)

This aspect of campus design, often overlooked and underappreciated, can be demonstrated in some edifying and historic examples of campus architecture. Here, certain architectural forms and shapes reminiscent of the traditional styles may evoke precedent; but the underlying theme of continuity and generational connections is also expressed in materials. The materials become visual reference points. Such designs can be persuasive campus placemarkers; especially when the stylistic canons and codes are corrupted, and only a sense of color and texture may remain as to indicate symbolic meaning and to provide visual coherence. Thus used, trans-style, continuity in materials strengthens a sense of place. In other instances, the utilization of building materials that are different from the existing palette can announce new institutional attitudes. The resulting architecture might then serve as heralds and icons of desired change, with equal place-marking effectiveness.

Universiti Kabangsaan Malaysia. Studies of vernacular architecture are used to generate building prototypes and campus design guidelines. Here the warm and wet climate and regional architecture affect the proposed solutions. Skidmore, Owings and Merrill, Architects. Dober, Lidsky, Craig and Associates, Consultants. (SOM)

King Abdul Azziz University. Saudia Arabia. Vernacular design treatments in the hot and dry desert region provide a design direction for the university building groupings. Skidmore, Owings and Merrill, Architects. Dober, Lidsky, Craig and Associates, Consultants. (SOM)

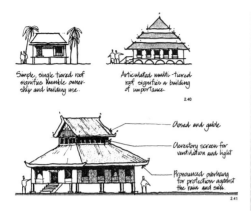

Simple, single-tiered roof signifies humble ownership and building use.

Articulated multi-tiered roof signifies a building of importance.

2.40

Closed end gable

Clerestory screen for ventilation and light

Pronounced overhang for protection against the rain and sun.

2.41

BUILDING SCALE

With the exception of palaces, few of the traditional buildings of Malaysia are large in scale. An appropriate way of achieving this smaller scale in the Sabah campus is by using the pavilion style of architecture, a style in which smaller, individual modules can be joined together to create large functional areas.

The pavilion style also provides flexibility in adapting to the natural environment. Individual modules are more flexible than single masses in conforming to the immediate topography and can even provide some advantages in utilizing natural ventilation and lighting.

Finally, the pavilion style will help to create a built environment of human scale. Buildings will be limited to a height that facilitates stairway access to all floor levels and that complements the existing scale of the natural surroundings.

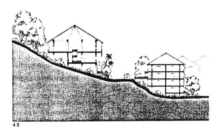

4.9

3.50

University Core Facility Courtyards

Beyond the gateway, a series of linked courtyards give identity to major core elements and to the Faculties of Sharia and Dawa. Arcades define these courts and provide protection from the sun. Shade trees, shrubs, and ground covers afford richness and variety for each space. Water elements in protected sitting areas add further interest.

3.52

Transition Courtyards

These areas provide a distinct transition from the major campus courtyards to circulation networks in academic and residential areas. Partially covered by arcades and roofed walks, they signal the beginning of the academic spines and give them identity.

Materials

Building materials are the elementary stuff of campus architecture. Wood, stone, brick, concrete, glass, metal—colored, textured, and formed, they constitute the design fabric, a building's immediately perceptible aspect.

Arguably, as climate determines habitation patterns, materials determine architecture. In the broad scale of human existence, admirable examples of the built environment are relatively recent in origin. Stone and baked clay architecture may be dated back 6,000 years. Works with steel and glass are less than two centuries old. The extensive use of processed aluminum in architecture is of recent origin. Each material required its own building construction methods so it could be used structurally, as a space enclosing fabric, and for decoration. Shapes and surfaces reflected the intrinsic qualities, at least until inventive minds, for fashion or economy, found ways to simulate the appearance of one with the materials of the other.

The identification and selection of exterior materials is sometimes overlooked in appreciating how designers give architecture a particular look. Finding Portland stone could be cut and transported in large blocks, Christopher Wren adjusted his designs accordingly, using "over a million tons" for St. Paul's Cathedral and for many parts of his London churches. The city's sense of place was strongly marked by Wren's choices, just as many campuses are today remembered because of a predominant building material, which at some time someone had to select. Why? Technical reasons, economics, aesthetics? How? And to meet what objectives?

Our interest here is the manner in which building materials serve as a metaphor of institutional presence; referential architecture, that is, design concepts in which consistency and continuity in materials on the building exteriors helps create a sense of place.

As will be documented, the visual results are like the treasured beauty found in certain vernacular architecture, where materials blend singular forms and rich detail into a readily perceived panoramic unity. Almost axiomatically, the best campus designers have sought to achieve this unity by connecting their work visually to the work of earlier generations by establishing a visual continuity through the use of materials, or imposing their own unity when the opportunity was presented, or by making a unique statement with contrasting materials.

The strongest campus design images are evoked when referential architecture is transformed into reverential architecture. In these instances—sometimes by mandate, sometimes through informal consensus—building materials are recognized as institutional emblems. The materials convey not just a distinctive sense of place visually, but the images also stir recollections and associations enriched by the institution's history.

Red brick, for example, suggests the Colonial American colleges. The material has been consistently used at William and Mary for traditional buildings and contemporary architecture. Three centuries of brick construction impart an ingrained image, comely and credible in Harvard Yard. The latest residential building (Canaday Hall, 1973) is joined in memory with the oldest (Massachusetts Hall, 1755) by this common material. Later, we examine how a modern material, concrete, was used at Harvard and the connotations for placemarking.

Referential/reverential architecture can be realized through different materials. The range of fabrics in the Southwest includes adobe (University of New Mexico), local stone (the University of Colorado, Boulder), and aluminum and glass (Air Force Academy). In the 1960s the University of La Verne wrapped two buildings in teflon-coated textile. The tenting gave the campus an image that drew tourists and students. On these campuses, placemarking through the use of materials is infused with allegorical and metaphorical significance.

Images of this kind can be created in campus sectors, as well as produced campus-wide. At Swarthmore College, the tweedy, gray, textured surface of its landmark building, Parrish Hall (Empire style, 1872) is echoed in a Collegiate Gothic chapel (1923), repeated in a modern library and dining hall constructed two generations later, and found in several residential halls whose dates span almost a century of construction. Draped over the college's south slope, in a vehicular-free precinct, the buildings and the landscape form a strong image, a campus design paradigm. In contrast, Swarthmore's north sector does not yet have this continuity, and the resulting campus design is less pronounced.

On the campuses cited and those discussed later, the visual continuity experienced through the use of materials also takes on a transcendental quality. A sense of place is charged with architectural effects that bind generations with agreement on materials, yet without denying each a chance to express and to celebrate their own values in an architectural style self-determined.

MATERIALS: MARKING NOT STYLING

In campus design, continuity in materials can be used to mark a place, honor antecedents, and connect generations. To demonstrate the point conceptually, it is desirable to unhook materials—as a specific, tactile, visual, design phenomenon, from their stylistic implications. Canonically, this may be heresy, rule-wrecking commentary which might enervate orthodox critical standards. As noted earlier, Collegiate Georgian is often associated with brick and Collegiate Gothic with cut stone. Those rules and conventions have yielded some alluring architecture in the past, as has comparable tenets devised for our own age. Sometimes, however, the desired effects mask dubious results.

Brick detail, Massachusetts Hall (1718), Harvard University. The oldest extant masonry building in Harvard Yard, several times renovated. (RPD)

St. Paul Cathedral district, London. The modern buildings attempt to provide visual continuity through colors and textures comparable to Wren's. (RPD)

University of La Verne. An unusual combination of modern materials and forms as institutional placemarkers. (RPD)

Parish Hall, Swarthmore College. (RPD)

Brick detail, Sever Hall (1878), Harvard University. H. H. Richardon's homage to history. (RPD)

Brick detail, Canaday Hall (1973), Harvard University. Architect Ezra Ehrenkrantz establishes visual continuity. (RPD)

Chapel, Swarthmore College. (RPD)

Dining hall, Swarthmore College. (RPD)

At Swarthmore College the strong sense of place is achieved through consistent use of materials rather than time-bound styles. The stone can be found in domestic and public buildings throughout region.

Greek Revival.

Transylvania College (1833), Old Morrison. (RPD)

Gettysburg College (1837), Pennsylvania Hall. (RPD)

Princeton University (1893), Clio Hall. (RPD)

White facades and hints of classical Greece mark time and place and a celebration of intellectual values. More often than not the Greek Revival building was a box with the classical columns and orders arranged as a temple-like portico at the front door. The geometric formula could be easily copied from pattern books. Elegantly proportioned, the structures usually were sited as free-standing designs on a green lawn; strong placemarkers then and now.

Thus, in the early 19th century, when money was scarce but idealism rampant, colleges would raise temple-like buildings, Greek Revival style. Economies lead to stagecraft architecture, edifices constructed with wood; sawn, nailed and painted white to look like the limestone, marble, or granite in classical architecture; and at Princeton, the reverse sequence when money and motivation permitted in 1893.

That the chaste, white, American structures had but a superficial relationship to Aegean architecture was ignored. The cultural values implied by the style "founded on classic myth, classic literature, classic art," writes its best interpreter, Talbot Hamlin, were as warmly embraced as the pleasure offered to those seeking visual relief from typical red brick Old Mains. Gideon Shyrock's flagship building (1833) for Morrison College (now Transylvania College) is a fine example; Pennsylvania Hall (1837), Gettysburg College, is another. The appearance of stone masonry building materials, faked and real, broadcasted the new attitudes and aesthetics. The "whiteness" marked both place and philosophy.

With this broad acceptance, why then did the Greek Revival fade way? Tamlin sees it as a derivative style where the conflicts between "clap-trap stage scenery construction" and the functional and economic advantages of industrial age building technologies could not be resolved. "Elaborations with the cheapest, most unsuitable materials in imitation of others more expensive to obtain and to work" were a major failing. The "emotional effect . . . was the essential thing . . . The whole cult of the picturesque was designed to disintegrate building techniques and lower building standards."

Parenthetically, to some extent, the cult of concrete as a 20th century material is suspect on similar grounds, not so much for its picturesque appearance, but quite the opposite, as will be suggested later.

HARKNESS QUAD/MORSE AND STILES COLLEGES

Relevant, then, to this discussion would be an instance of imagery—quality construction—utilizing materials that bind many generations visually and symbolically, and in doing so create a noteworthy campus design. The Yale campus provides an instructive example for that inquiry.

Of many architects commissioned to shape the Yale architecture, James Gamble Rogers was probably the most facile. He was capable and willing to give his clients whatever version of a sovereign style most suited the patron's values and the architect's persuasiveness, which in Rogers' case was considerable. Rogers was a plastic artist whose building facades are inventive and enjoyable to read long after the style he promoted was no longer fashionable.

As Wren did in the 17th century for fire-wracked London, Rogers went hunting for a stone that would give his architectural composition (Harkness Quadrangle, Yale University) a fresh surfacial quality. Rogers found his material in the old Plymouth quarries, East Weymouth, Massachusetts.

He arranged the stone in irregular chunks, untooled or smoothed on the outer side, and set with thick mortar, purposefully not polished and close-joined like "mausoleums and tombstones." In some of the Harkness quadrangles, he gave the building bases and gateways additional color and texture with a subtle tapestry of sand blasted bricks salvaged from old buildings. "Fine effects," noticed an

Branford Quadrangle, Yale University (1933). A segment of the Harkness Quad development designed by James Gamble Rogers. (RPD)

Morse and Ezra Stiles Colleges (1960), Eero Saarinen. Sterling Library tower is beyond.

Frank Dining Hall, Colgate University. Herbert S. Newman. A generation-binding building using materials and forms to recall an earlier campus landmark. (RPD)

The visual connections to the older Yale buildings were suggested in the color and texture of the building materials. (RPD)

early commentator, these "irregular courses of brick laid with careful carelessness in thick mortar."

Not all agreed. The Harkness designs, especially Rogers' eccentric vertical walls, agitated some critics who judged Rogers' work against what they considered to be more sober, reliable, and authentic interpretations of Collegiate Gothic. The latter were superficially derived from medieval models, but functionally far removed from modern college building requirements, practices, and codes.

Questionable then and now as a stylistic statement, the Harkness complex holds it own as a robust architectural landmark. The buildings have the added value as placemarker today because they inspired a progressive design concept that embraced continuity in materials.

Rogers repeated the textured facade in his Sterling library. Four decades after Rogers, Eero Saarinen incorporated his interpretation of the Harkness and Sterling buildings' color and texture in his audacious housing complex for Yale's Morse and Stiles colleges (1962). The irregular plan, with its nook and cranny spaces, expressed the Saarinen's wish to avoid repetitive cubes and squares on the site or in the building. The walls were made by placing pieces of granite in a mold, steel reinforcement was added, and concrete grout poured in under high pressure. Twenty-four hours after curing, the shutters were removed and the surfaces cleaned. The resulting vertical surfaces recalled Rogers', yet involved contemporary technologies and materials.

Saarinen's designs troubled purists. By attempting to define a modern interpretation of the older designs, in contrast to ignoring its presence, they felt he compromised modern architecture, as it was then defined. A tempered view now judges the results differently. Saarinen's work at Morse and Stiles is well connected to Rogers', and that in turn to earlier versions of Collegiate Gothic, and they in turn to European revivals and beginnings. The implied cultural associations and educational linkages were symbolically meaningful for Yale. Through materials, more than an interpretation of style and decoration, the new was coupled to the old. The linkages were expressed through two sets of buildings by two designers generations apart in most things, but sharing a fine eye for richly textured architecture.

The Rogers-Saarinen interplay illustrates a campus design technique that will serve well when there is reason to give a sector of an existing campus a distinctive image; or to celebrate an institution's place and history through the use of materials on an important building, when such materials can take on these metaphoric connotations. Herbert S. Newman's recent masterwork for Colgate University (1988) is an illuminating example of this principle of referential architecture. Frank Dining Hall utilizes shapes and forms that can be read as part of Colgate Hall, a 19th century edifice once the library and now an administration building. The selection of materials reinforces the sense of place visually in a becoming, generation-binding architectural gesture.

MATERIALS: METAPHORS OF TIME

Campus design images are visually stronger when the exterior building surfaces can be read as symbols associated with campus history, and thus help mark both

Colorado School of Mines. Late 19th century landmark building. (RPD)

Colorado School of Mines. Late 20th century landmark building. (RPD)

Free University, West Berlin. The everchanging cor-ten steel was selected to symbolize the advance of knowledge and the institution's status as a modern university emancipated from earlier traditions. (RPD)

Kennedy School (1974), Harvard University. Architectural Resources of Cambridge, Inc. design, with SBRA's 1930 river houses and Collegiate Georgian tower beyond. (RPD)

Kennedy School (1990). The 1990 TAC addition to the right. The hotel and housing designed by the Cambridge Seven to the left. All the buildings use brick as the local metaphoric placemarker. (RPD)

place and time. To each era, a material—an evocation readily apparent in the two landmark buildings at the Colorado School of Mines.

Harvard's red brick reminds us of the colonial beginnings. Large windows framed by aluminum suggest modern times and aesthetics. As an institutional metaphor, the combination of both serve well in the designs for the Kennedy School of Government. The metaphoric brick clothes new private housing and commercial buildings in the immediate environs, designs by several firms, a visually satisfying mix of campus and civic design. With slate and stone, the environs of the University of Edinburgh are equally joined visually to collegiate buildings new and old, a strong image in a handsome city worth noting.

The manifesto that accompanied the prize-winning competition drawings for the Free University of West Berlin (1969) championed change and flexibility, philosophically and physically. The client believed that the provision for change was essential for institutional viability. The architects and engineers responded with a clever arrangement of interior spaces that could be easily adjusted through flexible, modular partitioning and structural systems—"language technologique." Wishing to clad their buildings with a material as contemporary in outlook as the university mission, and as inventive as its campus plan, the West Berlin architects chose cor-ten steel for the exterior surfaces. The metal cladding on the outer shell would be permanent, but its surface would slowly rust, to give the facade a distinctive patina. The all-encompassing metal became an institutional metaphor, a marker of place and time.

Of the many possible materials, concrete would seem to be the metaphoric material for modern times, our 20th century. The clamp it has on technology and symbolism can be seen in thousands of college and university buildings worldwide: concrete poured, paneled, fabricated, stressed with steel for structural strength, sometimes bush-hammered for appearance. As a predominant 20th century building material, few college and university concrete buildings existed prior to 1940. These days, few are planned. The reasons are illuminating, though necessarily conjectural. They inform the definitions and importance of campus design imagery as offered here; but always with a necessary caveat.

In judging the efficacy of the built environment, an abstract ideal (such as materials serving as metaphors) may stimulate the imagination, and may generate a sense of place, but what counts most is the realized construction—such matters as functional fit, human scale, and a sensitive integration of site and environment. Against this standard, concrete architecture on many campuses is suspect. A brief review of why this may be so can offer insights for evaluating existing campus designs and for determining those not yet constructed.

CONCRETE: BEGINNINGS

Concrete's remarkable architectural qualities are as old as western civilization. The Pantheon testifies to concrete's durability, strength, and dramatic space-enclosing capabilities. Though these characteristics were noted in 19 centuries of architectural commentary that followed the Roman empire, the material was seldom utilized, mostly due "to an ingrained conviction that ashlar was the only respectable material for better class buildings." Brick was the second choice, when stone was unavailable.

Attitudes began to change in Louis XVI's reign. The desire to speed up construction and to economize on materials gave cause to imitate expensive architecture with mortar-bound stuccoed rubble which could be manipulated to simulate the exterior patterns of more costly buildings. A shortage of building materials after the French Revolution, the need for fireproof construction in dense urban areas, and an evolving tradition among French engineers for experimentation in technologies and materials provided both reasons and skills for fostering concrete architecture in 19th century France. Ranking high in these achievements is the parish church at Le Vesinet (1864), designed by Louis-Charles Boileau, the first modern concrete institutional structure.

At the beginning of the 20th century, concrete was typically employed in utilitarian structures: bridges, factories, and stadia. In Midwest farm towns, the grain silos were prominent landmarks, but not viewed as artworks; though they would later inspire painters and photographers. Though blessed by the avant garde as the choice material in the "vision of a new architecture" (a point well documented in Peter Collin's history of concrete architecture), most concrete structures were ranked low in aesthetic esteem, but not everywhere, however. In 1903, Harvard University completed its Soldiers Field Stadium, a pioneering enterprise, including what was at that time the largest single, continuous poured concrete structure in the world. Summing up the institution's architectural achievements at its 350th anniversary, historian Bainbridge Bunting labeled the stadium ". . . a masterpiece . . . functionally almost perfect, structurally innovative, and aesthetically advanced." Bunting believed the stadia "proved conclusively the aesthetic viability of massive ferroconcrete—the material Frank Lloyd Wright would use two years later at Unity Temple in Chicago."

The Harvard stadium project was one of three experiments in concrete buildings that Harvard faculty promoted and designed on the south side of the Charles River. Cary Cage and gatelodge (1897) and Weld Boathouse (1906) were not raw, large-span, buildings, but well proportioned, with an outer layer of exposed dark aggregate, accented with brick. The designs were the collaborative efforts of engineers and architects, Harvard professors, who championed concrete for its technical and artistic qualities.

Harvard's enthusiasm for concrete was somewhat at odds with popular critical opinion. Columbia's architectural guru, Professor A. D. F. Hamlin (1907), saw concrete as an "ungrateful and repellent material for exterior architectural effect." His outlook was shared by fellow academic Russell Sturgis, who hoped "that concrete would not replace stone for the artistic parts of our buildings." Underappreciated were concrete's plasticity for enclosing unencumbered large spaces; the manner in which aggregates could be used for texture and color; and the various ways that concrete panels and components could be casted elsewhere and then assembled to articulate and define the building facades and structural systems. Tony Garnier's Une Cite Industrielle (1918) demonstrated the potential. ". . . A signpost clearly marking a period now passed and opening up all possible hopes for the future," wrote Le Corbusier.

CONCRETE: THE 20TH CENTURY TRADEMARK

By the 1930s the tide changed, conceptually and in practice. Concrete buildings became fashionable topics, first in trailblazing magazines, and then in the mainstream of architectural journalism. In his influential examination of 20th century architecture, Sigfried Giedeon (1941) heralded concrete as one of the "trademarks of the new architecture." It was believed the material had intrinsic characteristics, truths, which when discovered would yield objectively defined architecture. The resulting shapes and forms would liberate designer and client from having to imitate or interpret styles from earlier generations.

Giedeon's history-as-manifesto (Space, Time, and Architecture) inspired several generations of designers and clients. As architecture, their successes and failures are still under scrutiny. Their concrete campus buildings are remarkably different than their predecessors, as campus histories and picture books now reveal. Less remembered in campus chronologies is the intellectual and artistic excitement that gave birth to these structures; an audacious awakening to a new aesthetic for a new world. The "rise and fall of the curtain wall," the "mystic of concrete"—the pros and cons of the material were well debated in technical and philosophical terms, as these lecture topics from old classroom notes would indicate.

Acceptable, indeed highly desired, concrete architecture provided much of the space that served the rapid and unparalleled growth and democratization of higher education following World War II. For many of America's community colleges, in many postwar British Universities, and in certain elite institutions where the new materials replaced brick and stone, concrete buildings became the signals of institutional advancement. Concrete became not just an acceptable material for the traditional forms of institutional architecture but an emblem of its age.

Of Harvard University's president, Nathan M. Pusey, it has been said (in a variation of an Augustan aphorism), that Pusey found the campus in brick and left it with concrete. In the mid-20th century, the use of concrete aesthetically, preached in the Harvard classrooms (Giedeon), practiced by Harvard's dean and architectural advisor (Jose Luis Sert), and embraced by the administration and patrons, found its embodiment in Harvard's tallest building, its most urban structure, and most artful edifice, the latter a tribute-giving monument by concrete's prominent 20th century designer, Le Corbusier.

How much is concrete architecture a metaphor of time and place?

> Lord Clark chose to conclude his television series "Civilization" in front of the residential terraces at the University of East Anglia, a stage set or perhaps a backdrop for the pursuit of learning in the present and the future. (Of the seven new English universities) he chose the one whose architecture has most consciously created a visual impression of experiment and inquiry, yet without the use of bizarre forms or materials, and notably without recourse to any academic architectural precedent.
>
> (*Building The New Universities*, 1972)

For the knowledgeable, the East Anglia concept had precedent (the paradigm of connected buildings); the specific forms were the architect's own; the ennobled material was concrete. Worldwide, from the mid-1950s through the 1970s, concrete was, in the main, the preferred chosen material for modern campus buildings. Bastion-like, many such assertive designs hunkered down on their sites with little regard to the surrounding context. Ornament-free detailing became a symbolic indicator, in contrast to traditional elaborated window and door trimming. Reputations were made on the basis of close tolerance designs for joining modern materials: glass, concrete, aluminum. Where swags and fluting once gave playful shadowing, the framing for the poured concrete etched and orchestrated light and shadow. In some instances, mechanical tools would hammer the concrete surface for texture and to reveal color gradations. Roofs were flattened, and the building verticals and horizontals sharp-edged, where they were not rounded sculpturally. These purposeful refinements on concrete buildings were powerful value-loaded designs, though now apparently dated and exhausted as cultural beacons.

However, apparently, some designers were unable to handle concrete materials technically. It would seem that construction methods could not keep pace with design intentions. Within a decade of their completion, three Harvard buildings "were experiencing significant enclosure problems. Solutions for the concrete deterioration were quite different in each case, ranging from patching to complete replacement of concrete facades." Observations and discussions at other institutions would indicate similar problems with buildings from this period.

On some campuses today, the appearance of concrete would seem to be not a material that manifests institutional advancement, but an error in aesthetic judgment. Further, unlike traditional designs, concrete architecture did not breed a complementary landscape. "To stand within (the quad) on a sunny day is painful to the eyes, for both pavement and the walls are white." Elsewhere, the heavy concrete planters which were expected to support trees, bushes, and plants, too often are now sterile and abandoned. The pride of using modern materials has given way to the depression of seeing stained, flaking, cracking concrete surfaces. When the site is wet and cloud-covered, moisture-dampened concrete is dreary and dismal. What was expected to be a scintillating architectural experience ends feeling like a visit to an Appalachian mining town on a grey winter's day. Cynics may have reason to say, that in concluding his version of civilization in front of the University of East Anglia, Kenneth Clark did pick an appropriate setting. But, in fairness, there are many examples of campus architecture which have been built successfully with concrete as the predominant material. Further, its increased utilization in the future may be necessary as timber and metal become scarcer and more expensive, reasons relating more to ecological imperatives than aesthetic interests.

A master of concrete, such as Sert, enlivens his Harvard facades with primary colors splashed on inset panels. Down river, the visual continuity afforded by concrete buildings at the Massachusetts Institute of Technology is impressive. "Materials can extend the memory of place, as well as mark it," says the Institute's planner, O. Robert Simha. On the East Campus, the feeling of continuity is carried forward from the original classical buildings to newer architecture with the utilization of a limited range of building textures, predominantly masonry architecture.

With comparable effect, Pomona College has achieved a similar unity. The campus design emphasizes the landscape. A century of concrete architecture is

Harvard University, Cary Cage (1897). The roofline inspired by a Janapese exhibit at the Columbian Exposition; the concrete materials, the faculty's experiment. (RPD)

Facade detail, Soldiers Field Stadium, Harvard University. In 1901 the largest ever single poured reinforced concrete structure. (RPD)

Detail, Weld Boathouse, Harvard University (1906). Concrete modified with elegant brick detailing. (RPD)

William James Hall (1963). A soaring tower on a souring podium; out of character with its surrounds. (RPD)

Four buildings from the era of concrete architecture at Harvard University: Carpenter, Holyoke, Gutman and Hilles.

Carpenter Center (1961). LeCorbusier. Significant only because Corbu designed it. (RPD)

Holyoke Center (1962). A fine space on the street level. Tough concrete architecture above. (RPD)

Trinity College, Dublin. (RPD)

Housing sector, University of East Anglia. (RPD)

Variations in the configuration of modern concrete buildings. As it weathers, the texture and color of the new Trinity College building is intended to blend with the nearby classical edifice. Being an entirely new university campus, the East Anglia complex leaves the challenge of visual continuity to the next generation.

Gutman Library (1968). A hard-edge concrete building softened by a welcoming landscape. (RPD)

Hilles Library (1965). Landscape again makes pleasant a dated concrete building. (RPD)

Massachusetts Institute of Technology. (RPD)

Pomona College. (RPD)

Concrete as a metaphor of modernity with visual continuity provided through the use of masonry materials which identify and sustain a sense of place.

directed to serve, not dominate, the scenery. Nonetheless, a building requiring architectural significance can be developed without compromise to campus design principles. The new gymnasium (1989) draws on the limited palette of construction colors and textures, yet emerges as a special thread in a tapestry of buildings and greenery which Pomona has come to prize as its campus design image.

At Trinity College, Dublin, the aging concrete facades take on a surfacial resemblance to the older, stone, 18th century Georgian buildings. If not intended, the result is nonetheless a harmonious ensemble. Concrete seems technically and visually appropriate in climates where masonry architecture mitigates potential damage from insects and molds, and where there are extreme variations in temperature and humidity. But if prizes and publicity denote current practice, which in turn would influence the next wave of campus architecture, then concrete as a metaphor of institutional advancement no longer is a "trademark" material. The facades of published work in the 1980s and early 1990s are embroidered with fine-grain masonry, such as brick; or animated by details that abstract traditional architectural shapes; or, the surfaces are textured with a mix of natural and manufactured materials. An unspoken rule seems to inform these designs: the materials in nearby buildings appear in the new facades to provide some degree of visual continuity, not contrast.

Strengthening Referential Campus Designs

Referential campus designs are those all-powerful images of place which once experienced are not easily forgotten. A discussion of methods and a further description of instructive case examples is best introduced by noting how campus design patterns differ from campus design inflections; that is, placemaking versus placemarking—a didactic salted by some theory.

Patterns emerge from processes that define the built environment in two dimensions (plan), or three dimensions (enclosed space). Inflections provide metaphorical meaning. Placemarkers serve as institutional symbols or emblems; but placemaking designs can also accomplish this objective.

In *Signs, Symbols and Architecture* (1980), Geoffrey Broadbent identifies four processes which he believes designers use to create built forms. The *pragmatic* process involves trial and error, like the evolution of the igloo or primitive reed hut. The *iconic* begins with an idealized form, which is then adapted to local conditions and construction practices. A wooden temple, for example, is erected in stone. *Analogic* designs are derived from models, a simulation of forms appearing in nature, such as shell architecture; or a concept appearing first in another medium, as de Stijl painting inspired Dutch architecture in the early 20th century. *Geometric* processes use dimensional formulas, that is, units which measure space and building components. These in turn are used in prescriptive formulas that generate floor plans, facades, and volumes; for example, Le Corbusier's Modular, or the numerical, and sometimes mystical, reckonings of a medieval master mason.

Without laboring the point, one will find that prototype campus designs, ensemble architecture, may emerge from comparable design processes. There are designs that evolve from trial and error; designs that reinterpret earlier models; designs that are inspired by site arrangements not originally found in the architecture of higher education; and designs based on geometrical concepts. The first and second are self-evident, the distribution of buildings, open spaces, and landscapes that are sui generis the typical, loosely structured American campus plan. Examples of the third include enclosed quadrangles and connected building enclaves that are derived from monastic models; or interpretations of Greek and Roman temple districts and forums. The fourth might be as simple a geometric ordering principle as the location of all highly utilized buildings within five minutes walking distance of a presumed centroid for optimum scheduling of facilities.

THE VERNACULAR AND OTHER CHOICES

Strong images can be induced when patterns and inflections reinforce each other through codes and canons that can be sensed by the uninitiated as well as those culturally knowledgeable. Collegiate Georgian, for example, will display a unity in site and interior space concepts, as well as materials and forms, and a detailing rich in symbolism—all enchained semiotically to convey a sense of place.

Arguably, the inferred meanings define the dividing line between building as a utilitarian object and building as an artform; or the campus as a place that facilitates specific functions versus the campus as an institutional emblem. The abstraction becomes real with the conscious employment of building materials for semiotic reasons; especially when the materials selected are visually dominant in panoramic settings that have a singular style, such as Duke University's West Campus; or when a selected material, such as brick, is used in varying styles throughout the campus, as at the College of William and Mary.

Some principles are reiterated: consistently used, materials can mark a place visually, symbolically and aesthetically. All three must play well to produce superior results. Metaphoric campus designs, meaningful for the memories they induce, enpowering architecture, should also be remembered for the pleasure they give, not their mordant assertiveness. The comely image may be difficult to achieve, but the methods are easy, if approached with a clear eye and a critical concern for the actual results.

Methods? In times past, the availability of local construction materials determined a building's surfacial appearance. Vernacular architecture in particular, spread over several centuries, had a family resemblance due to a harmonious use of regional stone, wood, and brick. Institutional buildings, secular and ecclesiastical, in the main, also drew on local plantations and quarries. Visually, the modest and the monumental were more alike than different. Whether seen in venerable, vernacular renditions such as the Cotswold villages, or urban designs created in a relatively short time span, such as 18th century Bath or Georgian Edinburgh, the purposeful application of a limited range of materials engendered ensemble architecture with a strong sense of place and time, universally accepted today as masterworks.

Compatible materials create a strong image worldwide, not just in Britain. Photographs of the backwater hamlets of ancient China, the remnants of Italy's peasant towns, and Sub-Saharan villages demonstrate this beauty. Nicely weathered, the enclaves are highly prized for their architectural harmony. What is true overseas is less evident in the United States, a younger country. The exceptional examples are equally prized, especially domestic architecture: silvery, shingled Nantucket; red brick Beacon Hill; pestled, stuccoed Art Deco apartments and vacation hotels in Miami Beach; Santa Fe's adobe residences. Here too, singular materials and building practices, preserved now by zoning and historic preservation codes, self-evidently serve as geographic placemarkers.

Myron Goldfinger distills these factors and considerations in his essay "Villages In the Sun" (1975). He saw in the vernacular architecture ideas which, if transformed into contemporary idioms, could reverse oncoming trends and attitudes which lead to apathetic, dull, repetitive, environmentally and socially insensitive community architecture.

Goldfinger's sermon was timely, though not new, nor startling. Gordon Cullen's philosophy of townscape covered the same ground (circa 1950) in a brilliant sequence of articles in the influential British magazine *Architectural Journal,* as did Bernard Rudosfsky in *Architecture Without Architects.* Their proclamations and insights are applicable to many aspects of campus design, especially at those places with a weak architectural heritage. How might the new strengthen the old and qualitatively improve such campus designs?

In these instances, the existing buildings, presumably uncommanding by most critical standards, would be treated (not ignored) as background architecture. The materials and details on the older buildings would provide visual cues for new designs. Views and vistas might be arranged in Cullenesque fashion. The resulting panorama would satisfy most eyes searching for the picturesque—a campus design objective which can be wrenched from the most humble and seemingly unpromising situation. To those who quibble that this is theatre not architecture: better a piece of contrived stagecraft than a visually dull campus.

The vernacular has always appealed to campus designers seeking unifying themes in their designs. Campuses with strong images have this consistency— their comeliness is palpable, purposeful, photogenic. The visual unity is further strengthened when designers orchestrate site, buildings, and landscape into coherent and connected designs. The patterns and inflections are worked together; sometimes campus-wide, as in the case examples of new campuses discussed below, or as in a campus sector, such as Saarinen's gesture to Rogers' earlier work at Yale, or the feel of brick at William and Mary, or the cut stone heritage that Benjamin Latrobe left at Dickinson College.

A campus well designed is a material well chosen. Brick and stone and painted wood—utilized in Colonial, Federal, Greek Revival, and Gothic architectural styles—these were the choice metaphoric materials during the first two centuries of American higher education. After the Civil War, colleges and universities grew in number, in tandem with westward expansion, pioneer settlements, and statehood. With the advent of industrialized building products, relatively cheap transport, and a design literacy nurtured by national magazines and the professionalization of architecture, dependency on local supplies and parochial styles was lessened. Choices were significantly enlarged, which in the broad spectrum of architectural time, gave (and gives) the current generation of designers the ability to select from an unprecedented and impressive range of exterior cladding. The import this has on the visual character of today's campuses, with the fashionable return of exterior color and textured surfaces, is not to be underestimated. A disciplined effort is needed to determine the timing and degree of continuity and change in the utilization of materials. Note the reflecting glass on the exterior facade of the Navajo Community College; an architectural gesture intended to demonstrate modernity, but too quickly a fashion now dated (Page 38).

In selecting building materials for exterior appearances, sometimes ordinary campus designs become enduring works of art when they are informed by an intelligent balancing of the client's expectations, the budget available, and a designer's prerogatives. The matching of concept and resources is an integral part of a design process—often methodically accomplished, but sometimes wrapped in charming intuition which can shadow hardheaded decisions as to what might be built and can be built. A Louis Kahn may hear building stones telling him what they wished to be architecturally; but there are other voices also speaking. The project budget and institutional politics, the influence of a finance officer, the outcome of design committee discussions, and trustee and donor preferences may also determine the eventual decision.

However the ideas are launched, experienced architects are able eventually to bridge reality's abyss—the gap between their beginning vision, the client's desires and resources. When the ideas are strong enough, vision will prevail. Two relatively recent instances illuminate this point. Both are new campuses, which since opening day continue to be well-regarded examples of modern architecture. The United States Air Force Academy (1956) utilized glass, aluminum, steel and concrete as its predominant building materials. The Rochester Institute of Technology (1970) was clothed in brick. Both are also fine examples of referential architecture, strong image campus designs.

THE UNITED STATES AIR FORCE ACADEMY

Over a thousand new American campuses open after World War II. Arguably, The United States Air Force Academy, Colorado Springs, Colorado, best represents the use of modern building materials and the power they have to suggest institutional and social values. The plans were announced in 1955, with the first buildings completed and occupied in August 1958. The months in between were filled with controversy about the designs in general, the chapel specifically, and cost overruns. Conceptually intended to be fingerposts for a new American architecture, the Acropolis for flight would convey "a national, not a regional character, the direct simple way of life, as styleless as the most modern guided missile . . . timeless." At the first public presentation, reported the *Architectural Record*, "assembled critics and congressman contemplated the glass and aluminum model buildings, boggled at the angular planes of the cathedral (sic), were awed by the scope and magnificence of the site and pronounced the whole presentation a solid hit. Thus passed, quietly, the eclectic era in government architecture." Not quite. And not quietly.

The uproar that followed the initial disclosures was intense, inflammatory, and impassioned. For a while, Congress held up a billion dollar defense budget, which included the $79 million appropriation for the Academy construction, self-evidently ransom for redesign. An "assembly of ugliness," cried one elected official; "a modernistic cigarette factor," said another; "an attempt to transplant New York City architecture to a Rocky Mountain area," complained a third. For Merton B. Tice, head of the Veterans of Foreign Wars, the designs were awful, "experimental architecture more suitable for a supermarket or factory than for a service academy." The negative opinions were shared by some presumably knowledgeable. "Shocking," commented Frank Lloyd Wright, "a fiasco . . . a glassified box on stilts . . . an imitation of modern architecture."

Surveying the criticisms, *The New York Times* editorialized that Congress would prefer buildings with "Greek arches, Roman domes and Gothic towers . . . variations blending Chartres Cathedral and Independence Hall." A modernistic campus conjured up "such radical images as Pablo Picasso, one-eyed women and melting watches." Above the fray, the paper understood "there should be objection to (schemes) that emphasize the 'functional' at the expense of the type of beauty that harmonizes with the setting." The *Times* offered no specific prescription or remedy, however, unlike Wright, who would start over with a competition among three leading American architects, with the final plans to be "approved by a jury of adolescents."

Not all commentary was churlish. The summer 1955 issue of *Art News* found the designs "impressive . . . twentieth century grandeur;" in keeping with the new attitudes about American architecture that was evident in the well-regarded embassy construction program overseas. The American ambassadorial presence in foreign lands was sheltered in modern designs that shed the traditional imperial styles associated with international status and diplomacy.

The political impasse over aesthetics could not wait long for tempered views to assuage the division of opinion. The necessity of getting the defense budget approved was essential for national security. At the same time that Wright and others were denouncing the Academy designs, President Eisenhower was convening a four power meeting in Europe to begin arms reduction, including delivery systems for the atomic bomb. The Air Force Academy's contributions to geopolitical strategies were more important than its architecture. Those guiding the resolution through Congress were wise enough to send that message through the back channels. They were also clever enough to identify compromises, make conciliatory gestures, and argue the issues on more (seemingly) pragmatic grounds than taste and fashion. The task was handled expeditiously. The outcomes illuminate the process by which controversial designs gain acceptance.

On the general aesthetic issue, Defense Secretary Talbot argued that "modified contemporary functional" architecture was necessary for economic reasons. An architecture comparable to West Point or Annapolis would cost "$250 to $750 million" compared to the $126 million appropriated for the Air Force Academy, he said. No real proof was offered. The idea of a prudent expenditure muted many criticisms. Parenthetically, actual expenditures soared to $190 million within one year. The final bill for opening day facilities two years later was approximated at $300 million.

Talbot moved the controversial chapel to the end of the construction sequence, with the implication it would be redesigned. The gesture pleased one senator who thought it "looked like an accordion, expandable with the student body." The eventual design, not out of character with the first concept, took 12 years to realize. It became an icon of modern architecture, a landmark building that draws universal praise and thousands of tourists to the academy site. On the question of glass, the metaphoric material that infuriated objectors, Talbot told Congress that the drawings in the first schemes were "only a picture of a picture." The new designs, revised within 60 days of the first presentations, would continue to be "straight-line modern," but have "forty percent less glass." Yes and no. As con-

Detail, USAFA Chapel, SOM. (RPD)

Detail, USAFA Academic Building, SOM. (RPD)

Detail, University of Illinois/Chicago. (RPD)

The Skidmore, Owings and Merrill Air Force Academy designs alarmed the public when first presented in 1955. Now much admired, the chapel is considered an icon of modern architecture. For some, the organization of the facades on certain of the Academy buildings are reminiscent of similar structures at the University of Illinois, Chicago campus, designed by the same firm; an indicator, perhaps, of style more than function.

struction proceeded some critic-placating modifications were made, but by then few were interested in measuring the amount of glass, or continuing a dialog (chapel excepted) whose tone and temper gained no headlines.

As a functional solution to the specific needs for training the cadets, the campus plan worked well. Despite the fact that the Air Force Academy did not become the national architecture that enthusiastic designers had projected, its real success was evident early. Reporting on progress in 1958, the young Russell Baker wrote: "From an amalgam of aluminum, glass and brilliant colors against the grandeur of the Pike's Peak, the newest service academy has caught the spirit of the space age . . . sleek, airy, and starkly functional . . . not a hint of West Point's grim Gothic or Annapolis's Colonial."

Carleton College. Seventy years of construction, three styles, with brick as the unifying campus design factor. (RPD)

RIT: UNITY AND VARIETY

The 1960 decision to relocate Rochester Institute of Technology from its crowded downtown quarters to a new 1,300 acre site at the edge of the metropolis was couched in stringent terms that would, in many circumstances, compromise the designs of most new campuses. Each major building was given to a different architect, who would work with a user group representing a constituent academic unit. By the standards of that time, the overall budget was low, $20 million for site improvement and $40 million for buildings. As designs proceeded the schedule was tightened, and had to be met for logistical reasons, as the move-in day became fixed.

The prospect of peril, however, was used to discipline the project designs. Through a cooperative effort managed by the coordinating designer, Lawrence B. Anderson, and with a location plan hammered out by landscape architect, Daniel Kiley, five different firms were able to produce buildings tailored to their client's programs, and at the same time fit them into an overall scheme. The outcome was "a successful example of collaborative design" as cited by the American Institute of Architects, which gave the project its 1972 Medal for Achievement in Architecture.

The central complex was envisioned as a megastructure, the flat site animated by courtyards and gardens, and punctuated by a seven-story administrative tower, with the overall design fused by a common exterior material, brick. A megastructure made sense in the northern New York climate, and was economic in terms of utility runs and land use. Brick was practical as it gave a unifying appearance to structures with different forms, window, and door patterns; which, in turn, were positioned because of interior functions, configurations, and massing dictated by the individual building programs. The facade's outside color and texture was not easily settled, however.

Project accounts describe lively debates about brick's symbolic meaning and aesthetic suitability, in as much as seven million units would be used. The initial choice was a handmade, textured model with an Ivy League pedigree; but this

Rochester Institute of Technology (1962). (RPD)

Rochester Institute of Technology (1962).
(RIT)

Brick, a traditional material associated with American higher education, encloses more than a million square feet of varying institutional functions at RIT. The comely rendition of a common material is considered a metaphor of institutional presence.

gave way to a smooth, production line, contemporary brick, suggesting modern technology. With that agreement, the task of detailing special sizes and shapes and finish was left to the coordinating architect. The brick was also used in certain interior arcades, on walks and walls. No transient theophany, the design inflection blended the vertical and horizontal planes harmoniously and was intended to symbolize the institution's purposes.

"An important achievement" noted an early critical assessment (1971). The campus plan became "the framework for bold compositional effects, bold vistas, beautifully scaled courtyards, . . . these architects have collaborated to establish and work within a common esthetic, which includes a shared vocabulary of structure, scale and materials to achieve a campus as unified as a medieval city."

The beginning ideas have coalesced into a significant example of campus design; once seen, not forgotten. Recently evaluating the design's efficacy as an institutional image, RIT's president wrote (1990): "The design of the Rochester Institute of Technology campus, which uses brick as a coordinating material, is as fresh today as it was in 1968 . . . new buildings have been added since then and a variety of architects involved, but RIT has maintained the integrity of original design concepts . . . (We are) architecturally distinct from many colleges and university campuses, trees have matured and, along with an array of plantings, have added to the total RIT campus environment. In the final analysis the design of the facilities supports RIT's image as a contemporary, progressive quality career university."

THEMATIC VARIATIONS

Occasionally, the use of materials can be modified and modulated without damage to an overall campus design effect when there are other visual clues that help reinforce a particular sense of place. Where RIT's building surfaces are deliberately controlled, and constrained, the buildings at California State University, Fullerton, are more animated, ranging from flat slabs to decorative scrolling. Coherence comes from a predominant building color and material, white masonry, which in combination with a vibrant green landscape, is effective placemarking.

To achieve that sense of place through the consistent use of materials, the University of Miami (Coral Gables) has codified the choices available to its building architects. New construction must conform to the campus design guidelines. The exterior look of some older buildings will be modified to approximate the colors in the guidelines when their time has come in the painting cycle. A regional material, coral stone, was selected for design accents. By varying the use of the stone in doorways, windows, and walls, background buildings can be distinguished from foreground buildings. The stone provides a geographic reference, linking university, site, and region metaphorically with a symbolic building material. Wren's St. Paul's precinct is an antecedent, where even the brain-dead work of the present generation blends into the cityscape through a common color. Similarly, Dickinson and Duke were cited earlier as campuses where stone is quarried locally and used extensively in the college buildings, thus generating a strong sense of place.

The Miami concept has several perspicacious precedents, such as the Auraria Higher Education Center, the City College of New York, and the State University of New York, Purchase. These are examined below in greater detail for the insights they offer on several aspects of campus development, including the selection of materials as a metaphor and modus operandi in campus design.

Auraria varies materials to mark its common-purpose buildings locationally. George B. Post's designs for City College of New York is a notable variation of Collegiate Gothic, critically underappreciated as a comprehensive campus design. As in the Rogers–Saarinen work at Yale, later designers at CCNY were able to echo some of Post's original site-inspired visual themes, thus strengthening a sense of place. The SUNY, Purchase campus uses modern building products to give a unified feeling to a campus designed by many firms under the aegis of a single master plan. The exterior materials were selected and applied as a simple ordering device, which, like RIT, permitted a group of architects to give each building their individual cachet, yet produce a design ensemble.

AURARIA HIGHER EDUCATION CENTER

Situated on 171 acres to the west of downtown Denver, Colorado, the Auraria Education Center merits attention as an educational model, as an urban campus, and as an encouraging example of how a campus design, with a strong design image, can evolve and adjust to changing conditions without diluting its initial vigor.

The single campus serves three institutions: the Community College of Denver, Metropolitan State College and the University of Colorado, Denver branch. Each has a separate mission and identity; all share classrooms, lecture halls, library, and support facilities. About 20% of all college students in the State of Colorado are enrolled in the Auraria Center. Most drive to and from campus daily, so large parking lots shape one edge of the campus, and rationalize the tight cluster of buildings and landscapes that form central campus. The opposite side is adjacent to the downtown core, with goods, services, and cultural facilities within walking distance. To the west the foothills of the Rockies provide splendid vistas, though occasionally blanked by smog.

Of the 1.4 million square feet of enclosed space, about 45% is new construction, of which about half is in buildings joined into a megastructure. Approximately 800,000 square feet was adapted from existing buildings. Several date back to the area's original settlement. They help give the campus a unique image. The historic buildings include: Emmanuel Art Gallery (1876), which was converted from a church that once served both Episcopalian and Jewish congregations; St. Cajentans Center (1924), once a Hispanic Catholic Church, now a campus cultural center; and the 9th Street Historic Park. The latter has 14 residences constructed in the 1870s. They straddle a Victorian street that was converted into a linear landscape, with the buildings adapted for university offices and support services. It is expected that the park concept will be extended so as to provide additional sites for historic residences that will be relocated from other metropolitan districts, when such buildings are threatened by urban expansion.

The campus design concept places the most intensely used facilities in the campus core area: library, student center, and physical education buildings. Classroom and laboratory buildings surround the core, with the historic buildings interspersed. A central campus walkway system utilizes the original village streets, some of which were closed to protect the core area from intrusive vehicular traffic.

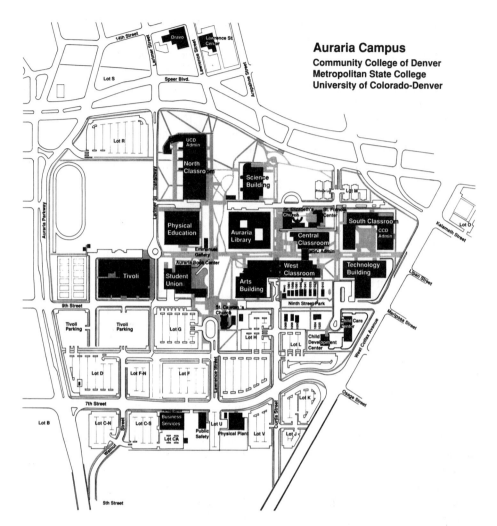

Ground plan, Auraria Center Campus, Denver, Colorado. (Auraria Higher Education Center)

The Auraria Higher Education Center campus is an instructive example of enlightened campus design. The main building complex and landscape are arranged as a pedestrian zone at one end of downtown Denver. The edges of the campus are well defined with street trees, signs and lighting. Parking is kept to the periphery in landscaped lots. A group of historic buildings, dating to the city's earliest days, have been adapted to university uses. In one instance, an entire residential block has been kept intact, with its domestic landscape. Landmark buildings, such as the library, are distinguished by eye-catching building materials. New purpose-built construction, such as the North Classroom Building, continues the linearity of the earlier campus design themes.

Library, (1977). Auraria Center Campus. (RPD)

North Classroom Building (1988) Auraria Center. (Hoover, Berg, Desmond, architects)

Auraria Higher Education Center, Air view. Fall 1990. (AHEC Facilities Management)

Future growth is expected to be accommodated within the present site boundaries. Low density sites may be converted to higher density uses.

New construction was planned to fit a 30-by-30-foot structural grid so as to facilitate and coordinate designs from different firms. The buildings have a strong linear quality, and rise three stories in height, with the upper floors occasionally stepped back to admit sunlight. The distinctive design palette was chosen to give the structures a contemporary look, and to provide a suitable background color for green plantings and seasonal flowers. The standard building materials include oversize brick, door frames, and windows tinted brown, metal and glass doors, and red roofs. The library, clad in light colored aluminum louvers, purposely stands out from the other academic buildings. The variance was intentional, so as to make the library a focal point in the campus design, visually and functionally. Through these principles, many architects have been able to add their individual interpretations to the original nucleus. The complex has subtly changed as new buildings differ from the first structures, in response to program, budget, and each designer's inclination to mark a place with their own inflection. The bland appearances of the initial buildings (pinchingly detailed, as a John Ruskin might describe them), have given way recently to more lively architectural expressions, as if the earlier achievements educationally should be celebrated with a better architecture. The campus landscape that blends the disparate structures and open spaces together is not yet complete, but promising in that both historic and contemporary planting concepts are envisioned, as well as outdoor artworks, signs, and lighting.

POST'S PROTEAN PROJECT

The College of The City of New York (now the City University of New York) was relocated from a downtown building to a topographically dramatic site, the equivalent of four city blocks, in one of those wavelike moves in urbanization that opened northern Manhattan, including the gentrification of upper Fifth Avenue and the construction of Central Park. Though underdeveloped, the college land was accessible by mass transportation and automobile. In 1887, funds were provided to build the largest American urban public university of its time, space for 6,000 nonresidential students. George B. Post won the competition for the architectural commission. The cornerstone was laid in 1903, and the initial construction completed within a decade. The outcome was an extraordinary campus design, in broad concept and small detail, which is barely mentioned, it not ignored, in most appreciations of college and university development. As to materials, the fusion of site and building is instructive for both its success and disappointment.

"It is worth noting," wrote Post in summing up his work at CCNY, "that the architecture was in every instance planned to meet the requirements of the College, and in no way was an attempt made to fit the requirements to the architecture." Words matched deeds. CCNY was a commuter's school. Student lockers were arranged in two tiers, as part of a concourse that also could be used as a lunch room, the whole providing social space for conversations and exchanges that would on conventional campuses occur in residential and dining halls. The Chemical Building, Post said, embodies "all that is the best in laboratory design, both in this country and abroad . . . the system of technical pipe lines, shown on

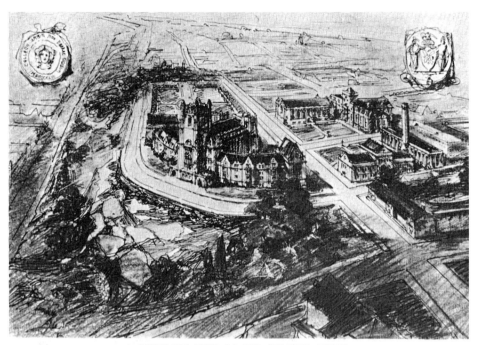

A BIRD'S-EYE VIEW OF THE COLLEGE GROUP.

Rendering of proposed development City College of New York. George B. Post. 1897. (Loeb Library. GSD. Harvard University)

Detail Campus Plan Study. South Campus Complex. John Carl Warnecke. 1977. (Author's Collection)

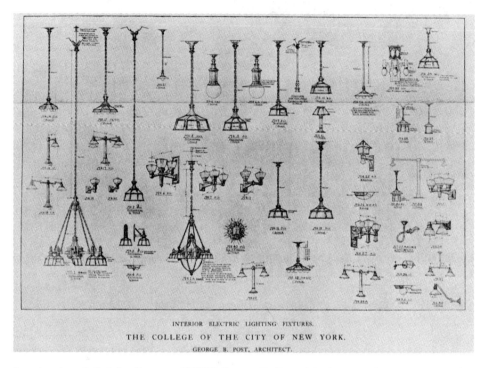

INTERIOR ELECTRIC LIGHTING FIXTURES.
THE COLLEGE OF THE CITY OF NEW YORK.
GEORGE B. POST, ARCHITECT.

Interior electric lighting fixtures, CCNY, George B. Post. (*Architectural Review,* December 1905).

Post provided a comprehensive campus design from site plan to the detailing of interior furnishings and fixtures. Post and his colleagues created a paradigm college campus design. "Conceived," he said, "and executed in its entirety, showing at every point the deep study and loving care of its designers."

Furniture designs. CCNY. George B. Post. (*Architectural Review*, December 1905).

the floor plans in different inks, resembles a color scheme for an Oriental rug." For 50 years, the rooms served well a distinguished faculty and undergraduate student body whose eventual contributions to American science and technology were second to none.

Post advocated incorporating every known industrialized technology in his CCNY buildings. The electrical work included wiring and devices for light and power, alternating and direct current, storage batteries for backup, public telephones, intercommunicating telephones, call bells, an electric clock system, and watchmen's clock system. As Thomas Jefferson would have his University of Virginia architecture communicate, by its physical presence, art and history, Post would also use his buildings pedagogically. The power plant was laid out, Post wrote, "so it furnishes a practical demonstration to the students of the most modern types of machinery for this work." His all-embracing designs included lamp-posts, sidewalks, walls, and gates, meticulously fabricated to Post's specifications.

Post wanted his buildings arranged as a conventional quadrangle and could not, because of site conditions. He attempted to clothe the buildings with the then fashionable Collegiate Gothic style and fell short. His exteriors would not meet fully the aesthetic standards then in vogue, however archly Post might argue. But, these failures may well be Post's achievements, especially if one enjoys a sense of place that is marked by designs that are not predictable formulas.

CCNY's topography was commanding, now and then, ". . . to the south," commented an early observer, "the great misty metropolis with its towering sky-scrapers, silhouetted against the sky." Part of the site was a curving edge of a plateau, a hundred feet higher than the city below. Here, Post anchored the Main Building. Across the street he placed a cluster of four smaller buildings, U-shaped. This apposition of forms gives the central area an unexpected charm, dramatized further with a massive academic block constructed in 1970. The building provides a pedestrian gateway to the older nucleus.

The colors on the facades of the new building pay homage to Post's visual concept which uses site materials to mark and celebrate a sense of place. Post shaped his exterior with stone excavated for the building foundations. The rock colors vary from warm gray colors to dark reds and browns. "Somewhat startling at first glance," thought Post, the composition ". . . is entirely harmonious, however and will improve with age." And, so it does. The inspired design rises from its own source, symbolically and literally. Foundation (the institution) is wedded to foundation (the building base). The outer building material encloses both coherently, cohesively, convincingly.

Parenthetically, the echoic orchestration of site and structure, through materials that have a common color and texture, is a campus design theme rich with placemarking implications. The stone that surrounds the approaches to Greek temples and paves the Gothic cathedral precincts, unifying both, may be seen as a precedent for this kind of comprehensive design. RIT's brick walks have this beauty, as would the stone walls and walks planned for the extension of Dickinson College.

Used in large masses, Post feared the CCNY materials would appear "cheap and monotonous." He found no comfort in Ruskin's opinion, that when used architecturally, stone should be enjoyed as nature intended, "irregular, blotched, imperfect." If Post had left the vertical surfaces alone, arguably, one might claim

Detail, Academic Building (1903), City College of New York, George B. Post. (RPD)

Detail, the 1977 CCNY South portal as constructed. The project architects picked up the color of the Post complex and the drama of the Warnecke plan. (RPD)

that modern university architecture would have begun with his CCNY work. Instead, Post opted to decorate the facades with white terra-cotta quoins, frames, shields and medallions, inside and out, Collegiate Gothic indicia. This "has proven so frequently of late its innate adaptability to work of this character," predicted Post. As it has too often, the lure of style marred an exceptional campus design idea. To burden Post with this retrospective criticism may seem unfair, until one sees the design initiatives soon seized by one of his peers at the University of Colorado.

BARNES' BINDER

Aluminum is also an architectural material associated with the modern times. It was extensively used for the first time in the construction of the Empire State Building (1931). The entire tower is aluminum, as are the entrances, elevator doors, ornamental trim, and 6,000-window spandrels, deplated to match the grey of the interspersed steel panels. Although the third most abundant element on Earth, aluminum was considered a precious metal until metallurgists discovered an efficient industrial processing method, around 1880 for pots and pans, and in the 1920s as a building material. The process for anodizing aluminum was discovered in 1920, but not applied for architectural components until the 1950s, when aluminum siding, baked panels, and custom designed trim and elements came on the market. Promoted as a material that resists corrosion and is readily malleable to designer's specifications, the long-term appearance of the material will vary with quality and cost.

Assuming the material was selected as a metaphor for modern architecture, but with the possible negative connotations of inexpensive residential siding, gasoline station facades, and low-budget schools, might idiosyncratic architects chosen for their flair and style, and image-conscious clients aware of such reputations, be put off by a campus image that imposed and controlled the use of aluminum in a high-style campus design? Would creativity be constrained and egos bruised? The ex-

State University of New York, Purchase. (RPD)

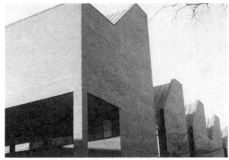

State University of New York, Purchase. A placemarking, disciplined palette of exterior materials giving visual continuity to disparate buildings. (RPD)

Edward L. Barnes expected that the facade materials would have a family resemblance; thus the giving each designer latitude on the inside and a disciplined campus design effect on the exterior.

California State University, Fullerton. (RPD)

University of Miami. (RPD)

The forms vary in response to function and style, but the materials are controlled as to color, generally white at Fullerton, and a range of masonry grays at Miami. The optical effect is a placemarker.

perience at the State University of New York, Purchase campus would suggest not.

Master plan guidelines established by Edward L. Barnes (1970) allowed each building architect to shape his individual commission as program would indicate and personal style encourage. The sites were defined by a formal circulation network and an open space concept, in a plan vaguely reminiscent of Jefferson's Charlottesville campus as examined through gummed eyelids. Visual continuity was achieved by limiting the exteriors to three materials: gray-brown brick, gray-tinted glass, an dark gray anodized aluminum. "With his laissez-faire attitude on form and his rigid rules on materials, Barnes is obviously (steering) a course between the insipidness of a Lincoln Center and the chaos of an Expo," noted critic John Morris Dixon. The success-d'estime (disciplined facades sited in a predetermined geometrical arrangement) is also reminiscent of Mies's work at the Illinois Institute of Technology, but with sufficient variation to mark the Purchase campus as a distinctive place.

Using materials to bind visually campus architecture from many hands, thus emphasizing its placemarking contribution, has been discussed earlier, as in Eero Saarinen's work at Yale; as was the use of color at California State University and the University of Miami. In some instances, such as Tufts University, where the overall campus design is weak and inchoate, materials can be used to suggest unity where none otherwise exists; a good placemarking example being the new student housing at Tufts University (1991). Reinforced by forms and detailing that recall older campus buildings, the binding is poetic, pleasant and persuasive.

Tufts University. New Housing 1991. (Architectural Resources of Cambridge, Inc.)

Materials: Design as Proclamation

Previous citations show how materials can serve referentially, that is, mnemonic devices that mark a particular place, time, and attitudes. The choice of materials can communicate and symbolize institutional continuity and advancement. The selection of building materials can also proclaim new purposes and ideals. More often than not, the signal announcing change is expressed in terms of style; a fracture line in design conceptualizing that is complete and unambiguous. Compare Barnes' Purchase campus to the placard designs of late Collegiate Georgian or Collegiate Gothic. But materials can also be utilized. Keble College, Oxford, is a fine example in this regard, and is also an instructive instance of aspiring and accomplished campus architecture, which in the unity of design detailing, interiors, and furnishings is a paradigm of comprehensive campus architecture. Keble's design objectives, the buildings' critical reception, and later fate are also instructive, thus rating special attention.

KEBLE COLLEGE

The original nucleus of Keble College (1868–1878) utilizes an architectural palette then unique for an Oxford College. The strong image was created by an extraordinary architect, William Butterfield, whose eye-riveting architectural composition, uncompromised by taste or context, demands attention, and stirs the critical senses as one passes through the university precinct. The stirrings were there on opening day and have not since diminished. Few campus architectural schemes have been subject to such contrasting options than Keble College. Few communicate so clearly a century later the client's intentions and the brilliance of the architect's solution. Few give such direct evidence of the visual delight that is yielded by a comprehensive design; that is, the harmonious interplay of edifice and site, structure and decor, spatial concept and plan, with the building details, furnishings, and landscape consciously integrated into the grand scheme. This

132

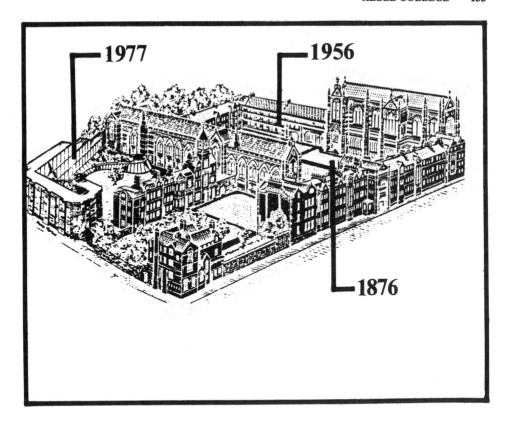

Keble College, Oxford. (Karen Berchtold)

Butterfield achieved in a group of buildings that were, as he desired, "red rags in a moral as well as a visual sense." The import of color will be seen shortly.

The resulting architecture at Keble has divided critics since opening day. "Actively ugly," wrote historian Nickolaus Pevsner; a view apparently shared by an Oxford undergraduate student society, circa 1960, "dedicated to the destruction of the Keble buildings—to qualify it was necessary to remove at least one brick." A coeval opinion saw things differently. Critic Kenneth Clark believed Keble was "one of the finest buildings of its date in England." Neither hybrid nor transplant, Keble stands apart from all other colleges in that living museum of campus design concepts called Oxford. As such, Keble gives cause for speculation about the staying power of those intellectual and moral verities that enfranchise new architecture and the obligation to continue those styles as metaphors once constructed.

For some, Keble matters not. John Steegman's (1950) acclaimed study of Victorian aesthetics ignores Butterfield and Keble entirely; though acknowledging that the "study of the history of Taste provides almost no constant values by which the student can guide himself." Chris Brook (1985), examining Butterfield's work semiotically, found Keble to be the epitome of Victorian thought. The architecture echoed its time and place, "an ordered imaginative and aesthetic event . . . (its) symbolic meaning becomes an inherent part of the physical world . . . (the designs were intended to be) architectural equivalents for non-architectural realities, (where) the emblematic is fused in the actual." A hundred years earlier, the *Illustrated London News* editorialized that the Keble designs would be "tolerable if ivy were encouraged to grow in profusion."

Paradigm, or paradox, or design parable, Keble College brings into play all the connected contingencies which give to life the strongest campus designs; schemes often discomforting to some, but a celebration to many. To note the circumstances that gave rise to Keble's initial success is to understand what may be required to achieve similar results in our own time. To see the beginning concept ignored and rejected by later generations is to appreciate the risks.

BEGINNINGS AND IMPLICATIONS

Favorable conditions at Keble included an institution poised for change; a social context that prized architecture for its ability to interweave function, aesthetics and symbol; and a designer dedicated to the client's philosophy, as well as one being sufficiently experienced to express and carry innovative ideas to reality. A chancy undertaking, to be sure, with success dependent on overcoming the many challenges inherent in pioneering campus designs.

Typical modern hazards include: an insufficient budget; designer arrogance, which in the excitement of presenting adventuresome architecture might actually subvert the client's intentions; and the client's own ability to differentiate between compromise and surrender as the design unfolds. To mediate these dangers, as discussed later, a disciplined facility program (architect's brief) will launch such projects with useful guidelines: purpose, size, room characteristics, building interior spatial relationships, site, budget targets. Nonetheless, innovative designs will demand painstaking review and revisions. The greater the departure from standard practices and conventional concepts, the more the project must be scrutinized and evaluated. The process is seldom smooth. Human factors weigh heavily when projects must move along from the initial conceptualization to construction. Thus, reasonable objections may be denied because it is inconvenient to address issues; or poor communication among designers and decision-makers may frustrate desirable dialog; or the psychological demands for getting on with the project may defer potentially beneficial discussions. Generally, when deficiencies surface, conceptually or in detail, workable compromises will produce better designs. But time and skill must be provided for those compromises to evolve. In the instance of Keble, all went well. The cause was compelling and the era ripe and ready for an architectural masterwork.

KEBLE'S CAUSE

At the start of the 19th century, Oxford lay fallow as an intellectual center. "An aristocratic exclusiveness" rendered "undergraduate life expensive and uncongenial to able men of humble background." The university was seen as an anachronism in an industrial age. Its Parliamentary art peers were able to delay the construction of a railway to Oxford until 1843 "on the grounds that it would threaten the morals of the student population." Nonetheless, the political and educational scene was ripe and ready for organizational, curriculum, and social advancement. By 1860, demographic increases added the weight of population to the pressure for institutional reform. The middle class was growing in number and literacy. The desire for higher education was keenly felt everywhere. Victorian beliefs that science and technology might be well nurtured by higher education led to the birth of new institutions in burgeoning industrial towns, the "civic universities." Oxford could not resist. The stock answer from older and entrenched dons resisting change—"Wait, Sir, until I am gone"—would no longer suffice. College rooms once vacant at Oxford were soon full. The waiting line for admittance lengthened.

Overlaid on fundamental forces calling for institutional change was religious ferment, ironically labeled, the Oxford Movement. Its proponents sought a return to the tenets and practices of the early Anglican Church and a dampening of state influence in church affairs. John Keble was one of the movement's chief spokespersons. Poet, priest, sometime teacher, the lamentations surrounding Keble's death included the possibility of establishing in his name at Oxford a college espousing his religious principles. The new foundation would at the same time give access to higher education to those qualified but unable to pay. Like 17th century Harvard, the new college would be organized to educate ministers, though not entirely. For Keble's supporters, this meant the gentry, poor, but well-motivated, some of whom might enter Holy Orders, devoted to Tractarian beliefs. The appeal was propitious and the purse soon sufficient to begin. The proposed new college would be the first at Oxford since Wadham (1610), two and half centuries earlier.

In purpose, curriculum, and physical form, Keble would be a complete departure from old Oxford ways, a countering of the complacent, the self-centered, and the effete. Not a college for everyone, mind you; John Ruskin's followers would eventually open Oxford for the working class, a social intervention that paved the route for matriculating women at Oxford in full status with men. For as the founding committee expressed its goals, Keble was not created "for persons of inferior social position, less cultivated manners, or of attainments and intellect below the ordinary level of the University." Nonetheless it was a big step forward in the "campaign for a less exclusive entry into higher education," even if only "for gentlemen wishing to live economically."

Fear of debauchery and the call for spartan quarters, for a student body presumably of high moral character and impoverished, informed the Keble building plans, as will be seen. All other matters architectural were expected to be celebratory. Religion was rites and rituals, a communion not grey with dread, but lively with Heaven's promise. Keble's visual surrounds were expected to be an expression of "sensuous pleasures at a time of rigorous (political) suppression." For the task at hand, the sponsors of the new college selected William Butterfield, an inventive and experienced architect, himself an active proponent of the Oxford Movement. Butterfield's life and work are so coupled with his time and social context that a few words about these matters are also instructive in introducing and appreciating his Keble College scheme.

SOCIAL CONTEXT

Victorian Britain was a building culture. "The architect," said Henry van Brunt (1886), "in the course of his career is (now) called upon to erect buildings for every conceivable purpose most of them adapted to requirements which have never before risen in history." With Britain's political and economic dominions to be found in every part of the world, invention and entrepreneurship were productively stimulated. Technology and wealth were transmuted into status through the architecture of town halls, museums, schools, hospitals, churches, railroad stations, banks, hotels, and central city enterprises; and not just in London. What Manchester does today, England will do tomorrow—so went a popular slogan. Keble College was intended to help educate this class, which aspired to organize and control new forms of industry, commerce, and culture; a group which Butterfield served notably in his church, school, and hospital commissions prior to Keble.

Born in 1814, Butterfield's career is almost coterminous with Victoria's reign, and the beginnings and ends of industrial Britain. His ascendancy as a Victorian architect parallels the general rejection of the late Georgian styles in favor of successive waves of architecture-as-craft, older styles revived and reinterpreted, and an episodic fondness for the vernacular and eclecticism. These ideas were stimulated by provocative writers, from A. W. N. Pugin through John Ruskin, whose prose was read and believed by an increasingly educated public, willing to debate architectural meanings, and ready to recognize architecture as a profession. It was a time not of constraints, but contradictions, given what might have become a national architecture based on emerging industrial technologies. Joseph Paxton's glass architecture and the Great Albert Dock bear witness to promises unrealized, while the House of Parliament and the Owen's Building at the University of Manchester epitomizes the seduction of revivalist styles.

Information that defended styles and defined building technology was not bound in limited editions dedicated to courtiers and cognoscenti; nor simplified and diagrammed in pattern books for the profit and instruction of semi-literate artisans. It circulated widely via the popular press and magazines, as well as in mass-produced books and reference works. The discourses, were well-salted with a sensible regard for responsible construction, "the complicated conditions of modern society," van Brunt again, "out of which eminently practical conditions of planning must grow elevations, of which the essential character, if they are honestly composed, can have no precedents in architectural history." Butterfield distanced himself from most of this sometimes arcane speculation. He would insist all his work had root in precedent. In truth, his designs were more original than derivative. The forms might recall some medieval model, but the color and textures that gave his facades their rich tapestry were fresh and inventive.

Through books and articles, Butterfield made known his views about architecture serving religion. He illustrated this congruence with plans and elevations of his own work, as well as establishing models for others to follow. His drawings for Instrumenta Ecclesiastica bears witness of a mind ready to grapple with details, such as sign lettering, church pews, and altar rails, as well as handling architecture in its largest dimensions. The questioning and probing mind, which is associated with the most prolific and dedicated campus designers, is evident in Butterfield's work. For his church work, he would observe and evaluate religious ceremonies, so as to understand how form should fit function. These traits too, contributed to his selection as architect for Keble College, where traditional ideas of student life at Oxford would have to give way to new philosophic and educational concepts. Professionally, Butterfield advocated the separation of the architect from the builder, disavowed the architect as a developer, and embraced the notion of the architect as an independent, objective professional: affording the client with designs, cost estimates, advice on selecting the building team, and providing site supervision.

Conscious of the craft of building, Butterfield's drawings gave directions as to the desired visual effects. He said there were no features in his design that were beyond the skill of an intelligent workman. Should there be uncertainty, he was quick to demonstrate on site what he envisioned. Appreciating craftsmanship, Butterfield was, in turn, appreciated by the artisans engaged to carry out his designs. During the Great London Building strike (1859), the Trade Unions nominated him as an arbiter. Thus Butterfield's reputation for hard work, extraordinary experience, and timely delivery did not go unnoticed by a client whose buildings at Keble College were to be funded by popular subscription; a reputation furthered by his earlier and successful encounter with Oxford craftsmen in his Balliol and Merton College commissions.

Butterfield's oeuvre, on one hand has been labeled "mysterious, glittering, beautiful, magnificent, novel, progressive, original." On the other, it was demeaned as "scandalous, tasteless, discordant, startling, eccentric and strange." The words are picked from an extensive critical literature. And, never at any given turn in these appreciations, in the episodic tides of fashion and taste, did there appear to be any unanimity in opinion about Keble, pro or con. In 1865, Butterfield's colleagues found him unworthy of the Royal Institute's Gold Medal for architecture, but changed their minds 19 years later. Modest, he would only accept the prize in private. Lesser lights were knighted, but not Butterfield. He died in 1900, then and now an enigma.

CUEING ON KEBLE

At Keble College, the social and cultural conditions had ripened for a dramatic departure from stultifying traditions. A refreshing new view of institutional purpose would replace an environment grown stale academically, and a splendid, though controversial, architecture would be realized. Time passes, but what endures?

Obviously Butterfield's Keble buildings have had to be modernized—refitted with new plumbing, electrical systems, and generally refurbished. Compared to earlier Oxford buildings and many constructed since Keble was opened, they age well, a tribute to Butterfield's knowledge of building crafts and construction techniques. These qualities hardly seem to matter in light of Keble's design expression, especially the campus design implications which brings these buildings to our attention, and merit this exposition. What, then, is this expression; and what role do materials play in this example of placemarking? What cues does Keble offer?

KEBLE DESIGNS

The 20 Oxford colleges previous to Keble's foundation (1868) date from 1245 to 1740. Masonry buildings, arranged in walled enclaves of gardens, courtyards, and quadrangles, they are a three-dimensional compendium of institutional architec-

The Victorians were skilled in planning and designing large building projects; accomplished in fitting institution's such as a university into classical style architecture, as in Manchester; and impressive in engineering works, such as the Liverpool docks, where forms were derived from function, with local materials identified with the locale. It was the age of the architect as the master designer, clearly evident in William Butterfield's Keble College.

Owens Building, University of Manchester. (RPD)

Great Albert Dock, Liverpool. (RPD)

Architectural alphabet from William Butterfield's Instrumenta Ecclesiastica. The facile designer would detail every possible aspect of his building projects. (RIBA Library)

The Butterfield palette, Keble College. (RPD)

Parks Road facade, Keble College. (RPD)

ture, from the medieval to the Neo-Palladian, with many inspired styles in between.

As in Venice and Fez, Oxford's beauty rises from collective efforts, centuries of architecture, whose all embracing fabric is immediately apparent, but not exhausted in poetic or pedantic distillations. "Domes and Towers! Gardens and Groves! Your presence overpowers The soberness of reason," thought William Wordsworth. For Matthew Arnold, the same scene was a "sweet city with its dreaming spires."

Oxford's panorama was more adventitious than planned. Each college acted as a separate corporation. Independent judgment was cherished. Architectural decisions came slowly. Imaginative schemes would be commissioned, then cancelled, or if in progress, drastically altered. As far as the records would indicate, there were no intercollegiate committees charged with coordinating construction so as to achieve some comprehensive effect. Modest designs and audacious building complexes nonetheless melded well with each other, beads on a string of accomplished enterprise several centuries long.

What most colleges shared in common was local building materials. As an ensemble, the university precinct glows with the honey-colored oolitic limestone that gives Oxford a distinctive sense of place: stone quarried locally; stone first shaped, carved and erected by master masons whose skills are deservedly memorialized in many a college archive; stone piled in classical designs by Wren and Hawksmoor, and in 20th century shapes by those that followed.

Catching the eye like the slash of red in Bruegel's *The Wedding Party,* Butterfield's new buildings emerge from the traditional Oxford scene with energy and vibrancy. Visually different from most preceding college architecture, occupying 4.5 acres north of St. John's College, Keble was large enough to dominate its site and environs on opening day and thereafter. Atypical was Butterfield's use of an assertive red brick, with the exterior elevations diapered and checkered with stone dressings and zig-zag patterns of yellow and blue brick. The polychromatic concept can be traced to Butterfield's epitome, All Saints, Margaret Street, Marlybone, London.

Some see Keble as a response to John Ruskin's praise for Venetian Gothic and its multicolored detailing. But Butterfield's work predates Ruskin's polemic. Where Ruskin would presume a hierarchy of forms and colors arranged in decorative patterns, Butterfield wanted "democratic ornament"; materials and their expression would convey "a life of continual struggle for independence." Color was a Butterfield hallmark. Those writing his obituary said, in this respect, "his eye was insensitive." Those viewing the Keble buildings will see subtleties in the arrangement of tones, tints, and textures which suggest otherwise.

For Butterfield, brick was a symbolic, as well as a practical, building material. He was irked by those who criticized his designs because they thought brick was humble. Purposefully, doggedly, Keble would demonstrate how wrong their judgments were. With his brick fabric, Butterfield imposed a dazzling, soaring, attention-gathering architectural composition unlike any earlier Oxford colleges. The countenance was neither referential nor reverential to the traditional use of ashlar limestone and earlier architectural styles.

Keble's floor plans were also different. Unlike the conventional Oxford quads, the range of student rooms at Keble were organized along corridors, not stairwells, "recognition that its members would not be served breakfast and lunch privately in their rooms," as had become the Oxford norm. Compared to accommodations to be found in many of the earlier colleges, the Keble student rooms were smaller and furnished without sofas and had no curtains. There were no suites for servants. All meals would be taken in the halls. The buttery was designed so beer could be served, but no wine would be available. A lack of privacy and comfort was supposed to impede indolence and hedonism.

Institutional philosophy, educational aims, and building program design were bound into Keble's comprehensive design. Spartan though the residences would be, the dining hall, library, and chapel were not so constrained. The latter's decoration has no rival as an example of Butterfield's fecund (some would say, feverish) imagination. As to site, residences, dining hall, and chapel framed a grassed quadrangle, the latter sunken like a dried pond, and from which the buildings seem more elevated than they would from a flat plane. Additional student rooms and a warden's lodge shared a second open space. In general concept, Keble was not unlike other Oxford Quads. To complement his building colors, Butterfield selected deep green foundation plantings, placed simply.

Stripped of conflicting judgments, passionate encomiums and damning deprecations, Keble is an impressive statement. Butterfield's designs say what they mean. Building materials, in vivid contrast with their surrounding context, proclaimed institutional change. The materials give Keble a charm and character uniquely its own. The design succeeds as an institutional metaphor, as a place-marker for a college intended to be different. Unfortunately, a word conveying dissatisfaction more than condemnation, the recent additions to Keble have ignored the metaphor that Butterfield so ably created. The 1977 buildings are arranged as a fortress-like wall along the southwest side of the college property. As the college guidebook acknowledges, they "make no attempt to blend with Butterfield's buildings." But, an important campus design lesson has been overlooked. By failing to reinterpret the fabric that Butterfield invented, generations are disconnected. There is little visual continuity between new work and old. Admittedly, the impressive original nucleus remains untouched, but the possibilities afforded by Butterfield's brick as a metaphor with meaning for Keble has been lost.

Detail, Examinations Building, Oxford, Post-Keble. (RPD)

University Museum, Parks Road. (RPD)

The University Museum Building was designed about a decade before Keble and the Examinations Building a decade after. Limestone architecture fits Oxford well. Among all the colleges, Keble is the splendid placemarking exception.

Detail Hayward Quad, Keble College (1977). (RPD)

Detail Butterfield's Keble. (RPD)

The late additions denied the past with a new scheme that missed the meaning and marvel of Butterfield's work.

Materials: Codes/Canons/Contradictions

Building materials can be selected and utilized to communicate institutional purpose and presence, through the image they create and the sense of place they reinforce. Butterfield's brick was an icon and symbol, that is, a representation of implied values, a formal sign that Keble was conceived as a different kind of College. The Keble quadrangle was recognizably Oxford. But the building facades were contrary to tradition. Brick was the gauntlet thrown to champion new values. For many people, not Butterfield and his client, the Keble architecture was discordant aesthetically, if not discomforting philosophically.

As icon and symbol, might brick be part of a universal architectural language, semiotic, which itself signifies certain values, easily perceived, and about which there is general agreement as to its meaning? If this were so, then campus design formulas could be established which would help realize predictable results. One would have a good answer to Joseph Hudnut's cri de coeur: "We need a new tradition which shall long at last deliver our universities from the vagaries of architectural secession."

Hudnut's plea was wrapped in a beautifully articulated essay, "On Form In Universities," (*Architectural Record*, December 1947). The article sanctioned the application of the International School, as interpreted by Mies Van Der Rohe, as a style suitable for higher education, but not to the exclusion of other campus design considerations. As dean of the Graduate School of Design, Harvard University, during the decade before and after World War II, Hudnut wanted to steer modern architecture through the shoals of rigid dogmatism, sensing, perhaps, the tyranny of "stripped and stark asceticism." He hoped the International Style would evolve "with an ever-widening range and a deeper human content." It would not then become, as the traditional styles did, another "formulae of motif and procedure." Hudnut's insights are still pertinent, and shed light on the search for campus design criteria and certitude. For Hudnut, form in buildings and form in campus plans would clearly express function. The designs would be principled to accommodate change, growth, and contraction. "When in doubt make free use of temporary construction."

Hudnut's ideal plans would be pliable enough to embrace, admire, and respect an architectural heritage, where it existed. He tempered this judgment, however. On one hand, Hudnut found a collage of styles appealing because it set "forth in dramatic form the sequences of temper and incident which have shaped the life they decorate." On the other hand, he was wary of history's limitations. Inherited styles are "strange costumes", "self-sufficient molds into which ideas are poured." The new campus architecture, as Hudnut saw it, would clear "our buildings of romance, ancient techniques, speculative esthetics, and (the) cant with which we burden them." For Hudnut, the welcomed purge would yield an architecture with "Variety and individuality, lyrical beauty and grandeur, wit and fantasy . . . not alien to a mode of building which is consistent with our genuine culture . . . and may also attain serene elegance."

Hudnut is quoted at length, because what he says about style could be true about materials. Accessible codes and cannons would furnish criteria for originating designs, as well as provide measurable standards for judging their efficacy. This does not appear to be the case—that is, a universal campus design language based on materials. The reasons why this seems to be so may help us to understand the limitations of materials as metaphor. The discourse will bring into focus and reaffirm the placemarking power of reverential architecture. As a start, some thoughts about brick (a humble and esoteric material, emblem and symbol) may help unscramble some paradoxes.

BRICK AS BRICK

Brick may be the most universal of building materials, with 6,000 years of known history. Suitable earths can be found in most parts of the world. The earths can be molded and burnt into various colors, textures, and forms. Shapes and sizes can be standardized and regulated. The outer surface may be decorated or left plain. Brick is fire resistant and has excellent thermal qualities. It is economical in terms of production cost, transportation, handling on the job site, and maintenance.

The first fired bricks were developed in the Near East, using manufacturing techniques that were then adopted by the Romans, and, via their empire, introduced to Western Europe. The Middle Ages occasionally used brick in domestic, sacred, and secular architecture, but not as extensively as in later centuries. In England, where our narrative is leading us, Roman building methods, such as baked tile, were forgotten for several centuries. Circa 1350 AD, brick was reintroduced architecturally with the Flemish immigration from the Low Countries. Showpiece architecture came into being with Tudor designers forming and shaping such exquisite works as Queen's College (1448) and Trinity College (1546), Cambridge. The unsymmetrical Tudor facades were embroidered with terra-cotta, laced with brick diapering, and strongly corbelled. The revivalist versions, popular on many American campuses in the 1920s lack the original visual exuberance and craftsmanship.

The Great Fire of London (1605) gave cause to substitute masonry architecture for wood and stucco in the capital city. Timber was in short supply. Public safety and the fear of conflagration were other compelling reasons to seek a new architecture. Codes, costs, and fashion favored brick. If campus architecture had genes, these three factors would be the DNA of thousands of American college buildings.

As to design in brick, from the Tudors to the end of the Hanoverian rule, brick was a choice material among taste-makers and master builders. Paradigm architecture, these concepts were readily transported across the North Atlantic. They were easy to emulate, relatively inexpensive, and the designs were filled with sentimental associations with the Mother Country, as documented earlier.

Thomas Mount is believed to be America's first brickmaker, 1636, in what is now Boston. The brick business prospered for the same reasons it did in Georgian London. Ruinous fires led the Colonial government in New England to regulate construction. By the mid-18th century "new buildings more than eight feet in length and seven feet in height" had to be erected as masonry architecture. There were few stone-cutters, so brick became the choice material. The manufacture itself was regulated, including size: "nine inches long, two & one quarter inches thick & fower (sic) & halfe inches broad". Jealous of the cachet and proud of the product, a later ordinance required the letter *B* to be stamped on all bricks that passed the Boston inspectors, who were enfranchised to cull out inferior goods. The enduring qualities of Harvard's earliest buildings may be traced to these beginnings, which provided models for three centuries of campus construction that followed in Cambridge and throughout the United States.

Around the beginning of the 18th century, taxes and fashion ended the second great age of brick architecture in England. The first (taxes) was a quick fix for funding the Napoleonic Wars; the second was snobbery. From 1810 to about 1850 ". . . socially downward as far as least as the lower middle class," brick was felt to give "a poverty-stricken appearance." By plastering stucco over brick facades in imitation of Paladin and Regency styles, status was gained through simulated architecture.

On many campuses in the United States, a similar technique was used to achieve a Grecian style, when funds did not permit white stone. In some places, the grey stone of Collegiate Gothic made its first appearance. As a predominant building material with symbolic connection to older traditions, brick gave way to these new fashions during the first decades of the 19th century.

In England, the taste for brick was stimulated again when the tax on bricks was removed and "people were beginning to feel that, although bare brick might (signify poverty) . . . stucco was much worse because it was dishonest!" There was universal distaste for the "Baker-Street style . . . (where) . . . dignity became dullness . . . mere speculators commonplace." Through mechanization and industrialization, the supply and quality of bricks increased exponentially. The third great age of brick architecture was launched. Victorian clients and designers were able to raise their houses and edifices in the material they believed best suited their taste and time. In the main Oxford would hold to its tradition of oolitic limestone. Cambridge, England would admit designs with brick, revivalist styles. The new English civic universities embraced the material enthusiastically, earning the sobriquet "the red bricks"; just as "white tile" and "plate-glass" would designate later English institutions metaphorically.

Whether industrial processes kept alive revivalist styles on the late 19th century American campuses, or the styles stimulated product development, is not

Royal Hospital, London, Christopher Wren. In plan and building design the progenitor for several centuries of college and overseas architecture. (RPD)

Washington and Lee College. The Wren influence two centuries later. (A. J. Lidsky)

Harvard's University Museum. 19th century brick architecture attractive in its simplicity. (RPD)

Detail, Baker Building, Alvar Aalto, Massachusetts Institute of Technology. Brick reinterpreted as a monocladding by a modern master. (RPD)

clear. But the use of brick was simplified by suppliers manufacturers whose catalogs encouraged architecture by formula. The Eastern Hydraulic-Press Brick Company would turn out three hundred million units a year. The company's 1895 brochure, *Suggestions In Brickwork,* illustrated dozens of design concepts, broken down so brick could be ordered in standard sizes and shapes, architecture by the numbers. To serve history, the hand-made wood-burned brick was again manufactured.

And again, fashion changed. Brick's best historian, Nathaniel Lloyd (1923) believed the "failure of the late nineteenth century brickwork revival was owing to the designer's failure to understand the material; and to the extinction of intelligent craftsmen whose achievements in earlier work was the fruit of long and intimate experience." Perhaps. Others suppose that new materials (concrete, glass and aluminum) would engender new styles.

More recently, the work of Louis Kahn, among other modernists, would suggest that brick is the universal architectural substance, flexible enough to be utilized in designs ancient, medieval, contemporary. Brick is appealing argues the German critic Gerd Zimmerschied because the module has human dimensions: "the length of a brick is approximately that of a human foot." He believes brick is the best architectural material as "a medium of personal expression." Eero Saarinen's chapel at the Massachusetts Institute of Technology would support this notion, as does Alvar Aalto's nearby dormitory, where brick is the Finnish architect's signature.

Up the ladder of respectability and down again, brick architecture waxes and wanes. As icon and symbol, brick's semiotic signals vary considerably. The contrasting messages it conveys today in institutional architecture on two sides of the Atlantic have been noted. Red brick has social connotations uncomfortable for traditional Oxford, where limestone masonry buildings before and after Keble College reign majestically; for some American institutions brick is an enpowering architectural gesture.

Materials: Bearers of Meaning

Brick, thus used as a metaphor of institutional presence, is an **invented tradition.** The importance comes from the specific cultural context that invests the material with symbolic significance. The design method may be universal. The importance will differ from campus to campus. Eric Hobsbawm defines such traditions as visible forms of institutional "self-assertions . . . which seek to inculcate certain values and norms . . . by repetition, which automatically implies continuity with the past . . . a suitable historic past."

Materials thus utilized are "bearers of meaning." The phrase belongs to John Onians. He uses it to trace the manner by which certain architectural effects (specifically classical building columns) have been interpreted and reinterpreted in western civilization from ancient Greece to 16th century Rome. In this slice of life, homage is always made to the beginning forms. They may be altered by later circumstances, though never beyond recognition. The alterations may be technical, such as adjustments made to utilize different materials; done in ignorance of the canons of taste that gave rise to the first forms; or the caprice of a designer that wanted to be free from previous architectural formulas but believed it appropriate to respect the past.

Onians writes: "Aware of their own needs, and understanding the desires, anxieties, and uncertainties of others, they (the designers) used (changes in the shape and placement of columns) to develop a shared knowledge and to influence ideas and actions . . . to find (one's) way through life." Image-conscious campuses have used materials for similar reasons. Referential architecture becomes reverential, as in the next five examples of institutions with an impressive sense of place.

THE COLLEGE OF WILLIAM AND MARY

Chartered in 1693, the College of William and Mary occupied its first building in 1702. When constructed, it was the largest building in the English colonies; four

College of William and Mary, detail. The mid-19th century reconstruction of the fire devasted Wren building. (RPD)

Brick paths through the woods. (RPD)

College of William and Mary. Contemporary housing, with brick as the generational binder. (RPD)

College of William and Mary. Contemporary academic building; brick for institutional reference. (RPD)

College of William and Mary. Library expansion. A celebration in brick with suggested visual ties to the earlier college architecture. (RPD)

stories tall, including dormered attic and half-basement, and 136 feet long. The structure anchors one end of the Duke of Gloucester Street, the spine of old Williamsburg, Virginia, the plantation's chief market town and capitol. Beginning in 1929, the town has been extensively restored as an idealized version of life in early America. Once dusty streets have given way to paved surfaces, the gardens may not be authentic, and the two hundred or so structures that constitute a living museum of town architecture have been modernized internally—how could they not be—but the overall impression of homage to a time and place is as impressive as it is favorable. The college's share of that homage is paid in brick.

As to the authenticity of the first college building itself, the question of origins and authorship remains unsettled in specific terms, but not in spirit. Having persuaded Queen Mary to endow a college for training missionaries, the Reverend James Blair returned to Williamsburg with an experienced builder, Thomas Hadley, and plans said to have been drawn by Christopher Wren. However originally constructed, a series of fires left to later generations the task of giving the building today's appearance. The worse conflagrations (1859 and 1862) reduced the walls to two-thirds the original height and gutted the interiors. What is seen today is the Collegiate Georgian's paradigm building, whose graceful proportions, composition, and detailing is the standard against which other such designs should be measured. A weighty criticism laid against such imitative buildings is that they are dated and stale as symbols and building technology. Worse are the hacked-out versions of Collegiate Georgian, which botched, bloated, and banal, give cause to condemn all revivalist buildings regardless of visual merit.

The phrase *good design* suggests there are standards against which an objective reckoning can be made as to what would constitute a successful architectural solution. The question comes into play as one examines the 62 major buildings that constitute the William and Mary campus today. The distance from the Wren Building to the western boundary of central campus is about two-thirds of a mile. On an architectural time line, the space between is filled with 300 years of continuous construction. Age alone bestows a special heritage. All the structures have been expressed in some form of brick architecture, for William and Mary, the metaphoric material.

As insignias, the buildings closest to the Wren complex were rendered in stylized versions of Collegiate Georgian. They frame a sunken garden that itself is Georgian in concept. Of the large structures to the west, the Stadium, Field House, and Health Center are marked with brick, as are several groupings of student housing, in contemporary designs. Should the metaphor be missed, some of the walks through the woods to these buildings are paved with brick.

The academic complex to the southeast earns comment as an example of generational designs in which a single material (brick) has been used in conjunction with modern interpretations of Collegiate Georgian. The ten major building—classrooms, faculty offices, laboratories, auditoria, library span the years 1957–1989. There are few design impulses from that period that are not represented in this illuminating complex; a period during which architecture became "exceptionally dense with original ideas, salutary hopes and fetching dreams." They range from the architecturally bizarre Rogers Hall (sheltering facilities for the Departments of Chemistry and Religion) to the recent addition to the main library by Perry, Dean, Rogers, where assertive brickwork is time-binding use of materials as an institutional metaphor.

STANFORD UNIVERSITY

On Stanford's opening day, its first president expressed the hope that "in every student shall be left some imperishable trace of the beauty of Palo Alto." "Each stone in the quadrangle," said David Starr Jordan, "shall teach its lesson of grace and genuineness." Well-endowed, possessing a benign climate and an extraordinary natural setting, the university has become, a century later, an eminent institution, educationally and architecturally.

Threatened by earthquakes, drought, urbanization, aesthetic fads—California's apocalyptic Four Horsemen of Campus Design—the Stanford's sense of place has been well-served by several generations of planners and designers dedicated to nurturing its image. The campus beauty comes from an interweaving of the best architecture the times would yield, a landscape that is responsive to geography's dictates, and the red tile roofs and buff-colored walls that recognizably mark Stanford as a special place. Historically, the roofs are a constant. The objective of continuing in new buildings the hue and color seen in the first exterior walls, however, has had to be adapted to physical reality—an adaptation with a price Stanford has been willing to pay to continue its role as a metaphor of institutional presence.

The original sandstone masonry was quarried south of San Jose and freighted to campus. "There a small army of stonecutters fashioned the intricate decorations" which give the first quadrangles a distinctive interpretation of Richardson-

Stanford University. Rusticated stone, ochre in color, arches, and red tile roof—the Stanford palette. (RPD)

Stanford University. Some visual themes restated, stucco walls, tinted ochre. (RPD)

ian Romanesque. Rectilinear buildings are joined by arcades; the latter a sequence of half-circle arches, set on short columns. The ground plan was influenced by Frederick Law Olmsted; the architecture formulated by Charles A. Coolidge; the total scheme favored by the founders. Stanford himself sent his engineers scouting for "the proper kinds of stone," he informed a newsman in 1887.

As did other industrial magnates of his time, such as James B. Hill, Stanford encouraged bold strokes in building technology, a prescient intervention as events soon proved. Steel railroad ties were used to construct the university museum, America's first reinforced concrete building. The rooms survived the whiplash from the San Francisco earthquake (1906), which severely damaged many other university buildings, including the museum wings, which were not reinforced. A similar tremor effected the buildings in 1989, though not as extensively. Fortunately, the university had rebuilt the old Quads so they would meet modern earthquake standards. The insides had been gutted and restructured, while the outer shell was preserved intact.

The original quarry was engulfed by subdivisions. Because the stone would not work well if stockpiled, and the supply was diminishing, the university invented a simulated sandstone made from concrete. This is used to replace portions of the old buildings, or for additions elsewhere. "Largely in response to the faculty there," says Stanford campus planner, Phillip Williams, "we formalized a concept of tan masonry and tile roofs in the design guidelines for the new Near West Campus. They wanted to reestablish architectural identity with the university rather than create a separate 'hi-tech' image." This criteria, color and texture, gives "respect for our roots" without compromising building functions and technologies. It promotes a transitional architecture "with substance and reason rather than a showcase for current fashion and architect's experiments."

HOKIE STONE

Like Stanford, Virginia Polytechnic Institute and State University occupies a valley setting, intrinsically attractive for a campus enrolling 20,000 students. Unlike Stanford, the development in recent decades at Virginia Tech has not yielded great

Virginia Polytechnic Institute and State University. Hokie stone used as an institutional symbol. (VPIU)

CHEMISTRY
ATRIUM

beauty, and in fact has compromised and eroded some of the early design concepts. The 1983 Master Plan addresses these deficiencies intelligently and skillfully by defining the entrances to central campus, by strengthening the edges of three architectural groupings that lie on either side of the historic drill field (a symbolic open space), by separating pedestrian and vehicular traffic, and through an in-fill construction strategy that will counter the tendency for further sprawl and visual dispersion.

Like Stanford, Virginia Tech has a symbolic building material—a dolomite limestone laid down 475 million years ago and now quarried north of the campus. The material shows up in a number of building styles, though not all-encompassing. The warm grey and tan stone typically is hewed into rectangular blocks. These may be carved, or joined with other materials, or laid up as a tapestry, with seams and grouting tracing the patterns.

THE UNIVERSITY OF NEW MEXICO

The building was insufficient in many ways. It was in no way suited to college purposes. It was unsafe owing to poor architecture. The roof was so heavy, that the walls, rendered weak by the numerous windows, were not able to support it. The building had been condemned and was repaired at the expense of several hundred dollars. It was still condemned and was not safe for use for another year, therefore, it had to be reconstructed. One architect wished to raze it to the ground. The plan was accepted to remodel it in the style of the dormitories.

(*New Mexico Weekly,* 27 February 1909)

As placemarking architecture, where construction materials connect generations with remarkable visual consistency, and where social and cultural values are evident in the building fabric, few American institutions communicate a sense of place more vividly than the University of New Mexico.

The first permanent building on the Albuquerque campus (Hodgin Hall, 1890) was built of brick and sandstone. The four story structure had a rusticated base, arched doorway, ventilated eaves, recessed windows, peaked dormers, and other details that were recognizably Richardsonian Romanesque; a universal university image at that time. "You know that building," observed a local historian, "because you have seen it a hundred times, from Indiana to Alabama." For New Mexico contractors, Hodgin was a demanding task. The successful bidder required modifications in the plans and specifications "to bring the price within the estimated ability of the Board to pay." On completion, the upper floors bulged. "The roof is too heavy for the building because the load is not well distributed," noted the inspecting architect. Iron rods were installed to tie the walls together.

In 1908, the structure, then called the Administration Building, was dramatically altered. All traces of its original exterior were erased and replaced with those physical characteristics that constitute the Pueblo style: flat roofs, rectangular windows, extended vigas, walls flaring at their juncture with the ground, softer versus hard edges, and the whole encased in adobe-like earth colors, seemingly monolithic, clearly sculptural.

The extensive reconfiguration was argued on several grounds: a final remedy for a seemingly unrepairable building, fear and prudence, utilization, economy, and style. The reasoning then seems as pointed and germane as it would be in similar undertakings these days. Bemused administrators might find comfort in knowing how little has changed in debating the rationale for a significant capital expenditure.

The former building had three outside entrances, the present building has more than a dozen, making it absolutely safe in case of fire.

The original building had twelve classrooms. As it is remodeled it has eighteen, a great deal of space before occupied by halls and stairwells.

This building was remodeled, made safer, and far more convenient in every way, two rooms added, and as assembly hall . . . built at the comparatively small cost of $19,302.15. The cost of the same, built according to classic architecture would have cost at least $25,000.00. Thus, we gained six recitation rooms, a fine assembly hall, and have saved the people of the Territory more than $5,000.00

Stylistically, the transformation was the culminating act of Dr. William George Tight's tenure as the university's third president. Tight saw in the Pueblo style a way of connecting the university to its regional history. The particulars that constitute the style are derived from Indian construction and Spanish Colonial archi-

University of New Mexico, Hodgin Hall, circa 1890. (UNM, Department of Facility Planning)

Hodgin Hall. Reconstructed in the Pueblo style circa 1908 in accordance with President William G. Tight's search for regional architecture. (RPD)

University of Mexico, campus view circa 1907. (Museum of New Mexico, Santa Fe)

tecture, thus combining sacred, secular, public, and vernacular forms into an invented synthesis.

A public institution, the University of New Mexico should draw sustenance from these cultures, Tight insisted. He used every opportunity not just to champion this belief intellectually, but to demonstrate it three-dimensionally. In 1905, the university power plant was wrapped in adobe architecture. Two new dormitories were completed in 1906 in plan and appearance adventuresome regional architecture. The women's building was named Hokona (Butterfly Maiden); the men's Kwataka (Male Eagle). Should the regional references be missed, Tight decorated the exterior stairwells with Hopi Indian pottery signs. In 1908, Tight was able to construct a temporary university exhibit for the Territorial Fair, proselytizing through architecture his design convictions. On campus, he enlisted the Alpha Alpha Alpha fraternity to build their chapter house to replicate the Santa Domingo Pueblo kiva.

Tight's belief that the built environment should manifest the regional heritage architecturally was a unique position for the universities to take at the hinge of the 19th and 20th century. Witness the development of new universities in Tight's lifetime and the styles selected by their founders and designers as symbols of values appropriate for higher education:

- John Hopkins University
  (Collegiate Georgian)
- Stanford University
  (Richardsonian Romanesque)
- University of Chicago
  (Collegiate Gothic)
- Massachusetts Institute of Technology
  (Beaux Arts Roman)
- Rice University
  (Modified Byzantine)

Given Tight's fervor for the Pueblo style, it would seem inevitable that the campus flagship building would have to sail under Tight's colors. The transformation was realized when the Administration Building's mundane architecture was erased. The new forms and materials were added and applied under Tight's direction. He won his crusade for an architecture that would ennoble a university by symbolizing its people, but the effort cost him his job.

Later generations ratified Tight's dictum. In their interval, 1935 through 1955, 38 University buildings were designed and constructed in the Pueblo style, 25 by one man, John Gaw Meem. His best work occurred in the Great Depression, when federal grants favored building projects that required large numbers of craftsmen and laborers; an opportunity Meem did not overlook when detailing his knowledgeable version of Pueblo Style architecture. He was able to introduce custom designed woodwork, ironwork, ceramics, and decoration, whose precedents could be found in historic New Mexican buildings. Blending all was adobe, real and simulated, Tight's thread through culture and visual continuity.

UNM, The Kwataka dormitory, circa 1910. (UNM, Department of Facility Planning)

UNM, the power house. One of William G. Tight's first essays in adobe. (UNM, Department of Facility Planning)

Symbol source. It has been suggested that the design concepts for first UNM Pueblo-style buildings were derived from the Smithsonian regional surveys reported by J. Walter Fewkes in 1896. Plate 272 may be the source of the Man-eagle wall painting on the Kwataka dormitory. (UNM, Department of Facility Planning)

UNM, Zimmerman Library (1936). John Gaw Meem's flagship building in the Pueblo-style fleet. The simulation of adobe, among other architectural gestures, provides visual continuity with Tight's themes. (RPD)

UNM, Bandilier Hall. A modest and persuasive interpretation of the Pueblo style in the adobe vernacular. As university buildings grew larger and functions more diverse, and attitudes about style changed, the continuation of the Tight-Meem philosophy was challenged. (RPD)

UNM, Science and Engineering Library. Materials and colors remain as referential architecture. (RPD)

Taos Pueblo, 1200 AD. (RPD)

University of New Mexico, Humanities Building. (RPD)

University of New Mexico, detail, Meem Chapel. (RPD)

University of New Mexico, detail, Academic building. The hard edge misses the placemarking feature of the regional materials, though the color and texture suggest adobe. (RPD)

In recent years, a reductionist process has influenced the exterior designs. To limit construction costs, mass-produced and factory-fabricated materials and elements were soon substituted for details and components once crafted by hand. The spirit of Tight and the skills of Meem's designs are acknowledged, but some of the actual work became vague as to origins, if not paradoxical in execution. In the Science and Engineering Library, for example, the referential and reverential is expressed in a color, a hint of an historic shape, and a gesture toward adobe. More forceful is the Humanities Building, clearly designed to suggest adobe, and shaped to echo the native forms of venerable Taos Pueblo.

UNIVERSITY OF COLORADO, BOULDER

Adobe is the material that transcends style at the Albuquerque campus. It evokes a special heritage, permits generational interpretations, and allows design transition from past to present. This is a favorable circumstance, as aspects of the original designs are identified and adapted, not directly imitated. In this respect, the University of Colorado (Boulder) is also a fine example of the transformation from referential to reverential architecture.

Colorado's first building (1876), now Old Main, was expected to be situated in a landscaped park, with pagoda, statues, flower beds, winding paths and roads, and shady trees—Currier and Ives Romanticism. During the early years, the reality was "a mile of mud," a harsh climate and inhospitable soil that was gradually tamed into a verdant quadrangle. Though no known drawings exist, the green was intended to be framed by buildings in various architectural styles. Students and visitors would come to appreciate the finer, or not so subtle, differences in Classical, Romanesque, Gothic, and Italiante designs.

As an ensemble the first buildings, quad, and landscape, with views to nearby Flagstaff mountain, form a pleasant image. The design is strong enough to be designated on the National Register of Historic Places as the North Quadrangle Historic District. But, the architectural distinction that earns Colorado special mention as a design metaphor comes from another source. The quadrangle includes Hellems Hall, Charles Z. Klauder's first building on the Boulder campus (1921), the starting point of a campus design concept that has informed seven decades of changing attitudes and values about what constitutes appropriate university architecture. The enduring quality is not a grand plan or style, but continuity in stone.

Born in 1877, Klauder was a disciplined and prolific designer. He died at age 66 at his drawing board, working over plans for a university faculty club. His professional obituary (*Pencil Points*, January 1939) placed him in the orbit of Bullfinch, Richardson, Hunt and McKim. "In his approach to his design, Klauder felt rather than remembered precedent; he moved about with the styles he used." Apprenticed at age 15, Klauder's skills and accomplishments had made him by 1917 America's best known institutional architect, and a logical choice for the University of Colorado regents who were searching for strong advice on building style as well as campus expansion. Little mind that the obituary erroneously placed his masterwork at the Colorado School of Mines, a mountain range away, in Golden, Colorado; it was Boulder that got the best of his genius.

The regent's difficulties can be summed up in one of many pleas that they were attempting to satisfy: a prominent Boulder citizen suggested that all funds be pooled into "one mammoth building" in which all the styles might be harmonized "in one grand symphony of stone."

Once engaged, Klauder proposed clothing the growing Boulder campus in Tudor Gothic. The conventional approach posed no problem to the regents inasmuch as it was a current fashion they desired. Too much so, countered university president George Norlin, sending Klauder back to Philadelphia with reservations about his parti, if not a command to redesign. Norlin wanted a campus design that symbolized the university's goal to be the preeminent institution in the Rockies.

University of Colorado, Old Main (1876). (RPD)

University of Colorado, Charles Z. Klauder detail. The selection of masonry materials provided seven decades of visual continuity, a major contributor to a strong image campus. (RPD)

University of Colorado. The Engineering Center adapts Klauder's forms to new ends and uses the texture of the local sandstone in the exterior walls as a design device for recalling visually the older architecture. (RPD)

University of Colorado, Klauder facade. (RPD)

Tuscany architecture. Said to have inspired Klauder's search for an appropriate style for Boulder. (RPD)

Chaco Canyon, detail, circa 1200 AD. Early American masonry architecture reminiscent of the Klauder work at the University of Colorado, Boulder. (RPD)

University of Colorado, Joint Institute for Laboratory Astrophysics. A distinguished example of referential and reverential architecture. (RPD)

Modified Gothic, introspective and safe, just would not do for an energetic and ambitious public university. The designs should speak to the important of science, engineering, and community service, and celebrate the region and people.

According to university legend, the train ride eastward gave Klauder time to imagine alternatives. A fluent draftsman, he sketched a dramatically different approach, inspired by Boulder's natural setting. It stirred memories of Klauder's travel through hillside Tuscany villages and farms. The architecture of that region had coherence and continuity; vernacular architecture achieved through the consistent use of stonework with steep, tiled roofs, intersecting at irregular angles. The shapes and forms thus created were accented and shadowed by a bright sun and blue sky, reminiscent of Boulder. Like the Tuscany hillscape, the university construction could be arranged with walls enclosing courtyards and quadrangles; the whole laced by walkways, accessible through archways, all orchestrated to reveal the views and vistas to the surrounding hills. If Collegiate Georgian resonates with fife and drum, Klauder's vision for Boulder was grand opera.

Klauder's design came to being at a time when the convential styles and design formulas, with few exceptions, had an exclusive claim on American campus design. Bush-Brown captures one such mode in a badinage that reveals the glory and the grievance. "Architects tossed chimeras of colorful stone, copper and terra cotta toward the sun, and craggy masses, dreadfully stunning by moonlight, were solemnly redolent of medieval piety far removed from the grimy furnaces, glistening rails and frenetic commerce where money was made for the new collegiate scene." For this kind of architecture, Klauder produced in Boulder as romantic a composition as he would later in Gothic for Princeton.

Particularly effective was Klauder's selection of Lyons sandstone as a predominant building material; in its panoramic presence, Boulder's equivalent of Oxford's oolitic ashlar. Quarried locally, it could be used in eight different ways, from rusticated blocks to a crushed rock filler for concrete aggregate. Thus, it was not as limiting in design expression as adobe, though as meaningful as a metaphoric material. Like Post's masonry at City College of New York, some of Klauder's detailing at Boulder hint at an architecture free of precedental references. The possibilities were not lost on his peers, who, honoring his work, saw in Boulder something "alive and vigorous, as to suggest a new approach."

As later events proved, Klauder's Tuscany derived concepts permitted large and complicated university buildings to be segmented into functional pieces and reassembled into refreshing and original architectural compositions. From 1921 through 1939, Klauder demonstrated the validity of his proposals in 14 major buildings and additions.

The Klauder concept is etched deep in the Boulder ethos. Few architects before, or since, would create on a single campus a broader range of building types: housing, engineering laboratories, museum, classroom and faculty offices, gymnasium, library, field house, and university club. Norlin's dream of regional architecture, remembered and associated with the university, was fully realized, not as a grand plan, but a sense of place uniquely its own.

The growth that followed World War II, during which time a campus designed for 3,000 students would have to accommodate 15,000, brought with it a necessary surge in construction, not all of its sympathetic to Klauder's concepts. The new architecture was lumpy; the detailing timid; the integration of building and landscape uncertain.

In 1960, counseled by Pietro Belluschi and Hideo Sasaki, the university leadership reexamined the question of planned development, architectural style, and landscape themes. Klauder's principles were reaffirmed, but modified to permit adjustments to program, budget, site conditions, the availability of stone masons, and the utilization of contemporary construction methods and building technologies.

Generally, the post-1960 buildings were responsible, evocative, and reasonable interpretations of Klauder's ideas. In some instances (Norlin Library Expansion), Klauder's designs were extrapolated so well as to be a Klauder clone. In some others, the designs were more gestures than adaptations; such as the Engineering Center, where the slanted roof, red tiles, and panelled Lyons sandstone display a family resemblance to other referential buildings. Fortunately the complex, commendable in general concept, is far enough away from Klauder's best buildings so that his exquisite detailing (now too expensive) is not missed.

Since 1970, 25 different architects have worked on 38 different projects on the Boulder campus. Klauder's influence can be seen in most of the buildings. A recent addition to the Joint Institute for Laboratory Astrophysics is all that one could wish for in reverential architecture. The design antecedents are acknowledged in shapes and forms. The Lyons sandstone in the facade is extended in color and texture to the surrounding pavement. A round window is located (humorously, not awesomely) within sight of one of Klauder's own versions of an appropriate sun shadowed aperture. Might Klauder have seen the archeological photos of Chaco Canyon's monumental masonary architecture seven centuries and several miles south of Boulder? The answer is yet to be determined, but the idea of converging designs, provocative.

Simon Fraser University, British Columbia. (Chris Hildred, Simon Fraser University Instructional Media Center)

Environs, Indiana State University, Terre Haute, Indiana. (RPD)

Landscapes

A campus without landscape is as likely as a circle without a circumference, an arch without a keystone, an ocean without water. Most campuses have significant acreage devoted to lawns, greens, and playfields. Areas between buildings have aesthetic, functional, and symbolic purposes which landscape defines and sustains. Landscape can serve as the skeleton for the overall campus plan, the interior circulation systems such as walks and roads, as well as provide a background for subtle and finer grain landscape motifs. The greenery includes the campus edges, gateways, gardens, arboretums, memorials, bell towers, fountains, outdoor sitting areas, signs, site furniture, and natural features on the site, including ponds, woodlands, and rock formations. These landscapes and plant material can abate noise, control dust, divert traffic, secure boundaries, afford privacy, and be arranged for pleasure.

The visual experience of the Indiana State University environs (Terre Haute) and Simon Fraser University (British Colombia) serve as polar contrasts; one on generous acreage enveloped in forest, the other in a decaying downtown neighborhood, where a tub of flowers and a street tree is an uplifting design statement. As land available and general geographic location will vary, so too will the landscape opportunities and campus design impressions. Arguably, campus design could be construed to be a sequence of visual impressions, generated by landscape components and experiences, which are arranged to produce a predetermined image and sense of place. The visual experiences begin in the environs as one approaches the campus, travels to the campus edges, enters the gateways and moves through the campus to various destinations. Page 226 outlines a campus landscape taxonomy. The individual components can be utilized for placemarking or placemaking. The list reflects an examination of several thousand campus landscape images—design icons, sacred places, grand spaces, as well as the modest nooks and crannies that humanize and invigorate campus life.

Differences in climate, sun-shadow patterns, soil, moisture, elevation, plant selection, and cultivation are fundamental factors that influence the size, appear-

Scripps College, Humanities Courtyard. Thomas D. Church, landscape architect. An instructive example of the landscape ethos that marks the Claremont Colleges as a distinctive place. (RPD)

Princeton University. From 1912 through 1942, the landscape designer Beatrix Jones provided Princeton with principles and patterns that continue to give the campus beckoning vistas and spatial sequences, courtyards, and beauty in all four seasons. (RPD)

ance, and quality of the campus greenery. More so than architecture, the land-scape can broadcast clues that locate a campus ecologically. To see, sense, and appreciate the differentials, consciously or otherwise, is to participate in a universal concern for habitat, natural resources, perhaps, world survival. A campus designed to illuminate such issues is consistent with higher education's teaching and research mandates.

Landscapes are art forms. Plant materials can be used in a painterly fashion, adding color and texture to architectural compositions, or as aesthetic objects in their own right. Certain plants are nature's clocks. Changes in color and leafing announce the passing seasons and, in some locales, the time of day. As a fragile but enduring art, this kind of landscape is found in abundance at Princeton University, where consulting landscape architect Beatrix Jones Farrand practiced as the "bush woman" from 1915 to 1943.

"Armed with an encyclopedic knowledge of plants, discriminating tastes, and unsurpassed skill in design, she cajoled trustees, browbeat deans, placated professors, conspired with head gardeners, and drove superintendents of buildings and grounds nearly mad with her spending." Then as now, Farrand's principles are instructive and commendable in their simplicity. She favored native species over the exotic plant materials, located in accordance with a plan that had a visual relationship "to existing lines or to possible future building sites." Evergreens were desirable against building walls so "the campus would look its best between September and June when the students were in residence." Pruning was a skill to be exercised aesthetically, and "unplanting" occasionally necessary to frame a vista. Farrand's efforts continued the exceptional work of James McCosh who served as Princeton's president for two decades in the 19th century. McCosh "delighted in planning new buildings and pathways" and was "instrumental in transforming an austere campus into an . . . environment of uncommon verdancy."

Greenery thus developed can become institutional symbols. Campus designs which encourage a landscape heritage will strengthen the notion of pride of place. Like mirrors to culture, the greenery could vary in meaning from campus to campus, as it does worldwide. Semeiotician Susan G. Carlisle sees the distinctive French forms "as faithful a guide to French attitudes as architecture or history." Nature is "raw material . . in need of direction . . . When the French treat a tree with little regard for how it might naturally grow," they assert "not only their right, but their responsibility to intervene for the tree's own good." For Carlisle, the "symmetry of French parks and the shape of French shrubs suggest . . . a Cartesian preference for mind over matter." In attitude, tree pruning is not much different than a French poodle's coiffure. Demonstrably, landscapes are culturally induced symbols rising from different sources and degrees of admiration as sacred or aesthetic objects. Compare France to Japan, where sacred manuals codify the six elements required for a traditional landscape: spaciousness, seclusion, antiquity, artificiality, water, and vista. The American campus landscape tradition is more laissez faire, reflecting, perhaps, a continental nation with pluralistic cultural influences.

Landscape can serve as an institutional metaphor. Bowdoin College's pine grove, cacti at the Arizona State University, the palms at the University of Miami, and the crab apple trees at Colorado's Fort Lewis College are prized examples of regional plants used for marking and exhalting a sense of place. Such traditions are visually rich, culturally significant, and historically meaningful. Fifty states

LANDSCAPE ELEMENTS

UNIVERSITY OF LIBERIA FENDELL CAMPUS PLAN

DOBER, LIDSKY, CRAIG AND ASSOCIATES, INC.

Climatological

PROTECTION FROM THE RAIN
and from intense sun in open areas.
For Example:
- Terminalia catappa
- Mangifera indica
- Samanea saman

PROTECTION FROM THE SUN
and with increased air circulation near buildings.
For Example:
- Delonix regia
- Cassia species

AIR CIRCULATION
can be directed and augmented, in and around buildings, with hedge and tree combinations. Wind can sometimes be increased up to as much as 26%.

Functional

EROSION CONTROL
Slopes and embankments are easily stabilized by fast-growing ground cover materials.
For Example:
- Elephant eats

ACOUSTIC CONTROL
Dense planting serves as noise barrier between the sound source and the listener. Roads close to classroom bldgs. should be buffered.

road | buffer | bldg.

SCREENS AND PRIVACY
psychological and physical separation are attainable.
For Example:
- Hibiscus species
- Bamboo species
- Nerium indicum
- Allamanda

Aesthetic

SCULPTURE
Specimen plants can be viewed alone as sculpture against a bldg. or landscape backdrop.
For Example:
- Cottonwood
- Draecena
- Artocarpus
- Pinus caribbea

CEREMONIAL AND SYMBOLIC ARTICULATION
of important objects or settings.
For Example:
- Delonix regia
- Samanea saman
- Roystonea regia
- Mangifera indica

TEXTURAL AND TACTILE RICHNESS
and color are incomparable contributions by plant materials.
For Example:
- Draecena
- Croton
- Acalypha

University of Liberia. Basic campus landscape principles applied to a regional setting. (Dober, Lidsky, Craig and Associates, Inc.)

170

Bowdoin College Pines. (RPD)

University of Miami Palms. (RPD)

Fort Lewis College Crab Apples. (RPD)

Arizona State University Cacti. (RPD)

Like building materials, plant materials can be adopted as institutional symbols and woven into the campus design as placemarkers and as well as placemakers. (RPD)

LANDSCAPE EXPERIENCES
HOBART AND WILLIAM SMITH COLLEGES
Dober, Lidsky, Craig and Associates, Inc.

Hobart and William Smith College Campus Design Studies. Landscape experience orchestrated to establish a sense of place. (Dober, Lidsky, Craig and Associates, Inc.)

have their official flowers. The fleur-de-lis is associated with French culture, the shamrock with Ireland, the thistle with Scotland, and leeks with the Welsh. Remember Shakespeare's Lancaster and York, their differences proclaimed with red and white roses emblazoned on shield, banner, and architecture? Ivy has taken on similar connotations for some colleges and universities. Williams College deliberately decorates its walls with a species that will turn from green to red to green during the school year—a living signal of institutional presence. Inspired by Frederick Law Olmsted, Jr., the Smith College campus was designed as an arboretum. Campus life is enjoyed in a series of connected landscapes which have come to be remembered and honored as a Smith image. About the same time, diagonally across the continent in Southern California, the Claremont Colleges were intended to be constructed "in a garden." The founders rejected formal architectonic plans in favor of horticultural settings. Here, especially at Pomona College and Scripps College, the botanical tradition continues with institutional conviction and pride, an image of regional beauty in the smog-bound San Gabriel Valley.

California may also take pride in the quality of landscape profiles that make each of the nine campuses of the University of California distinctive. Most of the campuses differ not only in the way they are structured organizationally for undergraduate and graduate instruction, research, and service but also in the physical forms that express and facilitate those differences. With the exception of San Francisco (the smallest and devoted solely to health sciences), these are multipurpose, megacampuses, enrolling 8,000 to 36,000 students. To decipher, compare, and evaluate their individual physical environments would be to write an encyclopedia on campus design. In their historic and current forms, there are few architectural or landscape concepts not represented. Proud Berkeley overlooking the Bay area; San Diego almost literally on the Pacific Rim; the open feeling of Irvine in contrast with the urbanity of Los Angeles; the new campus at Riverside with its grand lawn and courts; Santa Barbara well-marked with its red-tile roofs; these each have a sense of place; and in terms of an enveloping landscape and campus design concept, a jewel in any crown, the campuses at Santa Cruz.

GENTLE BE THE HAND

An architecture here must grow out of the problems, restrictions, and potentialities of the site. Usual relationships of building groups in a formal pattern may violate the topography beyond repair. Grading and reforming of the land there will be, but kept to a minimum. Tree-clearing will be inevitable, not because architecture forces it, but because the ultimate landscape demands it. There will be no indiscriminate removal of major redwood groves to accommodate preconceived architectural schemes. To a greater extent than any of us have faced heretofore, the buildings are less important in the visual composition than the trees. . . It would be foolish and highly undesirable to think that a new startling architecture will appear here. Any attempt of a designer to compete in grandeur with this site is doomed to failure. With the exception of areas especially preserved in their natural state the general effect in the main campus area must be one of sensitive collaboration between the designer and this spectacular environment, with the intention that neither shall impose unduly upon the other . . .

University of California, Berkeley. (RPD)

University of California, Riverside. (RPD)

University of California, Irvine. (RPD)

University of California, Santa Cruz. (UCSC)

Four university campuses pleasant and distinctive in their setting, landscapes, and architectural features.

(The plan) must be magnificent in conception, daring and forthright in its architecture—but gentle be the hand it lays upon the land.
(Random Notes on the Site—Typescript, Thomas D. Church,
Consulting Landscape Architect, Santa Cruz Campus
29 October 1962)

Located 75 miles south of San Francisco, the 2,000 acre site of the University of California, Santa Cruz campus unfolds itself like an oriental scroll with a physical form and educational mode unique in American public higher education. The sense of place begins at the south entry, where the historic ranch buildings that first occupied the site have been preserved and adapted for University use. From the gateway, campus roads carry traffic upward through grasslands and meadow to groves of trees—redwood and evergreen forests, which embrace the campus buildings. The climate and weather pattern, seldom severe, transform daily the scenic experiences, which include vistas to the Pacific Ocean below and the Ben Lomond Mountain above. The campus plan prepared by John Carl Warnecke and Associates (1963) is a vision fulfilled, yet awaiting completion.

The site is one of three experiments in university organization proposed for the University of California by Clark Kerr in his brilliant response to a surge in population predicted to begin in the 1960s. The Santa Cruz, Irvine, and San Diego campuses were to build big while appearing small, each with an organizational pattern distinctly its own. "We want to use bigness for all the advantages that it offers at the same time we retain a scale, physically and socially, educationally and administratively, that is human and, therefore, in the highest sense individual," noted Santa Cruz's first chancellor, Dean E. McHenry. The physical response was a campus design concept that provided sites for 20 residential colleges clustered on either side of core facilities such as libraries and laboratories, student center, and operations buildings. Like a superior plant, cross-pollinated, the intellectual advantages of the large, modern university (German in origin) were combined with the life style of the small college (initially seen as a West Coast version of Oxford, and more recently described as being "similar to the system at Harvard and Yale").

Warnecke's scheme anticipated 27,500 students by 1990. To date eight of the projected 20 colleges have been constructed. Enrollments total about 9,300 students, mostly undergraduate. The 1989 revised development plan concludes that "in order for the Santa Cruz campus to fulfill its goals and become a full-fledged member of the University of California system in terms of depth, breadth and quality of its teaching and research programs, it must grow with care and foresight to provide facilities for an enrollment level of no fewer than 15,000 students."

Critical mass, not population pressure, drives the plan forward. Site sensitive development, the image of a campus integrated into an ecological preserve, is the overriding theme in the 1989 plan. Over half the 2,000 acres have been set aside to be maintained in their natural state as protected landscapes, an environmental reserve, and land assigned for limited development such as a water storage tank. Outdoor playfields will utilize 88 acres. A total of 16,800 linear feet of new roadways are anticipated and space set aside for parking 3,887 vehicles. The specificity reflects caution and control over potentially intrusive elements. The 102-acre campus core will remain the focal area for centralized instructional and research fa-

Detail. Long Range Development Plan, University of California, Santa Cruz, John Carl Warnecke. The basic landscape concepts continue to guide university development, though many of the assumptions upon which the campus design was formulated in 1963 have not fully materialized. (UCSC Library)

cilities, and shared common purpose functions. The original arc of colleges and graduate student housing will be expanded to 241 acres.

New designs for the additional colleges are likely to be exercises in architectural imagination, with few preconceptions as to style and site arrangement, but similar in program intention: self-sufficient residential enclaves of 750 to 1,250 students, with affiliated faculty and staff, sharing the intellectual thrust of the individual college while participating in a university life vibrating in the Garden of Higher Education.

NATURE'S IMPERATIVES

Should there be multiple plantings to generate a landscape image, or plantings of single species to create singular strokes? The debate between designers seeking striking effects by using a single species and arborists desiring plant viability through species mixing is not yet settled. The Dutch Elm disease has decimated many a picturesque campus. Comparisons of photos of late 19th century college grounds in the Northeast and the same views today give ample evidence of landscape's vulnerability. Unlike buildings, which can impose a strong image in a rel-

Cluster college. Each Santa Cruz cluster college is differentiated architecturally. The all-embracing landscape serves as a unifying design theme. (RPD)

atively short time span, the better landscape effects require years to mature. Farrand encouraged Princeton to keep a stock of "large trees and shrubs in the nursery root-pruned and ready for immediate transplanting," should wind, age, or disease ruin the design patterns. But such strokes are of no help when the causes are systemic and endemic. Certain tree types used as design components to define axial compositions and en masse as design symbols now seem equally susceptible to disease and poor horticultural practices as were the American Elms. The amber light of caution should be obeyed when schemes are presented with single species designs.

Nature and nurture must be kept in balance. Good intentions are no substitute for informed opinions. For St. Catherine's College (Oxford), "Professor Arne Jacobsen designed everything, buildings, furniture, cutlery, the bicycle shed in a perfect circle, and the gardens." A corporation dump, "Marmite pots and sauce bottles of an earlier civilization," was transformed into a college site. The geometric matching of greenery and buildings became an icon of modern architecture, as such was determined in 1960, including one tree planted off axis "because nature is nature." Unfortunately, Jacobsen's first plantings would not hold, being unsuitable for the soil and microclimate. Fortunately, the second attempt is working. Jacobson's plan and proportions are not lost, though creepers and shrubs have lightened his austere architectural arrangements.

Design reasons must be matched with suitable methods, and for landscape, the long view is essential in conjuring an appropriate image. In these respects, the Simpson College (Iowa) experience is worth summarizing as an instructive example of landscape as symbol, as an insight to the consequences such concepts may have as art and ecology interface, and as encouragement for further efforts when such symbols are no longer viable. For almost a century, Simpson's silver

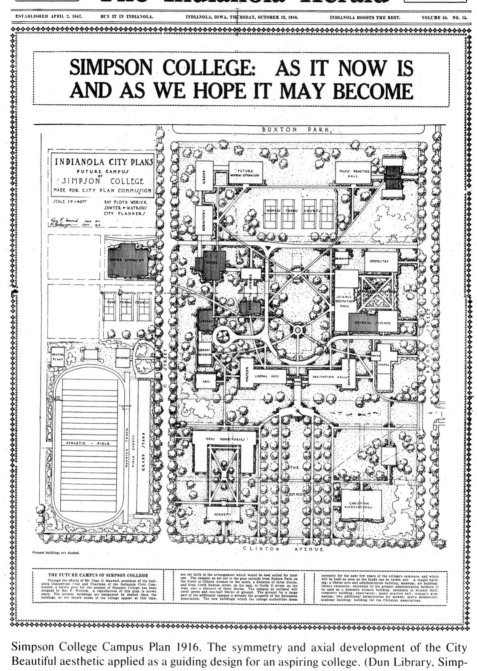

Simpson College Campus Plan 1916. The symmetry and axial development of the City Beautiful aesthetic applied as a guiding design for an aspiring college. (Dun Library, Simpson College)

maples have celebrated the campus presence in hymn, image, and campus design. The school's first two buildings "stood on land barren in winter and planted in corn . . . during the growing season." Shade trees were rare in that part of Iowa. The gift of young maples was most welcomed when a college trustee offered (May 1870) "seedlings the size of broom handles." Seizing an unusual opportunity, the college president declared a holiday and assigned each student the task of planting two rows of trees on the campus boundaries and clusters within. Comparable generosities adorn both the histories and the campuses of higher education. The magnificent elms that bordered Cornell University's East Avenue were the gift (1877) of "a plain farmer from a distant part of the country, a hard-working man of very small means . . . (who) would very much like to do something for the university." They were planted by Andrew D. White, Cornell's prodigious president, just quoted, whose lifelong interest in campus beautification are still evident in Ann Arbor and Ithaca.

By the turn of the century, the Simpson College trees had turned the prairie campus into a forested grove, giving the college a reputation for beauty known region-wide. The trees are featured in the college's 1916 campus plan, an orderly scheme that shows "Simpson College: as it now is and as we hope it may become." The plan is a fine example of the art of campus design as it was then characteristically practiced, conceptually and cartographically. The automobile had not yet abused the landscape. In the interest of symmetry, it was assumed the college's first two buildings could be demolished to create a rural version of the City Beautiful, an impulse not implemented.

At the time the plan was published, the maples were full size, legendary and soon to be honored in the campus song: "Riotous color . . . cool, shady nooks, whispering maples." The words and music rang out on graduation day 1990, but the silver maples were missing. The species was vulnerable to insect and storm damage. In a relatively short time, the campus looked denuded, the image diminished, and the havoc unexpected. Simpson landscape is gradually being restored, with less dependency on a single species; but the substantial visual impact of the silver maples—an all encompassing agglutinative for a century of varied architecture—will not have its equivalency in this generation.

The landscapes described so far are an art underappreciated in campus design today; too often seen as an extra to be added to the bottom line of the project budget, a sum to be reduced when contingency funds are expended. Perhaps this attitude reflects a society where ecological imperatives have been ignored and the instant effect commands more attention that the long term. Soundbites may have their architectural equivalent, but not landscape, whose maturation requires time, patience, and care. Recently an urban university, rightfully seeking a humanizing landscape in a visually impoverished locale, made a significant investment in landscape. Unfortunately, once installed, the funds for maintenance were insufficient for the species selected. The dying remnants added a nightmarish picture to an already architecturally tattered environment.

In truth, beautiful campuses are those well landscaped. Fortunately, landscape is again in its ascendancy as a contributor to campus design. The clarion cry for restoration is one of the profession's oldest. Stephen Blake, 1664: "The improving of a thing is to bring it from barrenness to fruitfulness; for bareness is a disease and improvement is a cure." Brown University is adding bulbs and flowering trees along the edges of its venerated greens. The older courtyards at the Harvard Busi-

The whispering maples. The thick grove gave Simpson College a design image that attracted students and tourists. (Dun Library, Simpson College)

The Simpson version of Old Main. The late 19th century building visible through the grove was preserved and renovated in 1987. The surrounding landscape has been developed with a broader range of trees and shrubbery so as to vary the design effects and lessen the possibilities of another ecological disaster. (RPD)

St. Catherine's College, Oxford. A lesson-giving example of a strong design concept upset by indifference to site and terrain conditions. The second version succeeded, though aspects of the design today have grown shabby through inadequate maintenace. (RPD)

Detail, the landscape revived at the Harvard Business School. The courtyards and paths constructed in recent years are fine examples of institutional landscape in a dense development zone. (Carol Johnson and Associates, Inc.)

ness School have been renewed and refreshened with a regionally viable landscape. The University of Illinois is extending northward the planting schemes which were inaugurated when the Dutch elm disease decimated the central campus. Cornell has a full-time professional to write guidelines for protecting and enhancing the campus landscape, and to coordinate and integrate new designs. Vassar College has prepared a comprehensive scheme to restore its historic landscape, a commendable, pioneering effort. The scheme (Sasaki and Associates) will enable the college to replace and resuscitate plant materials where they are critical to the views and vistas and to rationalize funding for mundane but pragmatic necessities such as site drainage.

The art of landscape is being replenished with fresh ideas, such as MIT's East Campus Courtyard and the Tanner Fountain just beyond Harvard Yard. The former uses monumental masonry materials on walls and horizontal surfaces, in conjunction with a slash of grass and trees, and a gateway that stirs recollections of Stonehenge, the latter, a 60-foot circle of field stones, moistened by mist in the summer and steam in the winter. The stones commemorate the clearing of the New England's woods and the ever changing surfaces the cycle natural processes, "the romance of a remote past, the mystery of places whose meaning is lost or dimly understood . . . and the desire for conceptual order in a complicated world," writes designers Peter Walker and Martha Schwartz. Not to be overlooked are interior landscapes, such as the Campus Center at Rochester Institute of Technology, providing comfort and delight, particularly in winter months. The

University of Illinois, the 19th century landscape which was dependent on large elm trees has been replaced with a studied vocabulary of hedges, grass, and smaller flowering trees. (Sasaki and Associates)

Vassar College. An extensive landscape restoration plan has been launched to restore the historic views and vistas and campus beauty. (J. A. Hibbard, Sasaki and Associates)

Southern Colorado University. Sculptured fountain, seats, and landscape—a pleasant respite in an arid land. (RPD)

Harvard University, Tanner Fountain. (Peter Walker and Martha Schwartz)

Massachusetts Institute of Technology, East Campus paving, landscape detailed as art. (RPD)

Rochester Institute of Technology, interior landscape. (RPD)

University of Vienna, arcade facing courtyard. (RPD)

Bates College, Library arcade. (RPD)

Old ideas refreshened, varying the combinations, new interpretations—these are methods which can be applied to devise placemarking landscapes. The patterned outdoor pavings at the Massachusetts Institute of Technology have their counterpart in a 19th century covered walkway at the University of Vienna. The Bates College arcade is reminiscent of Vienna, but expressed in a contemporary design, that also overlooks the adjacent landscaped quadrangle. The interior walkway at the Rochester Institute of Technology brings plant materials inside; the floor surfaces are patterned by the natural cycle of sun and shadow and artificial light.

Foothills College. (Peter Walker)

Southern Colorado University. (RPD)

Southern Mississippi University. (RPD)

Harvard Yard. (RPD)

Lawns and trees are used consistently as a metaphor for higher education—the campus, throughout the United States. On many European campuses, trees are used minimally, as design accents, and the ground plane typically is paved, not grassed.

University of Helsinki. Late 19c courtyard. (RPD)

University of Aachen. Late 20c courtyard. (RPD)

15th century arcade at the University of Vienna has its equivalent at Bates College—protected access space to see the landscape in poor weather.

CAMPUS GREENS: LAWNS AND TREES

> . . . this Lawn, a carpet all alive,
> With shadows flung from leaves . . .
> (W. W. Wordsworth)

Grass, trees, and fencing—this constituted the first landscapes of America's first colleges. Woodland areas were cut back, nature tamed, and the site organized for institutional habitation and buildings. The greens are hoary symbols, such as Harvard Yard, or the Lawn at Charlottesville, Thomas Jefferson's signature landscape at the University of Virginia. Today's versions provide a green ambiance for buildings, serve as an outdoor lounge, and furnish a stage for formal and informal institutional rituals. The image is captured in early drawings and lithographs, and more recently imprinted on greeting cards, calendar art, catalogs, and viewbooks intended to entice, recruit, entertain, and commemorate. A recognizable institutional placemarker, this kind of iconic greenery is duplicated by Hollywood set designers wanting to authenticate a typical campus mood. In these scenes, the lawns and trees will be displayed as the foreground for architecture or as a landscape with people engaged in daily life or special events.

Simulacrum and reality are not far apart. That much greenery will lie dormant and brown during most of the school year seems irrelevant. Spring's freshening blossoms and fall's vibrant colors are retainable memories. The greens have become metaphors for institutional presence; sometimes even seeded, grown, planted, and nurtured in environments hostile to their existence. The late summer cutting heralds the beginning of the school year; the last spring manicure is the prelude to commencement. The greenery may be the most enduring and prevalent of campus images. However, they are not a natural occurrence but a manufactured conceit, so prevalent on American campuses that they are taken for granted.

LAWNS SPATIALLY/SYMBOLICALLY/AESTHETICALLY

Though the lawn's provenance is misted in history, an appreciation of its origins will shed light on its endurance, application, and suitability as a campus design element and institutional metaphor. Lawns dimension outdoor spaces, as a floor carpet would a room. The method may have its antecedents in ancient Rome where villa walls enclosed pleasure gardens, some of which used ornamental grasses. These ground plans informed idealized concepts for the monasteries that emerged as educational centers in the dark ages. The monastic landscapes were developed to supply flowers for the altars, vegetables for the kitchen, and healing herbs for the physician. A typical layout included the garth, a cloistered space divided into four squares, fringed with grass and flowers. The space was traversed like a campus quadrangle, as monks walked to and from refectory, school, church, and work. At Mount Grace Priory, Yorkshire, the individual monk cells have their own walled gardens; sometimes flowered, sometimes grassed.

In principle, the Yorkshire concept is not unlike Thomas Jefferson's plans for the University of Virginia with the pavilions and ranges of rooms connected to the gardens. Most American Colonial Colleges simply dropped their buildings on a green mat, precedence for the open campus plan. Jefferson's campus design differed in this regard, being a U-shaped grouping of connected buildings facing five grass plots bordered with trees. The original nucleus was closed in by a Stanford White building in 1895. The Virginia lawn continued intacto, becoming as sacred a precinct as a public institution would permit.

Oxford and Cambridge's early colleges evolved from monastic settlements, or were developed from properties rented, purchased, or inherited. Many included gardens that were later integrated in the college's growth patterns. Few of these medieval landscapes survived changes in taste and aesthetic preferences. As buildings differ in style, so do garden designs. Merton College has Oxford's oldest collegiate enclosure (Mob Quad), begun in 1277 and completed about a century later. The record is not clear as to when the present emerald green square was planted. Awaiting stronger claims, Mob Quad would seem to be the oldest college lawn extant.

The Oxford experiences are informative in many regards, with citable precedents and interesting examples. William of Wykeham earns prominence as the first European planner to lay out a purpose-built campus design, New College, Oxford (1379). Here the older cloister was disengaged from its adjoining rooms to become a sheltered arcade for contemplative walks. The enclosed spaces was grassed and planted with trees. Once inside the college precinct, college members, staff, and visitors could enjoy a sequence of spaces designed for community activities, ceremony, exercise, reflective thought, pleasure, and utility. Thus realized, Wykeham's consciously designed landscape themes are as germane to campuses now as they were six centuries ago.

The grassy lawn as institutional icon: the design lineage can be traced from campuses on the rim of the Pacific (Foothills College), to the arid foothills of the Rockies (Colorado State University), to Iowa's cornfields (Grinnell College) and southern Mississippi's pine barrens, to the edge of Seneca Lake in upstate New York (Hobart and William Smith Colleges), to the older colleges and universities on the East Coast, such as Harvard Yard, and across the Atlantic to England. As Andrew Marvel would exult, these are places for "a green thought in a green shade."

Grass can be found throughout the globe, with over 9,000 species comprising 20 percent of the world's vegetation. Its utilization as a ground cover has strong connections with England: Shakespeare's Emerald Isle, bowling greens, cricket pitches, race courses, palace and manor grounds, town parks, and college precincts. Great Britain's climate fosters grass production, which early in English history was an agricultural necessity, and later a horticultural resource. From need grew art. Medieval and Renaissance manuscripts in mainland Europe do honor to the British tradition with drawings of the *plat anglais*. The lawn is a contrasting element in elaborate box, hedge, and flower bed arrangements. Mounded turfs, the lawn uplifted, become thrones in pleasure gardens, the seats for Madonnas and monarchs in Flemish paintings.

Bartholomew the Englishman codified these practices in his classic gardening

Mob Quadrangle, Oxford. The oldest surviving collegiate open space, more or less intact. (RPD)

encyclopedia (1265). Most medieval lawns were essentially meadows with mixed grasses and flowers, not often cut. But Bartholomew held:

> . . . the sight is in no way so pleasantly refreshed as by fine and close grass kept short . . . (which flourishing should) be beaten down with broad wooden mallets (and) trodden into the ground (to then) spring forth closely and cover the surface like a green cloth . . . Upon the lawn too, against the heat of the sun, trees should be planted or vines trained, so that the lawn may have a delightful and cooling shade, sheltered by their leaves . . . there should not be any trees in the middle of the lawn, but rather let its surface delight in open air.

Should campus design require a patron saint, Bartholomew would be a leading candidate. To his idealized lawn, Georgian horticulturists added scientific, aesthetic, and mechanical advances, and from Victorian England, the ultimate technology, the mechanical lawn mower. More so than any era, the Georgian affinity for greenswards stimulated both the image and invention of the lawn as a prototype design. The range of plant types was extended through imports from North America and Asia. Through trial and error, 18th century gardeners provided "ready-made mixes of six or seven grasses . . . with ten percent clover seed." The latter added nitrogen to the soil. The former produced the color palette much desired in North America. Parenthetically, today's obsession with weeds did not bother the Georgians. Herbicides were not used. The delicate tints and texture which weeds added to their lawn were thought to be part of nature's visual harmony, not a blight. This attitude about innate beauty might once again be encouraged, given the environmental stress caused by weedkillers and insecticides.

Georgian lawns were rough-cut with scythes and than rolled to felt-like smoothness. In some garden designs, shears were used to get a close-crop texture. Large tracts were tamped by horse drawn rollers. The animals feet were enclosed by padded overshoes to keep the hoof-prints off the placid green plane. The invention of the lawnmower (a by-product of industrialized clothmaking, circa 1830) make it possible for Everyman to garden like the gentry, and every collegiate quad to shear its outdoor carpets more often than before. Where earlier generations would tolerate high grass aesthetically, the cutting of grass blades to one inch heights became common practice as a desired art.

When England industrialized, cast iron parts, steam power, and cheap glass were appropriated for greenhouses, permitting year-round research on viable plant materials. Cheap books and magazines disseminated information on lawn production and care, a design influence comparable to the architectural pattern books. In bits and pieces, what occurred in England—design concepts, horticultural knowledge, practices and technologies—found its way to the North American campuses. Quickened by a common language and a mutual interest in civilizing nature, the English connections are evident on several thousand campuses from Antioch College to Xavier University; especially the manner in which Georgians would lay out their public buildings and estates—the arrangement of buildings on open lawns not pent up with trees. When the Collegiate Gothic gained prominence as a campus design metaphor, the grass-covered, enclosed English quad likewise would be used as a paradigm, as would the velvet greenery used as a garnish in Beaux Arts axial compositions that might have been drawn by Christopher Wren.

The Anglo-American lawns first seen along the Eastern seaboard have had, of course, to be modified in other parts of the country by climate, soil, and moisture conditions. But the determination to grow grass and create campus lawns has not been thwarted by seemingly adverse environments. Whether on the arid plains or in semitropical coastal states, some combination of seeds, fertilizer, and watering yield the desired greenery.

The enchantment with campus greenery may be argued on other grounds. Recent statistics indicate that an estimated 3.2 million acres of American land are cultivated as household lawns. The sea of grass reflects (claim some social commentators) the democratization of land ownership, celebrated first in Frederick Law Olmsted's design stipulations for his Riverside development (1868). Olmsted banned walls and enclosures. Each plot had a front lawn "that would flow together into his neighbors, creating the impression that all lived together in a single park." On typical campuses the greensward is the design element that unifies buildings and spaces. The lawn is an expected campus experience. "We wanted a melodramatic Harvard Yard, with green open spaces," notes designer Peter Walker in explaining his scheme for Foothills College (1957), where the California landforms and plantings were adapted to meet that end.

A campus design icon, the lawn seems immutable. After 245 years of discussion, the faculties at Christ Church College (Oxford) decided (1978) to enliven a prosaic quad with a Palladian greenery, first proposed by William Williams in *Oxonia Depicta* (1733). At the University of Idaho, the symbolic front lawn that

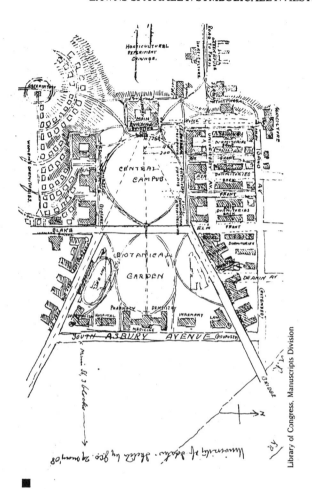

John C. Olmsted's plan for the University of Idaho.
*This sketch and a 25-page report were sent to President
MacLean in May 1908. The plan reflects Olmsted's fundamental
recommendation: acquire land, especially to the east.*

*"The greater part of the land proposed to be added east...is
relatively low and nearly level. It would be admirably well
adapted for the Athletic grounds and for ball fields and
Botanical Garden and any not needed for those purposes
should be improved and kept as a simple meadow, with a few
trees, so that the main group of University buildings would
forever have a handsome, dignified frontage; and so it would
be kept open to view from the railroad and the city."*

*The symmetrical layout of major buildings along a mall
and diagonal streets focusing on a primary building are
Renaissance design elements that found a home in the City
Beautiful movement that swept across early 20th century
America.*

University of Idaho, the Olmsted concept. (University of Idaho)

evolved from John Olmsted's campus plan (1908), considered by many an historic campus design element and placemarker, was endangered by a proposal to use the site for a new building. The cause celebre (1957) included the threatened resignation of the dean of the University's School of Architecture should the grass be violated. What was the outcome? Agreement to keep the acreage green. The author recalls (1985) the barbed-wide enclosure that kept untrampled the green grass that decorated the center of Fudan University (PRC). The lawn had become an emblem of Fudan's wish to participate in western forms of higher education; the greenery was the celebratory placemarker.

The grass wars continue these days. For some, the incessant conflict between asphalt for parking and grass for campus beauty seems endless, especially when pressures on the institution's physical plant budget has left once beautiful lawns tattered and worn. Poorly maintained landscapes have few friends when quotidian convenience vies with uncertain comeliness. What is true for grass is applicable to other plant materials that edge the lawns and adorn the campus. Increasingly, and sadly, that which was green, gracious, genial, if not grand, has been displaced by a bare, bald, and barren campus landscape. The annual "digging, dunging, cutting" has been forgotten. The image of campus as greenery has given way to the reality of an impoverished landscape; not everywhere but sufficient to be noticeable and worrisome.

The causes of this neglect are in part indifference, in part dire circumstances—the budget blues which have left campuses without sufficient horticultural skills to keep the landscapes alive. Of equal consequence are the constraints on augmenting existing landscapes. Thus desirable design initiatives are temporized in

Christ Church College, Oxford. The Georgian scheme implemented two centuries later. (RPD)

the name of economic necessity. On the positive side, hard times have generated campus plans that are marked not so much by a grandiose landscape scheme, but rather inflected by a "landscape ethic" which gives priority to saving and savoring existing plant materials and historic landscapes. In this context, a cultivated lawn or its equivalent and a viable landscape not only signifies a signal of institutional continuity and fiscal stability, but a campus that cares about its image, traditions, physical environment, reasons for being, and the people it serves.

These efforts could be advanced further by specifically designating someone in a prestigious and visible position to be responsible for the campus landscape. The office would become the focus for conserving and enhancing existing campus landscapes and promoting their enlargement and extension. The goal could be met by establishing and endowing a chair in botany, horticulture, or landscape architecture—an appointment that includes responsibilities as curator of the grounds. This would be consistent with the institution's teaching, research, and community service roles. Earlier generations ennobled the chaplain, the registrar, the dean of students, the librarian, the athletic director: officers with status, power, and influence. Why not a comparable post, respected academically, to look after the campus greenery?

Are lawns boring? Not intrinsically. In an inventive design, landscape architect Richard Haag softly blends a brick walk and grass into an unexpected version of a traditional quadrangle at Eastern Washington University, formerly Eastern Washington State College. Geoffrey Jellicoe's contemporary schemes for replanting Sutton Place (Surrey) give evidence of how grass can be arranged in small spaces and large—in delightful consort with walks, walls, trees, shrubs, sculpture, and water. Here may be seen a three-dimensional catalog of ideas worth considering for campus venues.

Eastern Washington University. (Richard Haag and Associates)

Some designers and planners believe that lawns and grass have exhausted themselves as a campus design metaphor. Some find the lawn's intensive demand for fertilizers, herbicides, and insecticides troubling environmentally. Some advocate a reduction in grassy lawns in adverse climates and in unfavorable soils. Cornell University's landscape architect, John Ulberg, believes that campus designers should consider the extraordinary range of groundcovers that are available as alternatives for grass. The materials are ecologically advantageous, require lower maintenance, and offer greater color and texture than grass. Ironically, the ecological imperatives led designer Carol Johnson back to the lawn's medieval beginnings, meadows and wild flowers, for the proposed new Emerson College campus. As Joseph Addison would write of his beloved Oxford, along these paths the "verdure of the Grass, Embroidery of the Flowers and the Glistening of the Dew" stokes the imagination.

CONTRASTING NOTIONS AND IMAGEABLE EFFECTS

An informative scan of campus designs produced in the last two centuries shows traditional landscape concepts being adapted to new conditions, with the differences exciting clients and designers to imagine landscapes in ways that contravene earlier theories.

Not all would agree with Francis Bacon (1625) that "nothing is more pleasant to the eye than green grass kept finely shorn." For a while, the rustic was prized at Oxford. Worcester College's medieval fishponds were converted to sylvan lakes. Nature was preserved, imitated, or simulated, giving cause for a codified campus design aesthetic, the 18th century picturesque. Cartesian site design compositions were "deformalized." William Hogarth's serpentine line would lead the eye on "a wanton chase" through a landscape with a nubby topology "Concave and Convex." The painterly instinct was undergirded by a pseudo-scientific rationale. Supporting the new landscape, natural philosophers would claim green was the color "most agreeable to the Organ of sight." The picturesque is a placemarker at such geographically distant campuses as Wheaton College and Tsinghua University. The lakeside areas are designers' artifices. The straight line is tabu. Nature is arranged and interpreted in ways suitable for inspiring painters and poets, al fresco. The resulting site compositions such as Lake Andrews (Bates College) are faithful to the word's original meaning—picturesque: a scenery adoptable or adaptable as a commodity worth having or viewing. In the 1920s, Carleton College wetlands were dug and shaped as two linked lakes. Bridged and edged with trees, the rustic image appears to be older than the college itself. At the University of New Mexico (1965), on an arid plateau a mile above sea level, Garrett Eckbo sculpted and landscaped a one acre artificial pond in the most unlikely of architectural settings. His inspired, popular, image-making design recalls an environment far removed from Albuquerque. With its waterfall, bog gardens, duck island, and fish, it makes no sense except as an evocative, emotionally charged campus landscape in the picturesque tradition. For the University of Miami, Lake Osceola is the campus open space.

To imprint the picturesque on Magdalen College, Humphrey Repton (1801) proposed reorganizing the medieval architecture by removing certain wings and roofs and romanticizing the adjacent meadow with a new landscape. The plan was shelved. A "preposterous absurdity" deserving to be "consigned to oblivion" said the influential Oxford antiquarian J. C. Buckler. His crusade for preserving the medieval scene helped promote the Gothic Revival, with a romantic landscape of a different kind, but no less stagecrafted.

Landscape issues were never treated lightly at Oxford, nor today on many American campuses with sacred spaces. Faculty and students will march to save a tree. Neighborhoods will organize to preserve a landscaped campus view. For some institutions, aesthetic differences are verifiable turf wars. The Merton College Memorials (Oxford) describe the bitter mid-17th century negotiations with adjacent Corpus Christi over abutting land; whether to leave the landscape in natural forms, or "the stiff Dutch clippings of trees then in vogue." Rock gardens were invented at St. John's College (Oxford), 1893. Professor Henry Jardine Bidder wanted a miniature version of an expansive picturesque landscape, with less fuss over controlling large acreage. His art form serves many campuses as a way of memorializing people and events graciously and economically. "However modest, don't attempt to move them once constructed," says one experienced campus planner.

In achieving a sense of place through landscape, the architectonic and the gardenesque are polar concepts, reflecting different strands of aesthetic history. The former, like the North Campus Plan for the University of Illinois, Urbana-Champaign, are calibrated arrangements of plant materials and ground covers, which in association with buildings, walls, and walks define and animate spaces geometrically. The latter, as with Colgate University's nine distinctive campus landscapes, emphasizes the intrinsic beauty and natural forms of the trees, plants, and shrubs; interpreting them ecologically in campus designs that reflect differing functions, terrain, and locale. The Illinois concept rationalizes the landscape with the linearity of the City Beautiful aesthetic. The Colgate venue approximates Henry James's Tuscany delights: ". . . compact and admirable, overflowing with everything that makes for ease, for interest and good example." And then there are landscapes which fit neither category, whose presence marks a place; nostalgic, memory-stirring imagery. Once discovered, these need conservation and nurturing.

SPECIAL PLACES: SCIENCE AS LANDSCAPE

Greenery for science and art; landscape's contribution to campus design rises above the quotidian with arboretums, natural areas, and gardens. These special places have an honored role in campus development, combining as they do instruction and research, while offering abundant beauty year round. The size, location, characteristics, and quality of these special places can inform the campus image.

Situated at the perimeter of Antioch College's central campus, the 940-acre Glen Helen woodland and stream preserve, with its dramatic change in grade, is a superb counterpoint to the nearby 19th century brick architecture and surrounding lawns. The Sanctuary at Sweet Briar College (Virginia), the Grassland Preserve (Washington State University), and Christy Woods (Ball State University) are small in acreage but formidable as an educational resource and a symbolic statement in an age where environmental issues earn front page attention. Useful

Worcester College, Oxford. (RPD)

Wheaton College, Massachusetts. (RPD)

University of Miami. (RPD)

Tsinghua University. (RPD)

Carleton College. (RPD)

Bates College, Maine. (RPD)

Ponds and lakes created to provide a picturesque campus landscape setting with regional variations that establish and inform a sense of place.

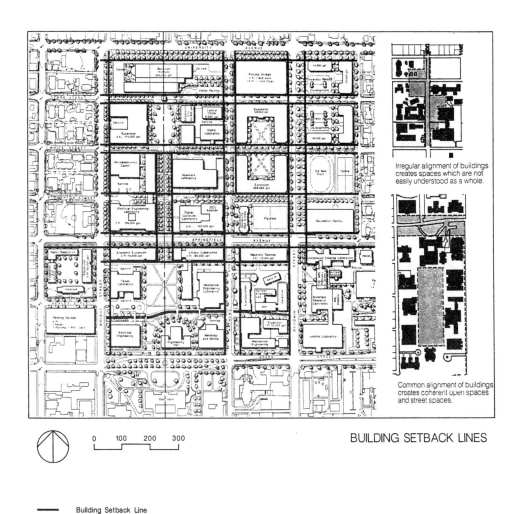

Irregular alignment of buildings creates spaces which are not easily understood as a whole.

Common alignment of buildings creates coherent open spaces and street spaces.

0   100   200   300

BUILDING SETBACK LINES

——— Building Setback Line

University of Illinois, North Campus Plan Studies. (Sasaki and Associates)

Landscape elements—roads, walks, trees, and new construction are positioned to create a strong geometrical campus design concept. Clarity and visual coherence is favored over a loose arrnagement of buildings and landscapes.

CAMPUS LANDSCAPE

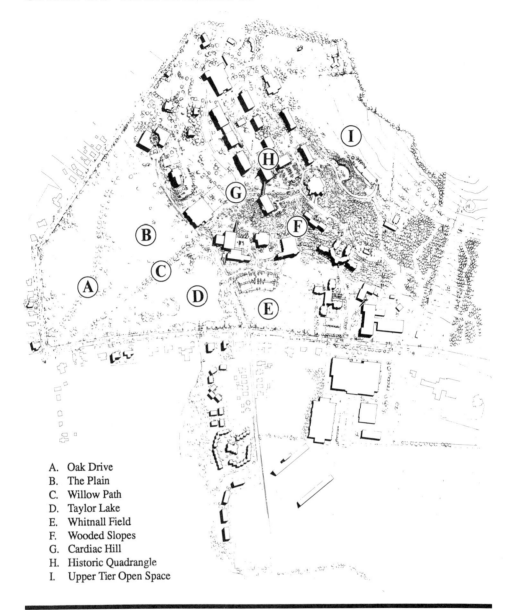

A. Oak Drive
B. The Plain
C. Willow Path
D. Taylor Lake
E. Whitnall Field
F. Wooded Slopes
G. Cardiac Hill
H. Historic Quadrangle
I. Upper Tier Open Space

COLGATE UNIVERSITY
CAMPUS PLAN STUDIES 1990
DOBER, LIDSKY, CRAIG AND ASSOCIATES, INC.

Colgate University landscapes. (Dober, Lidsky, Craig and Associates, Inc.)

Colgate University landscapes

Taylor Lake (D). (RPD)

Sinclair Community College, a formal landscape. (Edward Durell Stone Associates.)

Historic quad (H). (RPD)

Upper tier (I). (RPD)

Bucknell University, informal landscape.
(RPD)

Formal versus informal, the designer's choice helps generate the campus image. In contrast
to geometric campus design concepts, the Colgate University Campus is marked by an
interesting mixture of nine contrasting landscapes, which together create a strong sense of
place.

for field studies of birds, vegetation, plant populations, water and mineral cycles, and the mechanics of evolution, these natural areas provide an immediately perceptible contrasting landscape that heightens the awareness of other elements that constitute the overall campus design.

Landscape for science is a venerable collegiate tradition. Oxford's Botanic Garden is the world's oldest surviving. Founded in 1621, the Garden was created by filling the low meadow at the edge of the Cherwell River, near Magdalen Bridge with 4,000 loads of "mucke and dunge." The five-acre site enabled Renaissance scientists to acquire knowledge firsthand through direct observation of plant materials. Extended several times, the Garden today contains vine-covered walls, planting beds, specimen trees, glasshouses, and conservatories—precious for scientific reasons and as examples of horticulture as art. The Garden riverbank is accessible for informal recreation. The views north to Magdalen Tower are an international landmark in campus design.

Many campuses collect trees and shrubs for teaching, as they would geological specimens. The plant materials are often labeled, and sometimes located for the visual effect as well as natural viability and scientific relationships. Among those

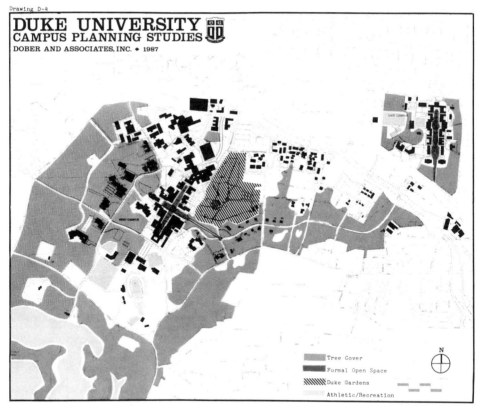

LANDSCAPE/MICROCLIMATE

Duke University, landscape features. The western tree cover is the place marking Duke forests. (Dober, Lidsky, Craig and Associates, Inc.)

Duke University, Sarah B. Duke Gardens. (RPD)

using this approach to campus design, Swarthmore College is outstanding. Here an affiliated institute, the Scott Arboretum, has spread over 5,000 different kinds of plants over 110 acres. A number of specimens—roses, flowering bulbs, crabapples—are laid out in gardens for seasonal display. Several major campus walks are defined by specimen trees, selected for their design qualities. In 1974, the Arboretum's reputation enabled it to obtain as a gift a rare collection of mature hollies. Over 400 plants were relocated from an estate 70 miles away. In conjunction with the adjacent Crumm Woods, the combination of formal and informal landscapes, and variety of plant material woven into the campus design fabric, engenders a superior sense of place—significant factors recognized in the articulation of the 1986 campus plan.

The Morrow Test Plots, at the University of Illinois, Urbana-Champaign, have effected the design of central campus. Buildings are positioned so no shadows would fall on agricultural experiments that have been conducted continuously for over 100 years. Modest landscape efforts can also be evocative and uplifting when science and art are melded. The new Botanic Gardens at the University of California, Riverside, are small, compact, and educationally and aesthetically enticing. The 39-acre site occupies rugged terrain on the eastern slope of the campus. Once-marginal land was surveyed and developed productively as a singular, placemarking, campus landscape. The first plantings were made in 1963 and now number over 2,500 species. The ecosystem supports over 200 species of birds, an instructive collection of local insects, mammals, reptiles and amphibians; as well as a seasonal flower collection and an herb garden.

The forests that surround Duke University, cultivated and managed for scientific purposes, help amplify Duke's strong architectural image. The tree cover

Botanic Garden, Oxford University. (RPD)

University of Illinois test plots. (RPD)

Swarthmore College Scott Arboretum. (RPD)

University of California, Riverside. (RPD)

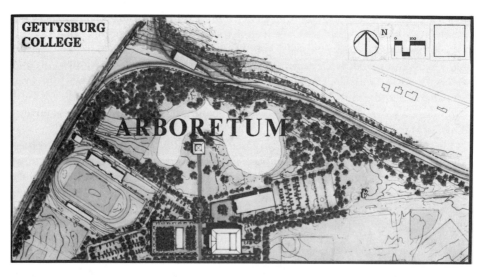

Gettysburg College Campus Plan. Relocation of a railroad right-of-way provided the opportunity to locate a new arboretum as the landscape edge for the central campus. (Dober, Lidsky, Craig and Associates, Inc.)

blankets the immediate surroundings. The passage through the woods from the west and south terminate with views and vistas of the towers and crenulated West Campus Collegiate Gothic buildings, or further on, the stately Collegiate Georgian at the east end. The formal open spaces in the quadrangles differ from the forest, and both are in contrast with the adjacent Sarah B. Duke Gardens. Here the seasonal flower beddings—8,000 tulips, Spring 1990—have become a national tourist attraction. The Duke and Swarthmore situations are special, as are their campus images. Few campuses are edged by forests, and few could afford to fund and manage expensive gardens. But variations on those campus design methods are possible as campus boundaries are defined with plantings; as landscape is used for instructional purposes; as memorials are encouraged; and as landscape is integrated with sculpture and artwork.

ART IN LANDSCAPE

Art in public places is not a new concept in campus design. Statues, archways, sundials, carillons, and decorative fountains are placemarkers that can be found continent to continent. Like a wise cook handling herbs, the campus designer will use these landscape components selectively in placemaking—for orchestrating surprise and revelation, for accent and orientation. Art work as campus design elements range from the smile-provoking scissors at Arizona State University, to an ancient archaeologically important stone ball in the garden adjacent Harvard's University Museum, to the abstract sculpture that decorates the lawn behind Princeton's oldest building, to the heroic scale monuments that are beautifully situated in the MIT landscape.

Beyond the traditional formats, two trends may be detected. The first is the outdoor museum, in which objects created as studio art are placed in the outdoor environment. The second is environmental sculpture, in which the setting inspires the artist to use hard forms (such as stone and cast metal) and soft forms (such as shaped earth and plantings) to create an overall setting that is generally devoid of representational meaning, or religious, political, or symbolic connotations.

Current interest in sculpture gardens deserves support. They may do for art what the botanic gardens did for science. The Franklin D. Murphy Sculpture Garden at the University of California, Los Angeles, leads the way as a fine example of the outdoor museum. In the 1960s, a dusty parking lot was reshaped by landscape architect Ralph Cornell into a gently, rolling green space. Inspired by the university chancellor, for whom the park is named, the design combines "the creative genius of sculpture with the constantly changing creativity of plant life" in a exquisite landscape where all can enjoy "the collaboration of nature and art."

DESIGN FOR MOVEMENT THROUGH LANDSCAPE

If nothing else, campuses are movement systems, time-tabled during the school day, predictable, though informal, in other hours. Most campus buildings, and thus circulation, can be located within a five-minute walking distance from the campus center, mega-campuses and mini-campuses excepted. The approximate 150 acres thus enclosed is best conceived as a pedestrian precinct. Vehicular traf-

Brigham Young University Bell Tower.
(BYU)

Princeton University gateway. (RPD)

Brown University gateway. (RPD)

Santa Fe Community College, gateway.
(RPD)

Stanford University, gateway. (RPD)

Oxford University, gateway. (RPD)

Gateways as art. Five versions of a landscape element that generates a sense of place,
memorable landscapes, and a welcoming campus design.

Franklin D. Murphy Sculpture Garden

Parking Lot 3

Underpass

N

Melnitz Hall

Circle Drive North

Circle Drive East

Dickson Art Center

Macgowan Hall

Frederick S. Wight Art Gallery

Research Library

Bunche Hall

Graduate School of Management

Parking Information

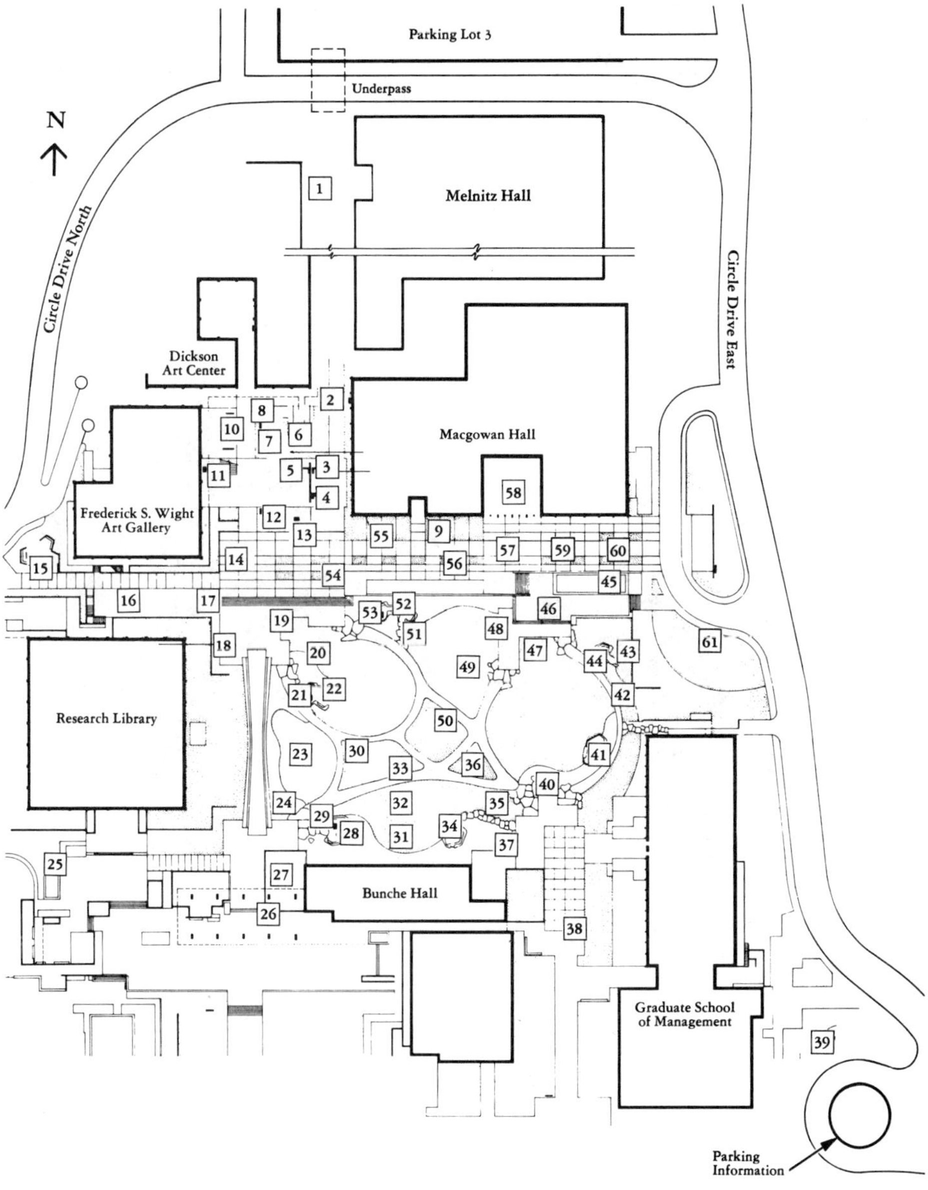

University of California, Los Angeles. Plot plan Franklin D. Murphy Sculpture Garden. An outstanding example of campus design. (UCLA)

University of California, Los Angeles. (RPD)

Arizona State University. (RPD)

Harvard University. (RPD)

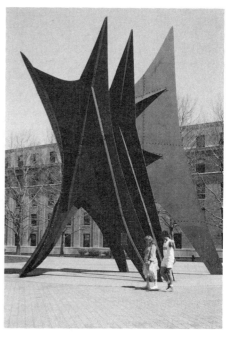

Massachusetts Institute of Technology. (RPD)

Sculpture as campus design placemarkers.

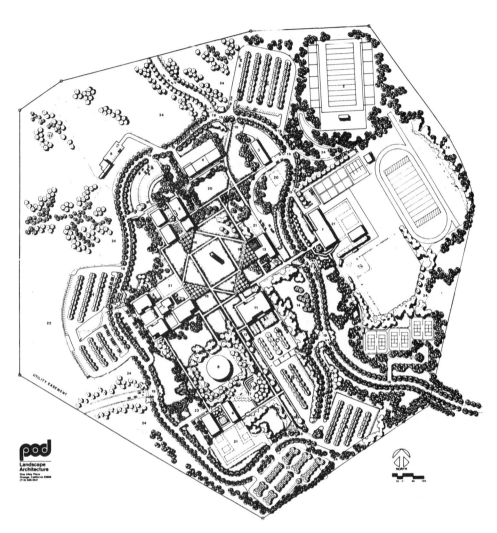

Mira Costa College. Circulation networks that structure the campus design. (The POD Group)

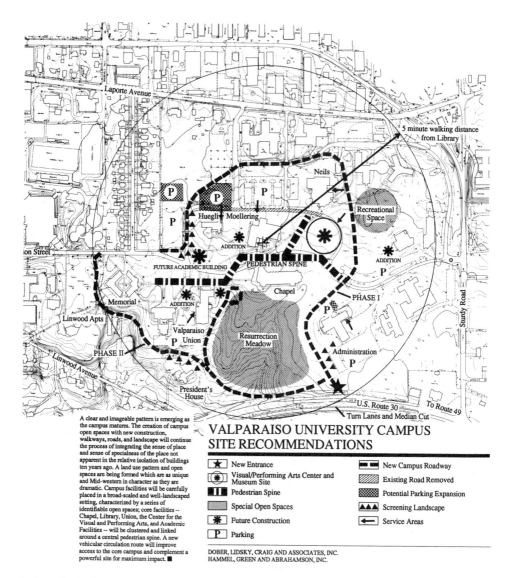

A clear and imageable pattern is emerging as the campus matures. The creation of campus open spaces with new construction, walkways, roads, and landscape will continue the process of integrating the sense of place and sense of specialness of the place not apparent in the relative isolation of buildings ten years ago. A land use pattern and open spaces are being formed which are as unique and Mid-western in character as they are dramatic. Campus facilities will be carefully placed in a broad-scaled and well-landscaped setting, characterized by a series of identifiable open spaces; core facilities -- Chapel, Library, Union, the Center for the Visual and Performing Arts, and Academic Facilities -- will be clustered and linked around a central pedestrian spine. A new vehicular circulation route will improve access to the core campus and complement a powerful site for maximum impact. ∎

VALPARAISO UNIVERSITY CAMPUS
SITE RECOMMENDATIONS

★	New Entrance		▬▬	New Campus Roadway
✳	Visual/Performing Arts Center and Museum Site		▨	Existing Road Removed
❚❚	Pedestrian Spine		▨	Potential Parking Expansion
▨	Special Open Spaces		▲▲▲	Screening Landscape
✳	Future Construction		←	Service Areas
P	Parking			

DOBER, LIDSKY, CRAIG AND ASSOCIATES, INC.
HAMMEL, GREEN AND ABRAHAMSON, INC.

Valparaiso University. Strategic planning for a new gateway and connections to the campus circulation systems. (Dober, Lidsky, Craig and Associates, Inc.)

fic and parking should be limited to that which is necessary for safety, service, and courtesy within the precinct, as well as reasonable accessibility for the handicapped and guests. Precincts of this size and character promote the constructive contacts and exchanges which are the essence of institutional life. They are small enough to instill a pride of place and identity with the institution as a whole, and, at the same time, large enough to foster and sustain those ever changing subcommunities which are necessary to enliven the college and university experience.

Mega-campuses can also engender these desirable qualities when they are laid out as a sequence of pedestrian precincts connected by appropriately designed circulation systems. The same principles can be down-scaled and applied to minicampuses, that is, institutions with significantly less than 150 acres.

In the main, campus designs can be categorized as those created before or after the dominance of the automobile as the principle mode of transportation. Within these paradigms, the quality of the campus design overall is directly related to the location, control, and appearance of the circulation systems. An automobile-age campus such as Mira Costa College can rationalize campus land uses, building locations, pedestrian paths, service drives, parking, gateways, and approach roads to generate an overall form. The network components are armatures for the campus landscape. In turn, their specific designs—the selection of plant materials, lights, and signs along the campus roads and paths, for example—become place-markers. Valparaiso University combined the siting of a new campus arts facility with the development of a new entrance road to give an enhanced design image to central campus, while at the same time preserving views, vistas, and open spaces associated with the university's sense of place.

Circulation design in pre-automobile age campuses tends to be untidy, if not unsafe and inconvenient. Typically, several growth surges probably have occurred since the institution's foundation. Old and new routes have to be tied to together so they serve current needs. Fortunately, the pedestrian network can be widened, relocated, and extended more easily than the requirements for vehicular circulation. The latter systems were too often underestimated, if not misunderstood, as to the impact they might have on the campus design functionally and aesthetically, and thus remedy can be anticipated and justified. Corrective measures may also be needed on new campuses. Arriving on campus for the first time (1989), the chancellor for the University of Massachusetts, Boston, Sherry Penney noted the anomaly of the broad front steps, which few were using because the convenient entrances were either "from the dismal, narrow bus lane, from the underground garage or from an open-air parking lot discretely hidden from the road. These steps to nowhere are a metaphor for a university that has been looking for an identity" since the new campus was opened in 1965, she commented. About the same time, across the continent, landscape architect Garrett Eckbo constructed a successful, placemarking entrance way for the University of California, Berkeley. The concept was informed by an insightful analysis of how the campus circulation could work so as to create a welcoming image at the campus periphery.

Expediency in handling separation of traffic may generate a strong campus image, as in UCLA's pedestrian bridge (Page 209). A methodical analysis of existing campus circulation will help reveal the problems and opportunities that the overall campus design should address from the periphery to the front and back doors of all buildings. Technical issues may require engineering assistance. But these considerations should not dominate the campus design—as they almost did at the

Rensselaer Polytechnic Institute. An elaborate computer-assisted analysis lead to a suggested plan that essentially ignored campus design features.

Circulation, landscape, placemaking, placemarking—the interrelationship of methods, concepts and results have been finely tuned at the Temple University and the University of Pennsylvania. Both are urban institutions in Philadelphia. Both have consolidated land holdings through street closings; have given precedent to the pedestrian over the automobile; and use landscape to define the broader campus design skeleton, and to provide a sequence of small and large green spaces that are threaded by paths that blend necessity and beauty into imageable designs. Disciplined but flexible, new buildings and spaces can be grafted to the form as change dictates. The first landscapes, simple and economic, have been enhanced as funds were secured. The designs have the vitality, variety, and vibrancy associated with ancient universities, without all-encompassing formal walls and intimidating enclosures. The landscape designs are sparkling, fresh interpretations of older traditions in campus design, a potential that has not been exhausted. The evolution of the "Diag" at the University of Michigan sheds light on their longevity and how they can be nurtured as institutional images.

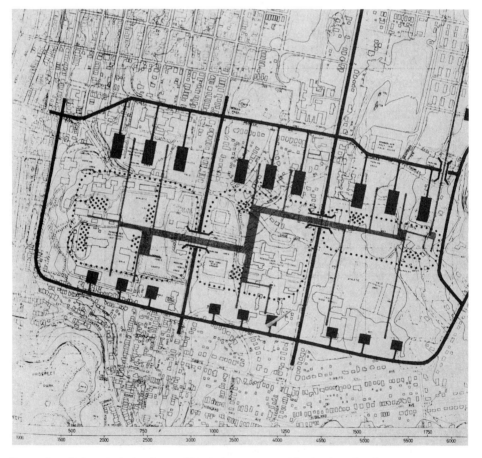

Rensselaer Polytechnic Institute. Circulation concept. (Author's collection)

University of California, Berkeley. Steps and landscape as gateway design concept. (Garrett Eckbo)

University of California, Los Angeles. An expedient solution to separating traffic produces a placemarking design. (RPD)

University of Pennsylvania campus

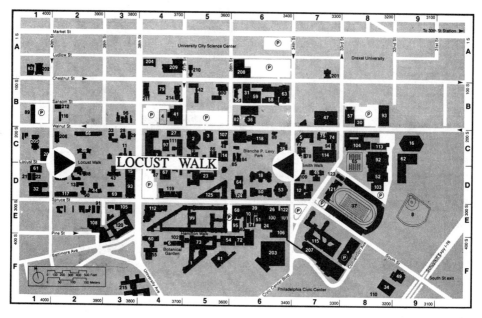

University of Pennsylvania, Locust Walk. A dramatic solution to street closings and campus circulation. (George E. Patton, landscape architect)

Detail, Locust Walk. Durable paving, lighting, trees: a campus design formula that works. (George E. Patton, landscape architect)

MICHIGAN'S "DIAG"

The Diag is the "heart of the campus today just as it was in the early days . . . the symbolic identity . . . imparting the spirit and the image of the University of Michigan," writes the institution's campus planner, Frederick W. Mayer. The central space in the university's original 40-acre campus was originally used to graze faculty animals, as the first buildings were on the campus boundaries, oriented to the street. As the campus expanded, smaller buildings gave way to larger structures, and the open area was crisscrossed by students and faculty on their way to and from classes. Around 1850, broad walks were built for circulation in poor weather. Soon thereafter, these paths were planted with trees under the auspices of university historian Andrew D. White, who as noted earlier, encouraged similar plantings at Cornell University during his presidency in Ithaca.

Michigan's original 40 acres was almost completely rebuilt in the 20th century. The campus was extended northward, with the Diag formalized as the armature. New construction defines a series of open spaces whose walks converge on the Diag. The "natural movement of students and faculty (becomes) a dominant force in the concept of architecture, function, and physical order (giving) identity and vitality to an academic environment." The principles thus articulated in the 1963 campus plan (Johnson, Johnson and Roy) continue to be applied with inventive variations, as in the recent Electrical Engineering Building. Here, a pedestrian corridor (designed with paving, street lights, landscape and benches) extends the Diag concept through the building atrium.

Strong image campuses are marked by circulation concepts that are tenacious and enduring. The range of buildings which give Washington and Lee University its early image (1845), with its walkway system, were reaffirmed and enlarged in the 1902 development plan, and again in the college's most recent campus planning efforts. The walk through Santa Cruz's woods and along Oxford's urban sidewalk are different because of the landscape context. The absence of landscape can be devastating.

University of Michigan. The Diag circa 1868. (UM Planning Office)

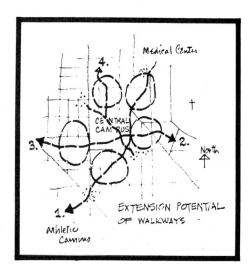

Concept drawing. The Diag extended as an armature in the campus design. (Johnson, Johnson and Roy)

PATH DESIGN

Paths connect buildings and spaces. They generate the placemaking skeleton which gives shape and scale to the campus design. Bent or straight, long vista or short span, paths give direction and order to the circulation flow. They unite, coordinate, and orchestrate the sequence of visual experiences that inflect a sense of place. Vectors and metaphors, paths have both utilitarian and symbolic purpose. A path well located is a campus design well constructed.

If path design were legislated, these would be the laws to be respected:

- paths intended to carry large volumes of pedestrian traffic during class changes should be wide enough to accommodate peak volume and lead from origin to destination without obstacle, deviation, or interruption;
- paths not serving a timetable may be more circuitous where terrain, spatial sequence, visual impressions, and a leisurely traffic flow is desired;
- paths should be designed so they are accessible to the handicapped, secure at night, passable in all weather, constructed of materials that are visually sympathetic to the environs through which they pass, and easy to maintain;
- paths should be designed and located in a hierarchy of volume and use; thus major walks can incorporate bicycle rights-of-way (where climate, site and custom permit) and accommodate service and emergency vehicles;
- minor paths can be down-scaled in these respects, but not neglected as opportunities to construct those byways which can make the journey from place to place visually different from the main paths;
- pedestrian traffic and vehicular traffic should be separated where possible, and conflicts otherwise mitigated;
- the intersections of major paths, and the spaces around them, should be designed to encourage participation in campus life.

Design details along the circulation network can evoke a sense of place. The

The Diag circa 1963. (UM Planning Office)

Landscape walks approaching Engineering buildings. (Johnson, Johnson and Roy)

Interior landscape. (Johnson, Johnson and Roy)

University of Washington. Tiered seating in an outdoor landscape. (David Walker, Peter Walker and Martha Schwartz)

University of Washington Engineering Plaza. (Richard Haag and Associates)

Massachusetts Institute of Technology. Seven decades of seating arrangements to promote contact, communication, and informal social life in pleasant surroundings. (RPD)

College and university campuses should be designed to promote contact and communication among those using the buildings and grounds. The circulation routes and adjacent open spaces are obvious locations for seating areas which promote that objective. Seating arrangements can vary from utilitarian and sculptural solutions to those that are designed as an extension of the building's architecture. Some recent designs demonstrate an interesting melding of contemporary art and function, producing strong placemarking and placemaking landscape images.

outdoor placemarkers in a typical campus landscape include paved surfaces, lighting, signs, display boards, bicycle racks, information kiosks, trash receptacles, fencing and billiards, benches and seats. Ideally, these components are selected and integrated into a visually unified campus design. To do so requires agreed upon standards, time, patience, and funding—easier to accomplish on a new campus than an existing institution, though the latter can be marked with designs which short on unity may be otherwise lovely and memorable. The subject deserves a lengthy treatment. Of many design components in the landscape of paths, two in particular should not be overlooked: signs and seats, devices for promoting communication and community.

Sign systems are important for several reasons: to help explain an intricate environment, to direct traffic, to indicate a destination, to commemorate people and events, to mark a place symbolically through a type face, logo, shield or other heraldic device.

Given the concept of the campus as a place that is intended to encourage contact and communication, the intersections of the pedestrian network are logical places for siting buildings and landscapes that serve and promote informal meetings, events, and conversations. Utilitarian objects such as outdoor benches should be designed or selected to facilitate these activities. Climate may effect seasonal use, safety may be a consideration, and maintenance will be a factor in choosing designs, as well as location. When designed with foresight and elan, the end product can be an art form unto itself, well worth a special effort.

Ideas for improvements can materialize from a systematic examination of the physical components that constitute the existing campus and an assessment of oncoming needs. The resulting opportunity diagrams serve as an agenda for specific campus design projects and as a coordinating plan. Five examples are shown: Temple University's path and edge system, the conceptual diagram for a pedestrian path system at the University of Bath, a gateway street at Duke University, a major campus right-of-way at Cornell University, and the path systems at Pomona College. Each are placemarking actions that also help structure the overall plan.

ECOLOGY AND CLIMATE AS PLACEMARKERS

> . . . the grass was fine,
> the sun was bright . . .

The above quote is a paean to campus landscape as poet Samuel T. Coleridge remembered it, and a thousand campus designs would emulate. For some the metaphoric image is more an epithet and epitaph than epiphany. Conservation biologists and ecologists are pleading for landscapes that are more sympathetic to local and regional ecosystems and conditions. In California, the driving issue is water, a resource in short supply. The response is Xeriscapes, the selection of plants, which once established, need little moisture other than that provided by nature. Pest resistant, heat and wind tolerant species include oleanders, toyon, lantana, eucalyptus, and bottle brush. A diverse group in terms of color, texture, size, and massing, this kind of palette places few limitations on the art of landscape design.

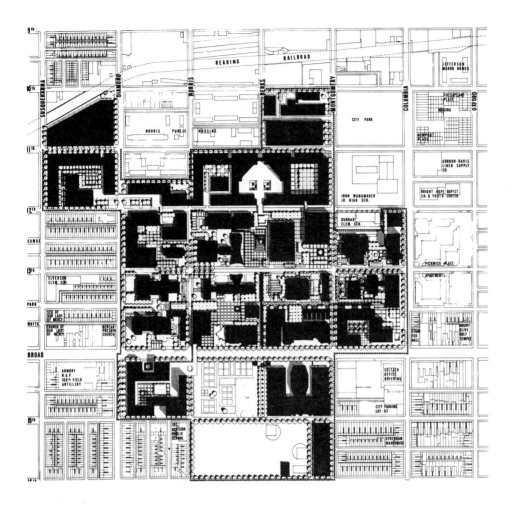

TEMPLE UNIVERSITY DEVELOPMENT PLAN
SITE PLAN
GEORGE PATTON LANDSCAPE ARCHITECT

Temple University. Landscape paths and edges defining a sense of place. (George E. Patton)

University of Bath.
Schematic diagram shows basic principles
of development plan.

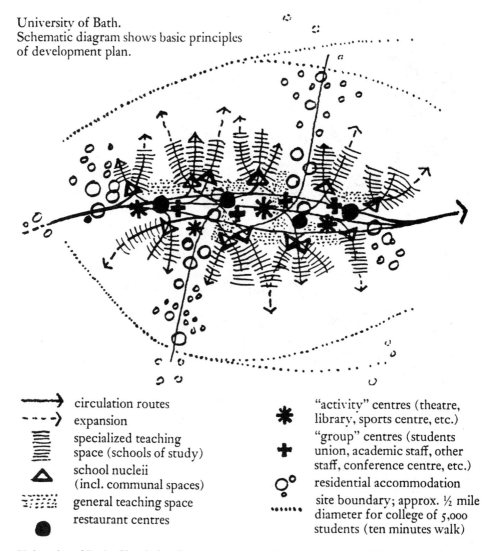

circulation routes		
expansion		
specialized teaching space (schools of study)		
school nucleii (incl. communal spaces)		
general teaching space		
restaurant centres		

"activity" centres (theatre, library, sports centre, etc.)

"group" centres (students union, academic staff, other staff, conference centre, etc.)

residential accommodation

site boundary; approx. ½ mile diameter for college of 5,000 students (ten minutes walk)

University of Bath. Circulation factors structuring the campus design. The skeleton for the campus landscape. (Author's collection)

University of Western Ontario. (RPD)

York University. (RPD)

Self-defining landscape opportunities.

Oxford University, walks. (RPD)

University of California, Santa Cruz. (RPD)

Urban versus rural. Site and situation determine viable, placemarking design concepts.

University of Illinois. Integration of bicycle and pedestrian circulation. (Sasaki and Associates)

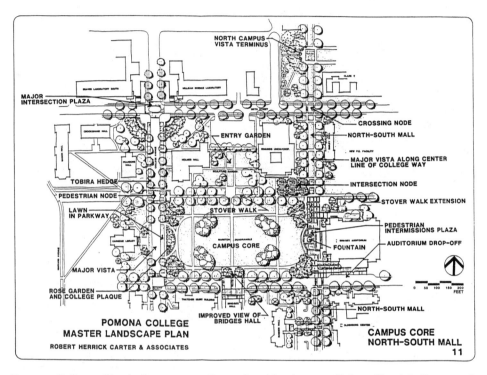

Pomona College. Site design concepts for regional landscape. (Robert Herrick Carter and Associates)

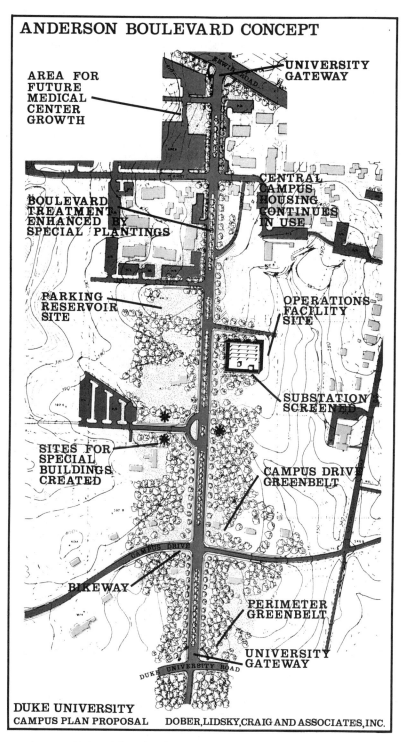

Anderson Avenue. Duke University Campus Planning Studies. (Dober, Lidsky, Craig and Associates, Inc.)

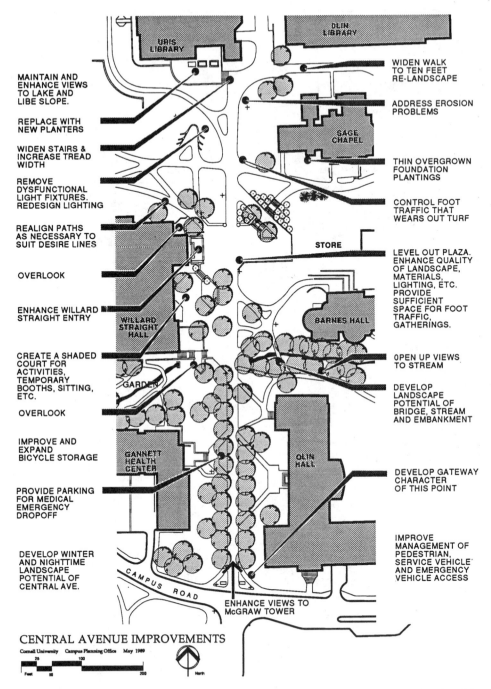

MAINTAIN AND
ENHANCE VIEWS
TO LAKE AND
LIBE SLOPE.

REPLACE WITH
NEW PLANTERS

WIDEN STAIRS &
INCREASE TREAD
WIDTH

REMOVE
DYSFUNCTIONAL
LIGHT FIXTURES.
REDESIGN LIGHTING

REALIGN PATHS
AS NECESSARY TO
SUIT DESIRE LINES

OVERLOOK

ENHANCE WILLARD
STRAIGHT ENTRY

CREATE A SHADED
COURT FOR
ACTIVITIES,
TEMPORARY
BOOTHS, SITTING,
ETC.

OVERLOOK

IMPROVE AND
EXPAND
BICYCLE STORAGE

PROVIDE PARKING
FOR MEDICAL
EMERGENCY
DROPOFF

DEVELOP WINTER
AND NIGHTTIME
LANDSCAPE
POTENTIAL OF
CENTRAL AVE.

URIS
LIBRARY

OLIN
LIBRARY

WILLARD
STRAIGHT
HALL

GARDEN

GANNETT
HEALTH
CENTER

CAMPUS ROAD

STORE

SAGE
CHAPEL

BARNES HALL

OLIN
HALL

WIDEN WALK
TO TEN FEET
RE-LANDSCAPE

ADDRESS EROSION
PROBLEMS

THIN OVERGROWN
FOUNDATION
PLANTINGS

CONTROL FOOT
TRAFFIC THAT
WEARS OUT TURF

LEVEL OUT PLAZA.
ENHANCE QUALITY
OF LANDSCAPE,
MATERIALS,
LIGHTING, ETC.
PROVIDE
SUFFICIENT
SPACE FOR FOOT
TRAFFIC,
GATHERINGS.

OPEN UP VIEWS
TO STREAM

DEVELOP
LANDSCAPE
POTENTIAL OF
BRIDGE, STREAM
AND EMBANKMENT

DEVELOP GATEWAY
CHARACTER
OF THIS POINT

IMPROVE
MANAGEMENT OF
PEDESTRIAN,
SERVICE VEHICLE
AND EMERGENCY
VEHICLE ACCESS

ENHANCE VIEWS TO
McGRAW TOWER

CENTRAL AVENUE IMPROVEMENTS

Cornell University   Campus Planning Office   May 1989

25   100

Feet   50   200

North

Cornell University Campus Landscape Studies. (Cornell University Campus Planning Office)

On several Florida campuses, planners and designers are reexamining past practices in light of the ecological imperatives. "For the past 100 years there has been a continuous effort to cover South Florida with exotic plants from the far corners of the world rather than use our own native plant resources," writes F. Terrance Mock. Under the guise of physical improvement and art, environmentally marginal trees, plants, and shrubs have been substituted for species that are hardy, attractive, and easier to maintain. The new landscape ethic begins with a simple premise: "stop telling nature what we want and start listening to what nature says we can have." The concept is not new to campus design. Many historic campus plans have been informed by a landscape that takes its cues from its locality. Broadly speaking, all campus designs can be divided into those which work with nature, and those which impose themselves on nature. The voices calling for ecologically sensitive campus designs have an audience willing to hear and act on their suggestions. The continuous greening of the campus affords additional opportunities.

Acceptance of the new landscape may be constrained by cultural perceptions as to what constitutes an attractive landscape. Native plant materials such as the original palette selected by Frederick Law Olmsted for Stanford University, "present a different image from those based on European or East Coast models," comments Phillips C. Williams. "They are usually more rambling, unmanicured and rougher on the edges." At Nassau Community College (Long Island, New York), a 19-acre tract on the college grounds has been identified as part of the original grass prairie that covered the island. To the uninitiated, the grass "looks like just one more weedy, shrubby, overgrown Long Island lot." The naturalizers, those interested in saving and using regional botanical heritages, are encouraging the college to use the native grass. They have documented that local variety costs less to grow than imported species, and "people will get a lot more enjoyment out of looking after a taller lawn filled with wildflowers that change with the season." The objective will require attitudinal, aesthetic, and legal change. Many Long Island communities regulate how high grass may grow, typically four to eight inches. A seemingly unkempt campus may have to be explained to the neighbors, as these and other examples of the new landscape promoted in public spaces.

Recent projects at the University of New Mexico, Gallup, and Stanford University are moving in that direction. Repeated drought cycles and the erosion of sandstone architecture, caused by irrigation water, have lead Stanford back to Olmsted's methods. For ornamental landscapes, native and adapted species are chosen over energy and water-intensive exotics. Rather than spend millions for an underground storm water system, the university constructed a wetland (1988) to act as a buffer from heavy rain runoff and as a holding area which can recharge groundwater supplies. Dubbed "Mem Marsh" in contrast to Stanford's Mem Quad, the site is being replanted with indigenous materials, including oak trees. The design advances the Stanford image: "a compact urban architecture set in the midst of open rural lands."

Harsh climates, an aspect of ecology broadly defined, will effect building forms and site arrangements, and thus be a factor in placemarking and placemaking. The proposed central area of the University of Alaska (Anchorage) was arranged to connect all buildings so as to permit a comfortable flow of pedestrian traffic in freezing weather. Sometimes these factors will appear in the microclimate and have to be dealt with retrospectively, as at York University, Canada. Downdrafts

Stanford University. Memorial Marsh with the iconic redtile roofs on the skyline beyond. (D. A. Atwood)

Xeriscape at the University of New Mexico, Gallup campus. When rain falls, the scrubby earth blossoms. (RPD)

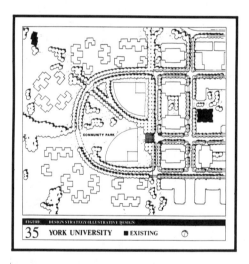

York University. New development advanced by ecological necessities. Also see p. 223. (York University Campus Planning Office)

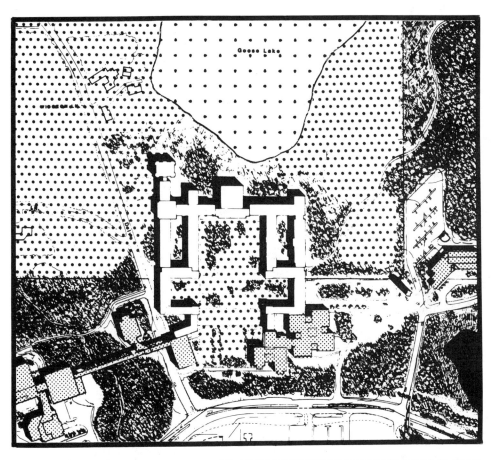

UNIVERSITY OF ALASKA
CAMPUS PLANNING STUDIES
Dober, Lidsky, Craig and Associates, Inc.

DETAIL AREA
▨ EXISTING BUILDINGS
☐ PROPOSED BUILDINGS

University of Alaska. Connected buildings in a harsh climate. Central Campus Plan.
(Dober, Lidsky, Craig and Associates, Inc.)

from a high-rise building accelerated debilitating wind conditions which could only be resolved by an extensive in-fill of new construction. Fortunately, there were other reasons to adjust the campus design, including the desire to enlarge the housing area to "intensify social interaction . . . in an area generally barren and inviting," and to encourage a landscape not stunted by an abrasive wind pattern.

LANDSCAPE TAXONOMY

The taxonomy is based on methodical examination of several hundred college and university campuses in the United States and overseas. The taxonomy is useful in evaluating existing campus designs and proposing improvements.

The principle components in the taxonomy are:

01. Periphery
02. Boundaries
03. Gateways
04. Ceremonial open spaces
05. Active recreation open spaces
06. Passive recreation open spaces
07. Gardens and arboretums
08. Building settings
09. Vehicular circulation routes
10. Pedestrian circulation routes
11. Campus crossroads
12. Sculpture, fountains, memorials
13. Outdoor furniture
14. Lighting
15. Signs
16. Plantings
17. Accents
18. Special Effects

As in any multi-dimensional design such as a campus, categorizing the existing situation by taxonomy components is not an exact art. Some visual effects are defined and explained by several taxonomy components. For example, a group of tennis courts is configured to meet competition standards; and would thus be categorized as active recreation. The space has a specific purpose: play. But because it is a pleasant place, the tennis court area may attract people who simply wish to sit in a landscaped setting, and thus, when so used, it is a passive open space.

The taxonomy is neutral as to quality; it doesn't explain cause and effect; for example, the selection of plant materials in terms of their suitability for climate or soil, or ease of maintenance. When the taxonomy components are deliberately employed and creatively arranged, the results are "high-order" campus designs.

PARK AS IN PARKING

Of all issues being addressed in campus development, few get as much attention in committees and campus design forums with so little evident results as parking. How sad to see a potentially attractive campus scene blemished by execrably located and atrociously designed parking. Too often in the guise of privilege and necessity, accommodations for the automobile have come to take precedent over all other campus design considerations. The time has come to put the park back in parking, for there are few campuses whose design would not be immediately improved if parking were treated as a landscape element. Some in-close parking is necessary for the handicapped, for visitors, and for those on campus who need ready access to their vehicles. Except in places with extreme climates, there are no other reasons for other kinds of parking to intrude into and abuse the central campus environment, defined as the 125 to 150 acres that lie within a five-minute walking distance from the presumed nodes, or center of campus—abuse physically with its reflection of glass and metal, abuse in safety terms, abuse as physical elements that are incompatible with the patterns of architecture and open space that make the campus an enjoyable place.

If campus design were a theological statement, there would be only one deadly sin: the presence of parking in the wrong location. In these instances, parking contributes to a sense of place the same way open sewers did to the medieval townscape. Parking should be treated as a utility, with supply and demand balanced by a rationale examination of need and alternatives. As a rule, campus buildings predictably drawing large numbers of spectators or audiences should be sited on the periphery of central campus with adequate parking nearby. Large campus residential enclaves might be similarly located. On mega-campuses, bus systems might be used to serve large parking lots on the campus periphery. Parking decks may also be justified on the basis of land values and its positive design effects. As recent projects indicate, the decks can be well conceived architecturally to fit into the local ambience. Where climate and terrain permit, bicycle use will help mediate close-in parking demands. On small campuses or large, as a campus design element, surface parking lots should be situated where they are least intrusive and lend themselves to a landscape that screens out their worst features. Trees, shrubs, paving and lighting have to be selected for safety and security, as well as for visual reasons. If conceived as "park-like," the fringes of the lots can be used for outdoor seating, play areas, and sculpture. Where the convenience of the automobile has precedent, campus design suffers most—and deserves the most Draconian resolution.

Q. Why prepare a campus plan?

A. For many reasons including:

- To help clarify, confirm or adjust institutional goals and objectives and priorities as they relate to the institution's physical resources, existing or desired.

- To help define the physical resources required to sustain and/or advance the institution's missions, goals, objectives and priorities.

- To describe and dimension physical improvements in general terms so as to have a reasonable sense of purpose, size, and probable cost.

- To express those requirements in a sequence that reflects institutional priorities and the realities of financing and phasing of development.

- To determine and coordinate the location of existing and future campus improvements so as to achieve a functional, attractive, and comprehensive campus design.

- To have a well conceived physical framework for making day-to-day physical development decisions -- a framework flexible enough to accommodate changing circumstances and conditions not foreseeable at the time the plan was formulated.

- To understand opportunities and initiatives that transcend immediate problems and solutions; so the institution will be able to act decisively when it is timely and prudent to do so.

- To document, for those outside the institution (donors, foundations, government, friends, accreditation agencies, and others), that the institution physical resources in hand, and those to be acquired, are well managed.

- To provide the institution with a sense of place that proclaims the College's purposes, distinction, and domain.

RPD

Why Prepare a Campus Plan. (Dober, Lidsky, Craig and Associates, Inc.)

As gate keepers for those who wish to live productive lives in the 21st century, colleges and universities will be viable institutions to the extent they can confront, resolve, and balance the forces of continuity and change. Campuses must be designed to anticipate and accommodate new roles, functions, and ideas, and at the same time carry on and integrate those traditional and conventional activities which deserve preservation and enhancement.

The abstraction becomes tangible as a design task since buildings and landscapes are the physical components which shelter, serve, and symbolize institutional life. Where historically all campus functions might be contained in a few buildings and a front lawn, most modern campuses are conglomerates, with many specialized buildings and landscapes. The actual number and type of components in a campus plan will, of course, vary with the institution's niche in higher education, mission, size, and related factors. Once constructed, some of the components will remain constant; many will change and be adapted to emerging conditions and realities; a few will be demolished. Young campuses will mature and older campuses will have their lives extended through new construction, as well as regeneration. In these circumstances, the articulation of an overall plan makes sense so as to connect and coordinate the various components which constitute the built environment, and to guide development toward predetermined goals, when and where they can be ascertained. Whether the yield is an informed diagram (the equivalent of a sketch on the back of napkin) or an elaborate visionary scheme (with computer-generated simulations of three-dimensional space and objects), placemaking is an essential first step in creating rational and pleasurable campus designs.

Placemaking and placemarking can be likened to a Mobius strip, with two faces connected and interdependent, but susceptible to showing a dominant face. It is the placemaking face that we now define and discuss in this section of the book. Placemaking and campus planning are synonymous phrases. As an activity, placemaking resembles town planning, producing the larger picture of the future, while

229

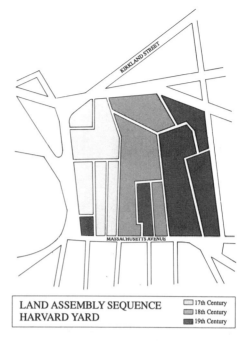

Development sequence, Harvard Yard.
(Dober, Lidsky, Craig and Associates, Inc.)

Air view, Harvard Yard. (RPD)

Cambridge University, The Backs. (RPD)

placemarking involves the specifics of campus architecture, landscape architecture, and site engineering.

TYPES OF PLANS

Because Clio, the muse of history, would prove it true, one begins the categorization of campus plans with a dividing line that separates serendipitous designs from the deliberate. Of the first, Harvard Yard is a good example. The campus image today seems complete and certain, but the actual deposition of buildings is not in accordance with any growth plan that is known. The last land parcels were acquired 200 years after the College's founding. A series of site-sensitive decisions placed buildings where there was a consensus among those who made such decisions at the time of construction. The result is some quirky and interesting exterior spaces, including a subtle change in topography, now pronounced by the plaza that caps an underground library. Brick is the visually predominant architectural material, unquestionably strengthening a sense of place. Lawns and trees fill the space felicitously, more by historic accident than predetermination. Walls, gates, and buildings that define the edges of the Yard came late in the sequence. Their presence cordons campus from city, perhaps more of a placemaking gesture than any of the other actions. The river bank colleges at Cambridge University are equally good examples of places that grew serendipitously.

Deliberate campus plans range from those that work with a clean slate to those which must integrate new and old. The plans can be grouped as follows: new campuses, sector plans, insert and add-on plans, and plans for regeneration. In the first two instances, designers should have no difficulty in integrating placemaking and placemarking. Some bravura examples have been cited earlier: the University of Chicago in the Collegiate Gothic style; the Rochester Institute of Technology in a contemporary mode.

In the second two instances, designers typically have to modify, manipulate, and/or mutate an existing environment. Most campus design commissions in the coming decades will fall into this latter category. The design opportunities are obviously more limited than on a new campus or in developing a campus sector. The objective of creating a distinctive campus is nonetheless achievable in as much as both new campuses and old can be effected by a common theoretical approach. The method involves the location of the physical components which constitute a campus (buildings, landscapes, infrastructure) in order to achieve a physical pattern which is functional and attractive; with forms that are appropriate for the institution's purpose, size, resources, and organization; positioned to reflect the best aspects of the particular site, locale, and environs; with an overall design that is as complete as possible, as early as possible; but amendable and adjustable to new conditions. In these schemes, the site arrangements and design inflections are located to encourage contact and communication among those using and visiting the campus, and to generate an image and sense of place that promotes and promulgates the institution's presence, domain, and values.

As earlier examples and citations should reveal, each phrase in the above lengthy prescriptive sentence is loaded with placemaking and placemarking significance. In simpler terms, $I = (PMK)(PMR)$. The strength of the Image (I) is related to the compounding of Placemaking (PMK) and Placemarking (PMK).

What follows now is an amplification of terminology and definitions, and an outline and discussion of placemaking processes and procedures, and plan implementation.

NEW CAMPUSES

The prospects for new campuses in North America are limited by demographic trends which indicate that most states and provinces have sufficient institutions. The exceptions are high growth areas such as California, where several new campuses are scheduled to be constructed in the near future. Drawing on its considerable experience in developing new campuses in the 1960s, California planners expect to develop three new campuses by the year 2000. The effort began with a task force charged with the responsibility for defining the academic dimensions of an ideal campus. The criteria suggested included a curriculum and organization that would attract a multicultural educational community, working and living in a "protected environment for continuous educational research and development," with studies centering on the existence of the "human endeavor" in an ecologically and politically livable world, producing students who were "self-motivated inquirers," instructed by a faculty committed to the idea of periodic "self-assessment" and of testing their abilities to teach.

The physical side of the California effort included a sophisticated site selection routine that was intended to take the wrinkles out of a politically competitive process. An institution of higher education is a prized regional economic and cultural resource. The criteria and countdown to a final site determination are a model endeavor, a high point in rationale planning (Page 233).

Overseas, the private sector may yield some unique opportunities as wealthy patrons and special interests seek to institutionalize their aspirations with a new campus. The prospects for new public campuses are considerably bright in countries not yet economically mature, and dim in those nations where the population growth is stable and university development well-evolved, such as Western Europe.

Excerpts from the Perkins and Will studies (page 234) for a new campus in Saudi Arabia (1990) indicate how such campuses are being currently represented graphically. The sample drawings from SOM's master plan for Northwest Frontier University (Pakistan) incorporates the four key steps in developing a plan for a new campus: site analysis, educational organization, site location, phasing. Each step, or course, requires considerable detailed study. There is no single template that will serve all cases. Differences in climate, curriculum, and capital alone give cause for considerable variations in design concepts.

While four-year institutions in the United States are likely to remain stable in number, community colleges may increase. Among recent examples, the waterfront campus of the Seattle Central Community College (1989) is a good example of a single building site and Santa Fe Community College (1990), a multi-curriculum educational enterprise. Santa Fe is informative for several reasons, recapitulating as it does many useful campus design ideas reviewed earlier. The site organization makes visible and accessible the academic offerings. The building grouping encloses and defines a central landscape—the mythic lawn and trees of higher education, and contemporary sculpture. The remaining terrain is left in its

Evaluation Factors and How They Will Be Applied

Step 1: Potential Areas	Step 2: Candidate Areas	Step 3: Potential Sites
Step 4: Candidate Sites (50-60)*	Step 5: Preferred Sites (15)*	Step 6: Recommended Sites (8)*

At each step areas and sites will be evaluated against factors listed at left. 'G' indicates measures that will eliminate certain areas or sites. 'C' indicates qualitative measures for remaining sites. Dashes indicate factors not measured at this step.

Factors Steps	1	2	3	4	5	6
1. Transportation						
■ Airports	G	-	-	C	C	C
■ Highways	G	-	-	C	C	C
■ Transit	-	-	-	-	C	C
■ Traffic capacity	-	-	-	-	C	C
2. Demographics						
■ Adequate population	G	C	-	-	C	C
■ Employment opportunities	G	C	-	-	C	C
3. Housing						
■ Owner-occupied housing and land	-	C	-	.	C	C
■ Rental units and land	-	-	-	-	-	C
4. Geotechnical						
■ Exclusionary conditions	G	-	-	-	-	-
■ Foundation conditions	-	-	G	-	C	C
■ Hydrology	-	-	G	-	C	C
■ Seismology	-	-	G	-	C	C
■ Topography	-	-	G	-	C	C
5. Site Appeal						
■ Visual resources	±	-	-	-	-	C
■ Land use control	-	-	-	-	C	C
■ Adjacent land use	-	-	G	-	-	C
■ Cultural amenities	-	-	-	-	C	C
■ Recreation	-	-	-	-	C	C
■ Commercial land	-	-	-	-	-	C
■ Education	-	C	-	-	C	C
■ Health Care	-	C	-	-	-	C
■ Emergency services	-	-	-	-	-	C
6. Public Support						
■ Public expressions	-	C	-	-	-	C
■ Growth policy	-	C	-	C	-	C
7. Environmental						
■ Enviromental site assessment (hazardous material/ waste)	-	-	G	-	C	C
■ Cultural resources	-	-	-	-	C	C
■ Noise, odor	-	-	-	-	-	C
■ Climate	-	C	-	C	-	
■ Biological resources	-	-	-	-	C	C
■ Water supply and quality	-	C	-	C	-	C
■ Air quality	-	-	-	-	C	C
8. Site Availability						
■ Easements	-	-	-	C	-	C
■ Ownership and use	G	-	-	-	-	C
■ Assembly	-	-	G	-	-	C
■ Relocation	-	-	G	-	C	C
■ Public access	-	-	-	C	-	-
■ Size and configuration	-	-	G	-	-	C
9. Utilities						
■ Utility availability	-	-	-	-	-	C

G= Go/no-go criteria   C= Comparative criteria (excellent, good, fair)   Dash= Not applicable

*Numbers are approximate

University of California. New campus site criteria. (Author's collection)

Central area. Umm Al-Qra Campus, Perkins and Will (1990). (Steinkamp/Ballogg by permission of Perkins and Will)

Seattle Central Community College. (The Miller/Hull Partnership)

Santa Fe Community College. John Greer, architect. (RPD)

Santa Fe Community College. Architect John Greer arranged the new campus (1991) as a set of connected buildings defining and embracing a major campus open space. Lawns and trees are a gesture to American campus design traditions. The selection of building materials and architectural detailing proclaim a sense of place associated with the Southwest. (RPD)

Academic Physical Organization

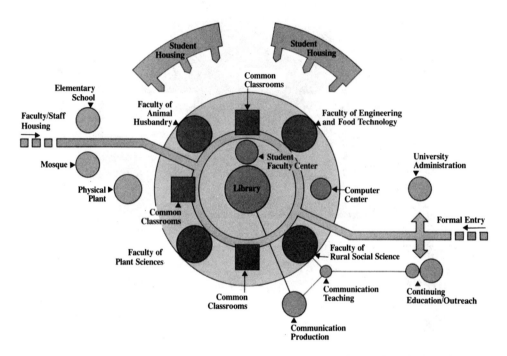

Organizational diagram and concept design. Northwest Frontier University, Pakistan. SOM architects. W. Porter, consultant. Dober, Lidsky, Craig and Associates, Inc. consultants. (SOM)

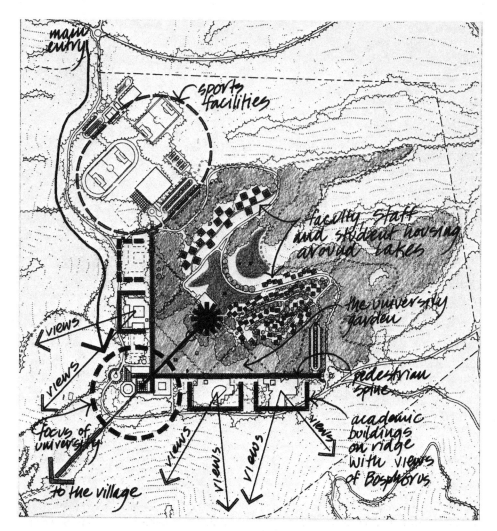

Master Plan Diagram (1991) Koc University. Istanbul, Turkey. The proposed new campus is organized in response to programmatic requirements and fitted to the site to take optimum advantage of views, vistas, microclimate and terrain influences. (Arup Associates)

natural state, dry and arid. The contrast heightens the awareness and delights of the central area. The architectural forms and materials are referential and reverential, drawing on the Santa Fe historic idiom, reminiscent but not literal. The gateway expression is welcoming and simple, an instant landmark. Temporary buildings (a necessary matter to accommodate large enrollments, while phasing in new construction) are positioned outside the central area. The overall campus design glows with intelligence, conviction, and aesthetic merit.

SECTOR PLANS

Sector plans guide the development of large-scale new construction, conceived and coordinated like a new campus, but situated on and integrated into an existing campus. The master plan for the Stanford University engineering and science complex (1988) is a typical example. It brings to one site a variety of academic disciplines and research groups who would benefit from proximity to each other. Through this relocation and expansion, space on central campus is then opened up for other groups. The site arrangement is intended to evoke the image of the older Stanford quad. Faculty participating in the planning also insisted that the eventual building architecture avoid the "hi-tech" look, and emulate some of the texture, color, and forms of the university's historic structures.

The long-range plan plan for the University of Miami (1989), page 239, identifies three special development sectors. One is a multipurpose educational sector for buildings and activities (museums, theatres, etc.) drawing visitors to the campus via the adjacent highways and mass transportation. The facilities are also within walking distance of central campus, and are positioned to shape and animate one edge of Lake Osceola, a campus landmark. The second sector is a student housing enclave, whose pattern, density, and layout are complementary to the adjacent residential neighborhood. Construction will enable the university to meet its goal of becoming an international university by providing additional students the option of living on campus. The third sector is a long-range development zone for activities that are complementary to the university's missions, such as research organizations, with the potential for income from rental property. The sectors are interwoven into an overall campus design concept that sustains and enhances the image of a university in a South Florida landscape setting.

INSERTS AND ADD-ONS

These kinds of campus plans are not fueled by larger enrollments but qualitative objectives. Whether a small college such as Mt. Vernon (Washington, D.C.) or a mega-campus such as Carnegie Mellon University, the institution scans its horizons and probable resources and identifies a series of physical improvements which will strengthen its niche in higher education. Three kinds of actions are typically taken: the insertion of new construction into the existing campus fabric, add-ons to existing facilities, and major renovations. The location, scale, and sequence of improvements are best handled by establishing an overall plan. The

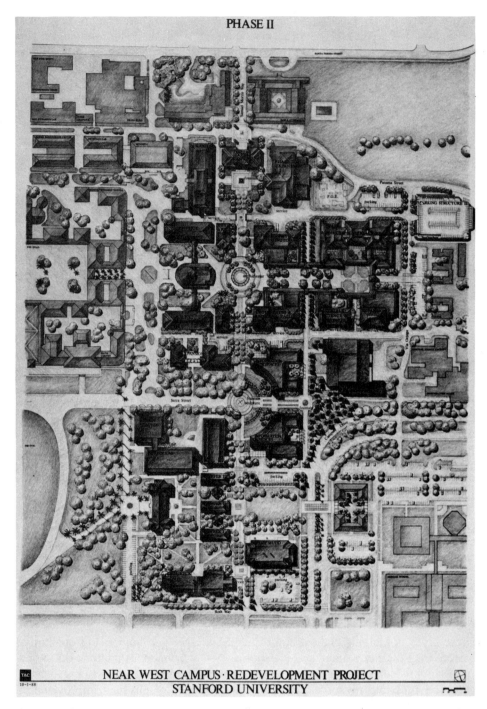

Stanford University. Sector design concept, North West Campus (1988). TAC. (Stanford University)

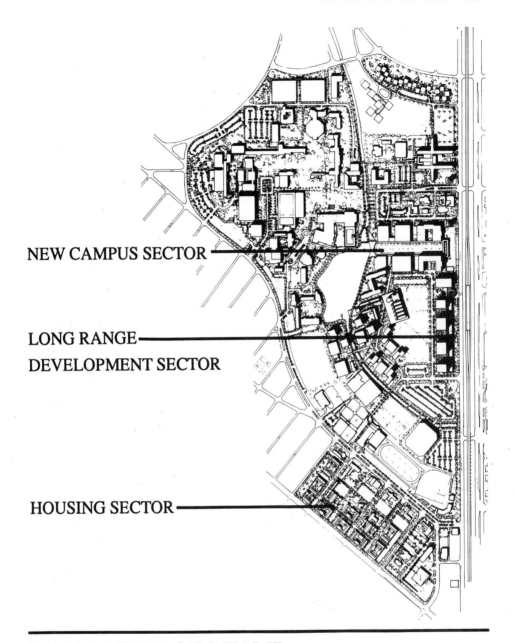

NEW CAMPUS SECTOR

LONG RANGE
DEVELOPMENT SECTOR

HOUSING SECTOR

UNIVERSITY OF MIAMI
CAMPUS PLANNING STUDIES 1989
DOBER, LIDSKY, CRAIG & ASSOCIATES

University of Miami. Sector developments, campus design concept (1988). (Dober, Lidsky, Craig and Associates, Inc.)

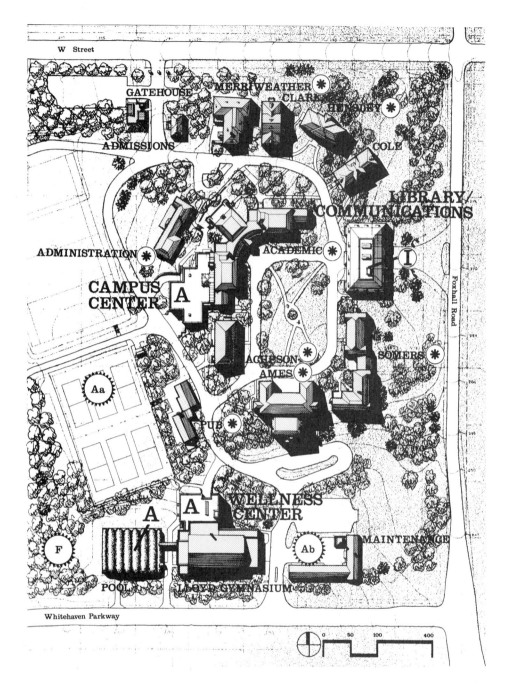

MOUNT VERNON COLLEGE
PLANNING STUDIES 1989
DOBER, LIDSKY, CRAIG & ASSOCIATES, INC.

[✱] SIGNIFICANT RENOVATION

[A] ADD-ON

[I] INSERT

Mount Vernon College, campus plan. An insert and add-on camus design concept. (Dober, Lidsky, Craig and Associates, Inc.)

plan can demonstrate project feasibility, confirm site location, help reach agreement on phasing, and indicate how the individual projects contribute (one hopes) to the institutional image and sense of place.

To work well, this kind of planning has to be orchestrated so that all the campus constituencies participate in the planning process. The existing campus has to be deciphered and evaluated, and alternatives explored and adjusted to economic, physical, and educational realities—routines described more fully later. The yield is worth the effort, as in the imaginative solutions that mixed new housing and the utilization of a large stadium area at Carnegie Mellon University.

Backed with administrative conviction and certainty, and the insider's knowledge of what is possible, projections and proposals can be given approximate shapes and forms and simply diagrammed to inform others of intentions and relationships. The 1924 Harvard University development plan (page 55) was cited earlier as a workable concept. The illustration on page 243 is a diagram of possible physical development at the Massachusetts Institute of Technology. The diagram serves as a coordinating plan for locating projects and/or reserving sites not yet fully defined. Undergirding the MIT diagram are several decades of on-going planning by an experienced professional staff. This permits the institute to delve deeply and quickly into a project specificity when the time has come to move from a general proposition to project feasibility, programming, and design implementation. When this occurs, the diagram is adjusted. However, most institutions do not have a full-time professional planning staff; thus the importance of a systematic examination of site and environs as a necessary step in creating insert and add-on campus plans.

Each campus has its own physical personality. It can be understood and communicated in detailed site analysis drawings or summarized in a simple diagram of significant conditions, such as the Carleton College graphic, page 244. The inserts and add-ons then determined will flesh out the campus plan with informed acknowledgment of the work of earlier generations, but adjusted to new circumstances and expectations.

As outlined later, fitting and testing various options is also a necessary step—frustrating to some who want quick decisions, comfortable to others who realize that add-ons and insertions must be examined as to their total impact on the built environment. At Dickinson College, after testing several schemes, it was evident that adding space to existing science facilities might work functionally, but would seriously compromise the visual character of the historic campus. An alternative site was found for a new chemistry building, which in combination with smaller additions, renovations, and space reallocations solved the problem. Further, the site decisions had wavelike effects on other aspects of the campus plan, clarifying sites for expansion of the campus union and library and justifying investment in the surrounding landscape. Inserts and add-ons usually are projected for the older sections of the campus because they allow existing activities to continue in situ; or have a programmatic relationship to nearby structures, or sustain a logical campus land pattern. Adding new space is particularly challenging when the context is venerable and historic, affecting buildings as well as landscape. Recent developments on Brown University's Green offers insights on various methods for handling growth and renewal in these circumstances.

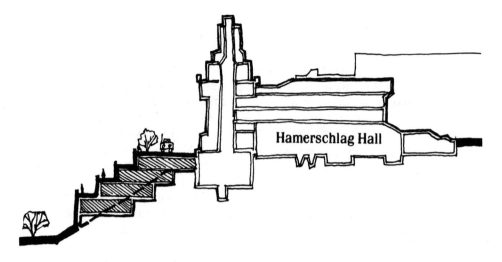

The scale and significant architectural massing of Hamerschlag Hall is respected in the siting of the new Electronic Technologies facility. The stepped new building is conceived as an extension of Hamerschlag's base and reinforces the hillside.

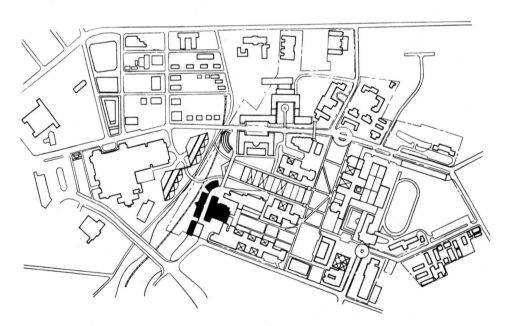

Carnegie Mellon University, campus design. Add-on concept. (CRS Sirrine, Inc. Consultants)

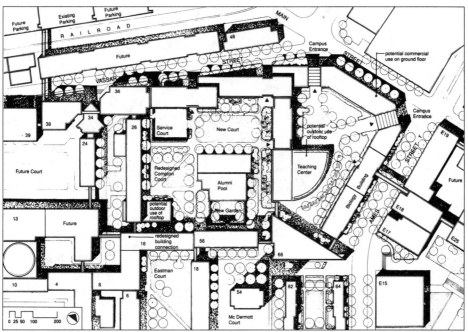

Figure 4. Illustrative Plan of Northeast Sector Development.

Massachusetts Institute of Technology. Strategic development diagram, northeast sector. (MIT Planning Office)

The development concept links the new construction to the older buildings so as to advance a cherished campus design principle on MIT's East Campus—connected buildings. The concept provides all-weather protection for moving people and equipment, optimizes the opportunities for assigning and reassigning contiguous space, and situates buildings so as to define landscaped courtyards, and rationalizes the location of service docks and the symbolic front doors to the sector complex.

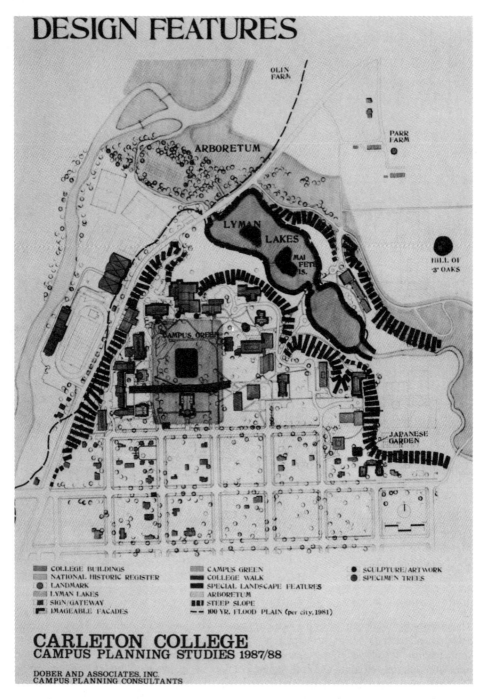

Carleton College, detail, campus planning site analyses studies. (Dober, Lidsky, Craig and Associates, Inc.)

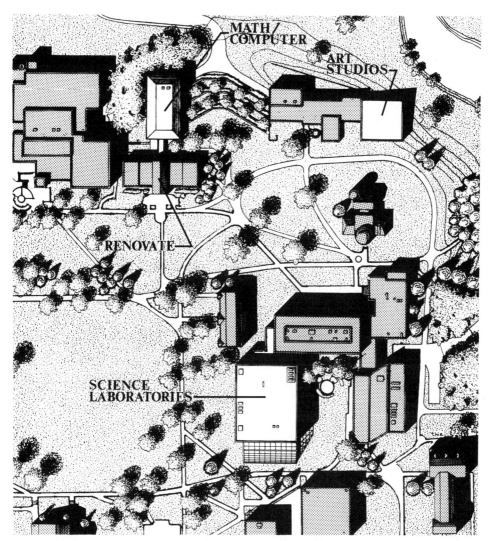

DETAIL AREA • CARLETON COLLEGE CAMPUS
PROPOSED CONSTRUCTION
1990 CAMPUS PLANNING STUDIES
Dober, Lidsky, Craig and Associates, Inc.

Carleton College, 1990 central campus development concept. (Dober, Lidsky, Craig and Associates, Inc.)

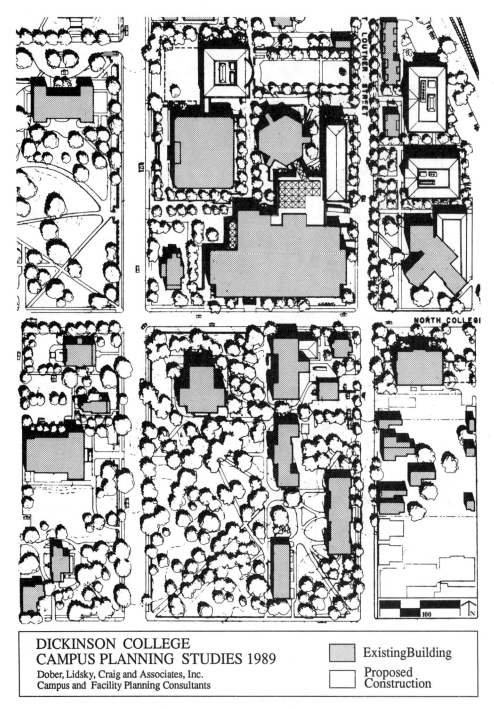

DICKINSON COLLEGE
CAMPUS PLANNING STUDIES 1989
Dober, Lidsky, Craig and Associates, Inc.
Campus and Facility Planning Consultants

ExistingBuilding

Proposed
Construction

Dickinson College 1989 Campus Plan. Adding and inserting new construction in a tight land situation. (Dober, Lidsky, Craig and Associates, Inc.)

THE BROWN UNIVERSITY MODEL

Brown University's central campus is a living museum of American collegiate architecture. For two centuries, each generation has contributed a good example of the architecture of its time. The clustering of the buildings around the Green (page 249) is considered a fixed element in the campus design. The surrounding development is a mixture of high-density modern buildings and 18th and 19th century domestic architecture. The latter is a design heritage which Brown has pledged to preserve and use. The resulting ambience is prized, protected, a principle contributor to the Brown image. For these reasons, there is very little flexibility in rearranging the campus design, yet renewal must be accommodated. Buildings age. Functions change. A vital institution cannot remain fixed in its own carapace, however treasured it might be as history and admired as the art of architecture. A campus is not a place to be pickled for posterity. Strategically, Brown has used different methods to adjust image to reality. The inevitable tides of change are not ignored. The approach admits improvements without debasing the ambience, as follows.

The exterior of Faunce House (Brown's equivalent of a campus union) is maintained intact. Inside a series of renovations have been carried out to adjust old space to new needs, and to refreshen the decor. The Green-facing side of Rogers Hall was constructed in 1862, the rear in 1911. The outer shell of the former was preserved, the back section demolished to create a site for inserting a new auditorium. The frontpiece (a sterling example of plain, period architecture) was reconfigured for classrooms, and as a lobby and support area for the large hall. New and old brickwork are nicely melded in an architectural gesture that respects the past without condescendence to the future.

Though a premium price had to be paid for the exterior stonework, the extension to the John Carter Brown Library was designed so the ensemble (the first space and the recent enlargement) appears to have been constructed at one time. The interior of the original main reading room, evoking 19th century scholarly life and research techniques, remains as it was in the beginning. The addition provides a 21st century setting for the collection, protection, conservation, and use of rare books, maps, and documents printed before 1800, describing the desettlement of Europe—the library's main mission.

The relocation of geo-chemistry from Rhode Island Hall to a new building (1985) followed a decision not to stress the historic Green structures with functions they were never intended to accommodate, such as high-tech science. The new building is inserted into a land use zone adjacent the Green designated for such construction in the university's long-range plan. Rhode Island Hall is now a low density administration and academic building. The interiors of Hope College (1822) and Slater Hall (1879), Green buildings and Brown's earliest student residential halls, are scheduled to be renewed as part of a $51 million campus-wide housing restoration plan.

In microcosm, the Brown experience on the Green embraces the full range of actions expected as most colleges and universities in the coming decade: selective demolition, inserts, add-ons, renovations, restorations, and space reassignment. Through careful planning, such proposals can be advanced so that designs and funding are tailored to the particular issues to be resolved in each case; and at the

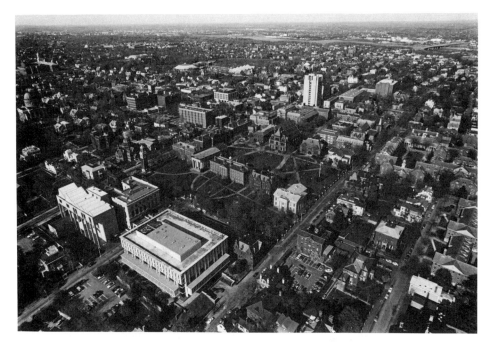

Brown University, air photo. (John Foraste, Brown University).

Brown University. Historic district buildings used for academic purposes. (RPD)

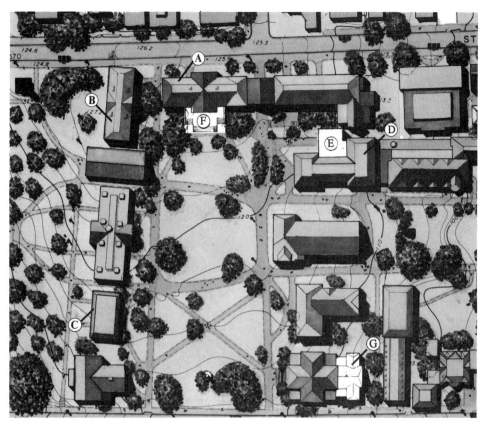

BROWN UNIVERSITY
CAMPUS PLANNING STUDIES   1989
Dober, Lidsky, Craig and Associates, Inc.

Brown University. Central campus development concept. (Dober, Lidsky, Craig and Associates, Inc.)

The Green is preserved as a central open space. The surrounding older buildings are given new life through a variety of actions that respect their architectural importance, projected functional requirements, and the budgets available for renovation, reconstruction, and additions. Improvements in buildings A, B, C occur within their existing shell. Building D replaces an obsolete structure with a new design, whose modern exterior interprets the materials and detailing in adjacent architecture. Sites E and F are designated as opportunities for a new generation of landscapes. Building G is a major addition that continues and emulates the massing and detailing of the building to which it is attached, a faithful and expensive gesture.

Brown University, Faunce House. Restoration plans by Goody, Clancy architects. (RPD)

Brown University, Rogers Hall, Solomon Teaching Center. Clancy and Goody, architects. (RPD)

Brown University, John Carter Brown Library Addition. Hartman and Cox, architects. (RPD)

Brown University, Hope Hall. Historic structure scheduled for regeneration. (RPD)

same time there is an overall strategy and policy that coordinates development to enhance the institutional image and safeguard a sense of place.

By creating a campus-plan context for inserts and add-ons, an institution will get best use from existing land and buildings. Each proposal can be adjusted and adapted to sustain an overall campus design concept—either an existing paradigm, or one that surfaces from the studies. There are economies available through the rationalization of infrastructure and landscape investments. In many instances, this kind of campus planning will reveal longer-range initiatives which an alert administration and board of trustees will want to work on: development in the campus environs, street closings, land acquisition, the seeding of ideas, and the removal of impediments for the next round of physical development.

REGENERATION PLANS

There is a fourth category of campus plans that merit attention because they address the mundane and neglected aspects of the campus environment and integrate such improvements with the traditional projects that bring excitement and energy to placemaking. The word *regeneration* is used to indicate an institutional commitment to a comprehensive approach to making the entire campus attractive and functional, not just selective aspects as in inserts and add-ons. Comprehensive measures, as we would define the term, include the above plus the systematic reduction in deferred maintenance and the acceleration of building and site renewal. These last items are the least glamorous of undertakings, but for most American campuses and many overseas, now the most essential.

Spatially, American higher education grew sixfold from 1950 to 1990, from approximately 500 million to about 3 billion gross square feet. This extraordinary achievement, culturally and socially unprecedented, was buffeted by circumstances which have left a considerable portion of the architecture in poor condition and worsening. With few exceptions, both affluent and modestly endowed institutions have facilities that are significantly blighted, outdated, or in disrepair. In the main, institutions have not been able financially to set aside money to address this fundamental issue. The economic dimensions of this problem and consequences it has for the built environment cannot be ignored. In 1990 the capital value (replacement costs) for higher education was estimated to be $300 billion. A prudent annual funding rate for repairs, renovations, and replacements of that which was wornout was estimated to be two to four percent of total replacement value. Recent funding has been approximately one percent annually—a disastrous shortfall that explains, but does not excuse, the dilemma.

At a three percent spending rate, annual physical plant capital expenditures would be about $9 billion, or approximately $750 per student, 1990 dollars, assuming a statistical base number of 12 million students which was the approximate national enrollment in 1989. College and university facility improvements have not been budgeted to this level. A change in attitude and accounting practices is necessary so that the foundations and walls of higher education will not tumble—philosophically and literally. As to the backlog of necessary improvements to reach a reasonable level of functional sufficiency and condition, that price has been estimated to be $60 billion (1990). A significant resolution of this seemingly intractable problem is likely to require some combination of the proactive campus

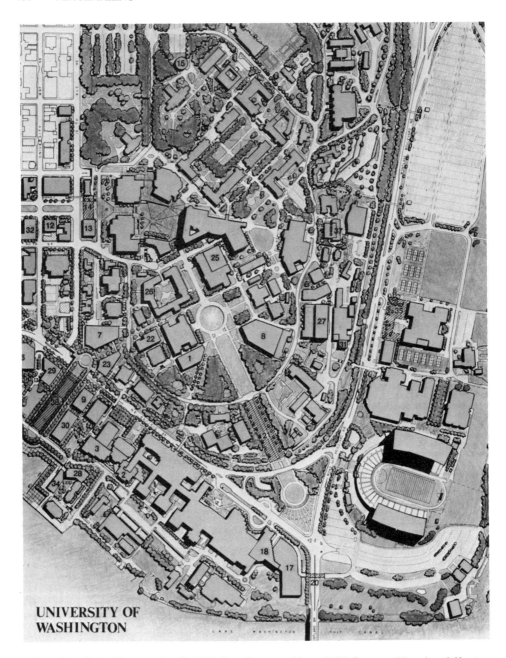

University of Washington, detail. 1990 Development Plan. (UW Campus Planning Office)

planning now shaping the University of Washington and the hardscrabble tactics that have been adopted at Gettysburg College.

At Gettysburg College, regeneration planning searches out ways to piggyback funds for reducing the backlog of disrepair with monies gathered for proposals that will visibly raise the quality of campus life and clarify the college's physical image. For example, the dowdy main college dining room is enlivened with a trendy new decor. The morale-lifting drawings excite the campus. The funding is increased to replace worn-out kitchen equipment and mechanical systems, which might otherwise have low priority. A new elevator is inserted into an historic, landmark structure, thus making all the space accessible, and helping to justify building-wide renewal. A clever scheme for adding space to a set of physical recreation and athletic buildings increases their building utilization and appearance; both measures help gain acceptance for funding repairs for plumbing and HVAC systems. As demonstrations of responsible planning that has an immediate effect on campus aesthetics and functions, these achievements give Gettysburg the confidence to proceed on other fronts, such as the exchange of land with an adjacent railroad to obtain a better land-use pattern, and in turn, the ability to landscape the campus edges. Each of these individual actions are taken with a view of implementing the college's broader and longer-range development objectives, and the immediate problems of addressing quotidian plant renewal.

In scale and complexity, the University of Washington's 1990 General Physical Development Plan has few equals. Forty major projects are anticipated, covering the full range of renewal, replacement, and new construction. The plan recognizes that some portions of the physical plant are not renewable and will have to be written off, including minimal architecture that had to be constructed at a time when funds were scarce, or conceived when design fashions and functional solutions were mismatched. This confrontation with reality justifies as much as 2.2 million square feet of new construction; much of it to be assigned to science and engineering. Some of the space is arranged to frame an eye-catching new campus open space overlooking the Seattle harbor. Other projects are in-fill and add-ons that respect campus site patterns considered historic, including the remnants of a World's Fair which proceeded the university on the site. The 1990 plan represents wholesale regeneration, with a unique programmatic basis that may herald the beginning of a new kind of American mega-university. If completed, the campus will accommodate a projected 20,600 faculty and staff by the year 2001—one of the largest such concentrations on any campus worldwide. Any increase in student enrollments during this period will be channeled to nearby satellite campuses administered by the university.

PLACEMAKING PROCESS

Placemaking process and product are intertwined. Many historic campus design methods and reasons are still valid, as documented; but planning as a procedural process that orchestrates multiple interests is of more recent origin. Once upon a time, a noble air view of the campus (as it might be) would give focus and inspiration to campus development through a dramatic rendering (informed by a few and drawn by the anointed). Whatever their merits might have been, plans thus articulated in that fashion today would be judged and dismissed as folly, fancy, or

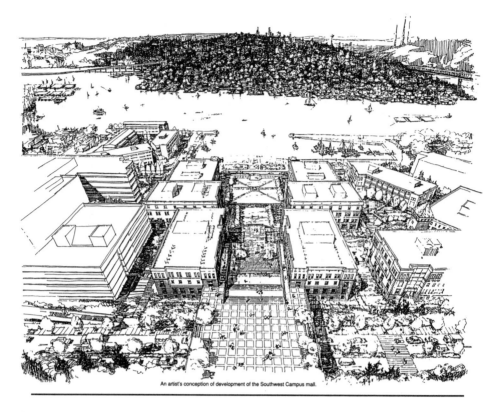

An artist's conception of development of the Southwest Campus mall.

Campus design concept. University of Washington campus planning studies. (UW Campus Planning Office).

expedient schemes. They would be quickly shelved as lacking the necessary psychopolitical realities of collegiality and shared governance which higher education has come to prize as a right and ritual. Those leading the planning efforts should not underestimate this aspect of their work. A deep-rooted plan has many benefits. The designer's dreams, where persuasive, are more likely to be realized, because participation strengthens the willingness to see good ideas through to their ultimate conclusion.

Whatever type of campus plan is being developed, the plan's legitimacy and longevity is directly related to achieving: (a) campus-wide understanding of the physical characteristics of the area under study, (b) general agreement as to what improvements should be represented in the plan; and (c) confirmation of their location and the sequence of development. The give and take of collaborative campus planning requires a sequence of studies and understandings that enable placemaking to proceed in an orderly manner. The processes and steps may be simple or intricate depending on the scale of the plan and the number of issues to be addressed. Some plans will be useful when only a sketch; others will come to life only when elucidated in ample detail, both in the physical expression of the future and the reasoning that supports those conclusions. The nine-step sequence below can be utilized in most situations, new campus or old. The framework can be fleshed out with routines, inquiries, and reiterations as determined when the

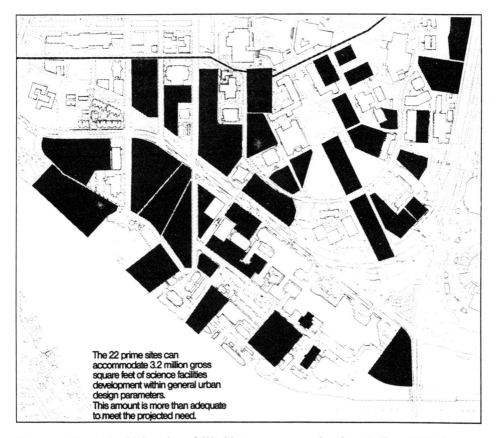

The 22 prime sites can accommodate 3.2 million gross square feet of science facilities development within general urban design parameters. This amount is more than adequate to meet the projected need.

Site capacity study. University of Washington campus planning studies. (UW Campus Planning Office)

planning is started, or adjusted when the beginning process has to be amended to account for the unexpected.

Nine-Step Placemaking Process

1. A plan for planning
2. The campus plan agenda
3. Site and environs analysis
4. Progress report
5. Alternatives
6. Synthesis
7. Reviews and revisions
8. Documentation and dissemination
9. Implementation

Step One—A Plan for Planning
The critical first step (a Plan for Planning) should be well organized. For best results, the process and sequence must be endorsed by those who ultimately de-

cide what can or may be built, as well as the planning participants themselves. There should be a well-articulated sequence of activities, with a clear calendar of events, and a lucid division of labor and responsibilities among committees, study staff, constituency representatives, and consultants, should such be engaged. The mandate to plan and participate should be issued publicly by the institution's senior leadership. The study sequence should be arranged to invite and provide campus-wide discussions at an hour and in settings which will inform the campus of the study findings, alternatives, and conclusions—with the goal of receiving comments and suggestions, endorsements, or demands; as to the latter, better early than late.

Typically, an acceptable plan will emerge when there is general agreement as to the facts and findings and a consensus about their meaning and consequences. The method requires a tempo and patience appropriate to collegial deliberations, especially those dialogs beloved by academics and treasured as their prerogative. In this decision-making environment, there are no short cuts. The train of reasoning runs smoothest with a stated destination, an authorized ticket, a clear track, a convenient timetable, and a welcoming invitation issued to all who wish to journey.

Step Two—The Campus Plan Agenda
The campus plan agenda is like the engine that drives the vehicle; the libretto that structures an opera; the hypothesis that informs an elegant piece of scientific research. Utilitarian, imaginative, rational—a program that defines institutional purposes and needs for the campus plan will reflect all three facets of conjecture and certitude.

Programming techniques now available to generate the campus plan agenda combine modern management techniques, operational research, theories that link design and behavior, and participatory planning methods. Computer applications permit the manipulation of extensive data and statistical modeling. The background information—the policy framework—is often summarized as an academic plan or labeled as the institution's strategic plan. The specific facility requirements are then quantified, rationalized, and listed in order of priority. The literature describing programming methods is extensive, including space standards and criteria. The programming effort should be tailored to the type of campus plan envisioned, a matter best determined in the first step of the planning sequence. A well-formulated program lengthens the shelf-life of the campus plan and will yield information essential for viable, placemaking campus designs. A general method for producing the campus plan agenda is outlined below, after the description of the remaining steps.

Step Three—Site and Environs Analysis
The objective here is to disaggregate, decipher, and evaluate the physical characteristics of the site and environs to reveal and appreciate those aspects of the site under study which may inform the proposed plans. New campuses excepted, most of the future campus design exists, awaiting conservation, extension, and enhancement. Table 1 lists and defines 12 pieces of information that should be gleaned from site studies. The information should be summarized in a series of drawings on an accurate base map. A segment of a typical base map sheet is shown below, with a sampling of typical information as it might appear in a sum-

The process at work. Reviewing campus development alternatives. Auburn University. (Author's collection)

mary report. The facts and findings should be displayed so that all the participants will have a reasonable understanding of the campus and environs as a physical place with measurable dimensions and attributes. Without a proper base map, the information will be distorted, and the interpretations and judgments based on those findings tainted and compromised. The advent of computer-assisted graphics and simulations provides new tools for this older process; but the graphic products have not yet proven to be as portable or as accessible for group discussion as the conventional wall-sized drawings and slides. In certain cases, a topographic model may be helpful.

New campus or old, site discussions and location decisions should be guided by a rigorous examination of terrain and locale. Acreage available, site configuration and campus design features, micro-climate, access, topography, infrastructure, the nature of the surrounds—these are influential campus design factors. Presentations and discussions of existing conditions can serve as a conduit for exchanging opinions and attitudes about the built environment as it exists, and as it might be modified. Typical considerations as summarized in plan documentation are shown on pages 228 and 255. On an existing campus, a thoughtful analysis of site and environs may also uncover certain site issues and ideas that should be added to the campus plan agenda, for example: a conflict in pedestrian and vehicular circulation; an older and well-located landscape that deserves resuscitation; lighting for safety and security; a view or vista worth framing with landscape and buildings in the oncoming campus design.

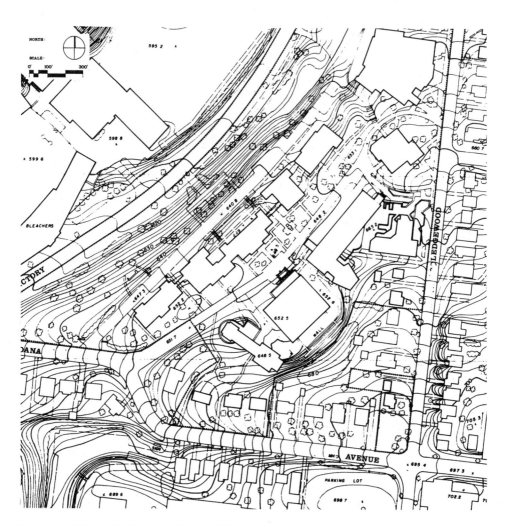

Base map. Xavier University. (Dober, Lidsky, Craig and Associates, Inc.)

A dimensionable base map is an essential tool for placemaking, whether preparing a generalized scheme or a more detailed plan. The base map should indicate topography, the configuration of buildings and structures, the location of roads and paths, and significant tree cover. Since the campus and community boundaries typically need attention, the base map should include the land immediately adjacent the area under study. The base map can be used to record the analysis of existing conditions as outlined on page 259.

Table 1   Existing Conditions Analysis

01. Environs
02. Institutional land ownership
03. Campus land use patterns
04. Predominant building use (functions)
05. Pedestrian circulation*
06. Vehicular circulation*
07. Parking
08. Topography
09. Campus open space patterns
10. Campus landscape
11. Major infrastructure
12. Special physical features and issues

*Including handicap accessibility.

Step Four—Progress Report

Tactically, at this point in the study, it is usually beneficial to make a major progress report to the campus constituencies, organized as follows:

a. the mandate for planning
b. the beginning goals and objectives
c. facility and site requirements, to date
d. summary of site and environs analysis
e. recap of major findings, to date
f. a list of alternatives being considered
g. a statement that the purpose of the meeting is to obtain reactions about the work to date, and to elicit views and ideas about other alternatives that should be considered as the study proceeds
h. the identification of the person to be contacted should there be additional comments and ideas to be communicated after the meeting is adjourned
i. a recap of the remaining work and schedule.

Some may fear that this kind of progress report is an open invitation to delay and obfuscation. If the work to date was reasonably articulated, with genuine involvement by representatives of the campus constituencies, the fear is unfounded. If there are fundamental grievances and disputes about process, priorities, program matters—then these have to be eventually resolved anyway. The progress report is an opportune time to begin mediation and resolution.

Step 5—Alternatives

Each campus site and situation is unique. As stated earlier, institutions vary in their size, organization, missions, resources, and so on. This complexity is likely to yield alternative solutions—hence Step 5. Usually this aspect of the process focuses on location issues; the agenda for the campus plan having been settled earlier, and the physical character of the campus deciphered and understood by the planning participants.

Constructive contention is a hallmark of vital institutions. The articulation and discussion of alternatives is productive for several reasons other than tradition.

By presenting and discussing options and choices, the main features of the best solution will be revealed, as well as the criteria for making that determination. The discussions evoked by comparing alternatives can be channeled to create the consensus necessary for an institutionally acceptable plan. As in the instance of the 1987 Allegheny College Campus Plan, a cluster of alternatives can be graphically dimensioned to reveal significant differences, page 263. The two options would both shape the campus core, and intensify its utilization, but differed in the location of two major buildings, parking solutions, campus design features, and cost. With the ideas explicated in public, it was then possible to find general agreement as to what should be depicted in the campus plan.

In the 1990 University of Washington planning process, a number of alternative sites were identified as having the physical capability of accommodating new science and engineering facilities, page 255. The choices varied in terms of combinations of new and old space; impact on campus landscape; and programmatic relationships among those assigned to the space. After review, the most promising options were combined and modified and then incorporated in the plan.

The 1982 Campus Plan for Colorado College featured one alternative for the location of a campus union in the final public document, while the process reserved a second-choice site as backup option. The first choice was an example of "bold-stroke planning," page 264. It was intended to test the political feasibility of closing a major community street that had long divided the campus physically. The second was a safe option, which in time proved necessary. Other aspects of the public plan, such as the location of a new science facility were not shown as options, as the location selected was functionally best and not politically problematical. With the outcome of the street closing uncertain (but worth pursuing), the availability of alternatives helped settle a well-honed and institutional-specific development strategy.

Step 6—Synthesis
With the agenda settled, the site and environs understood, and alternatives examined and reviewed, the planning process then synthesizes the work to date and articulates the placemaking plan. The graphic representation will vary in accordance with the complexity of the plan, as indicated in earlier definitions and examples. At the least, the campus plan drawings should express: (a) goals and objectives, (b) the physical character of the existing site and environs, (c) the location of all physical changes and improvements, (d) the sense of place and image being established or enhanced, (e) the price to be paid and the value to be received, and (e) the implementation sequence.

Step 7—Reviews and Revisions
Once drafted, the synthesis should again be presented in public, with the goal of making those revisions that common sense, consensus, or institutional leadership would direct.

Step 8—Documentation and Dissemination
Within the resources and time available, it is desirable to prepare a summary document of the undertaking and to disseminate the findings and conclusions to the largest audience possible. The study materials and summaries should be deposited

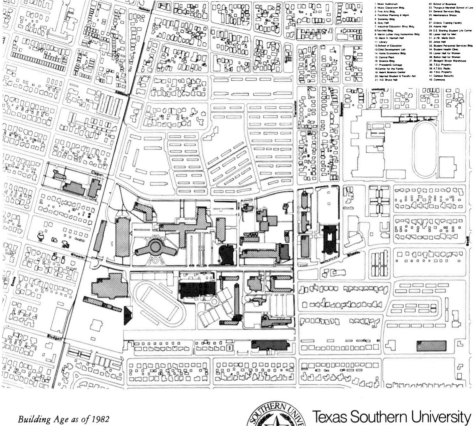

Building Age as of 1982

■ Currently Planned or Under Construction
■ Less Than 10 Years Old
▨ 10-20 Years Old
▨ Over 20 Years Old

0   100   500   1000

Texas Southern University
Long Range Campus Master Plan

Campus Planning Consultants

Moseley Associates, Inc.
Lockwood, Andrews & Newnam, Inc.

Building age, site analysis studies. Texas Southern University Long Range Campus Master Plan (Moseley and Associates, Inc.)

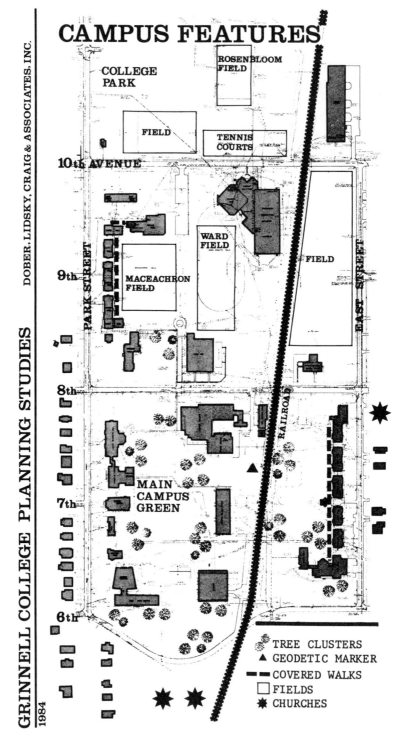

Significant features, site analyses studies.
Grinnell College Campus Plan. (Dober, Lidsky, Craig and Associates, Inc.)

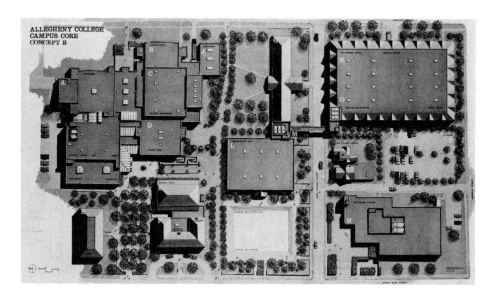

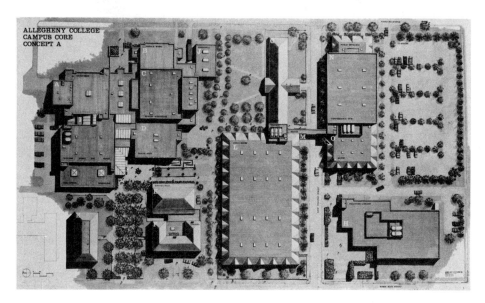

Alternative concepts. Central campus development, 1988. Allegheny College Campus Plan. (Dober, Lidsky, Craig and Associates, Inc.)

Alternative concepts can be used to clarify institutional goals and objectives, to help conceptualize and communicate campus design proposals, to illustrate and test various site configurations, to understand phasing implications, and to animate the participatory planning processes with a simulation of reality. As the technology for computer generated images improves, the number of such alternatives, and the opportunity for this kind of client and consultant interaction, will be measurably advanced.

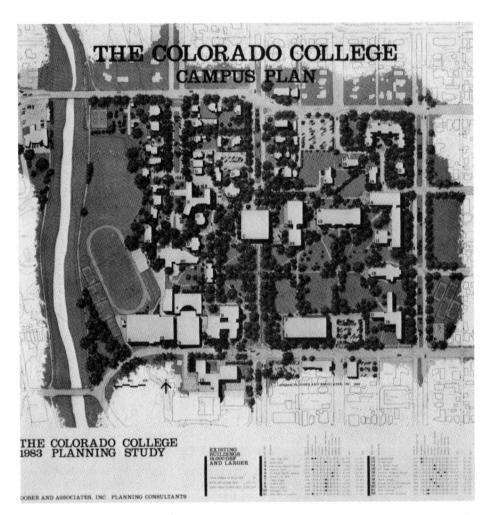

Bold-stroke diagram. Central campus development concept. Colorado College Campus Plan. Building (C) closes the street which divides the campus. (Dober, Lidsky, Craig and Associates, Inc.)

in the institution's library or campus planning office as an archival record and for the use of those who want to use the documentation later.

Step 9—Implementation
The best campus plans are those that lead to early action—an immediate reward for those who have labored and a proof of the plan's viability and acceptance.

The above nine-step routine is applicable to existing and new campuses. For new sites, there would be less attention to on-going operations, and the establishment of an institutional profile and the determination of needs is likely to require a greater effort.

As to who decides the final outcomes, presumably the process fits the concept of shared governance and responsibility. A consensus emerges, and where it does not, institutional leadership and trustees act decisively in a prudent and productive manner.

Intrinsically, a campus plan is a snapshot of a changing picture. The focus and coverage and shelf-life of the plan are directly related to the effort put into the process outlined. For most institutions, the development of a campus plan is an episodic event. On-going and continuous planning is desirable. This requires a professional staff and an institutional willingness to participate in that activity. Not all can do so. In the absence of such an administrative structure, the campus plan can be kept alive by periodic review of its assumptions and outcomes, adjusted to recent events, and summarized by an annual report to the trustees by the chief executive as to progress and impediments.

ESTABLISHING THE CAMPUS PLAN AGENDA

Process is easy and creativity plentiful. The most difficult task is determining what should be represented in the campus plan, including cost, priorities, and sequence of development. Some campuses are large enough to have their own zip codes. A few are small special purpose institutions occupying a sliver of land in a dense urban setting. The routine outlined in Table 2 can be adapted to most situations.

In terms of facilities, the campus plan agenda should list and dimension new construction, additions, major renovations, demolitions, significant space reassignments, and an accounting of deferred maintenance. The descriptions should include purpose, a sense of priority and urgency, and probable capital costs, however approximate these may be.

In general these days, the trend on existing campuses is to fix and facilitate the use of existing buildings, rather than promote new construction. This does not mean there may not be a case for new space, but the rationale for the proposals must be consequential and considerable, not conjectured or contrived. The general procedure can be stated as follows: what we need minus what we have equals what we must obtain. As suggested in Table 2, the best place to start is by defining the institution's niche in higher education via an institutional profile. The profile can be gleaned from institutional self-studies (which are conducted periodically for accreditation), an academic plan (which may be formulated for specific purposes, such as a legislative requirement or in anticipation of a capital campaign), or on-going institutional research, or prepared especially for the campus plan study. The alert campus designer will also seek to identify the institution's peers,

Table 2   A General Procedure for Determining Facility Requirements to be Represented in the Campus Plan.

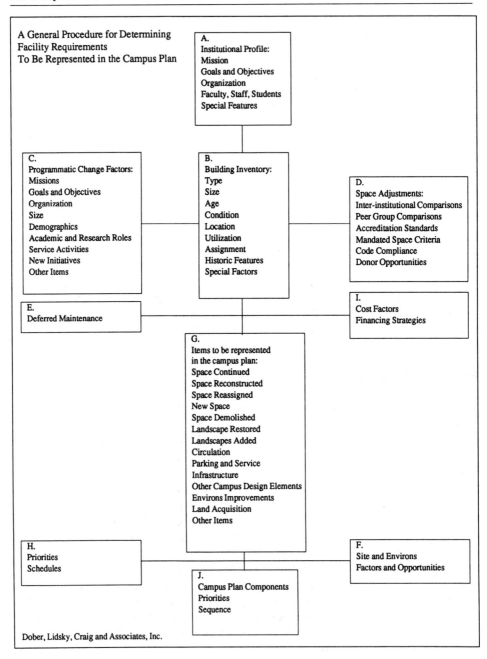

A General Procedure for Determining
Facility Requirements
To Be Represented in the Campus Plan

A.
Institutional Profile:
Mission
Goals and Objectives
Organization
Faculty, Staff, Students
Special Features

C.
Programmatic Change Factors:
Missions
Goals and Objectives
Organization
Size
Demographics
Academic and Research Roles
Service Activities
New Initiatives
Other Items

B.
Building Inventory:
Type
Size
Age
Condition
Location
Utilization
Assignment
Historic Features
Special Factors

D.
Space Adjustments:
Inter-institutional Comparisons
Peer Group Comparisons
Accreditation Standards
Mandated Space Criteria
Code Compliance
Donor Opportunities

E.
Deferred Maintenance

I.
Cost Factors
Financing Strategies

G.
Items to be represented
in the campus plan:
Space Continued
Space Reconstructed
Space Reassigned
New Space
Space Demolished
Landscape Restored
Landscapes Added
Circulation
Parking and Service
Infrastructure
Other Campus Design Elements
Environs Improvements
Land Acquisition
Other Items

H.
Priorities
Schedules

F.
Site and Environs
Factors and Opportunities

J.
Campus Plan Components
Priorities
Sequence

Dober, Lidsky, Craig and Associates, Inc.

Study sequence. Establishing the campus plan agenda. (Dober, Lidsky, Craig and Associates, Inc.)

in as much as this information also helps position the institution as to function, scale, and type of facilities required.

A second piece of essential information is the existing building inventory, Box B, Table 2. This is a summary of the type, size, age, utilization, condition, tenancy, location, and historic features of all space own and operated by the institution. The information is typically summarized by building, net and gross square feet, and function. The latter should be stated in terms of the building taxonomy shown in Table 3, as this permits inter- and intra-institutional comparisons and evaluations. A typical building condition summary, suitable for campus planning purposes and project planning, is illustrated on page 261.

The quality and reliability of the statistical profiles will vary with the type of plan being prepared, the availability of information, and the institution's experiences in generating and using such data. Sometimes the data are mandated by laws or encouraged by external groups who wish to encourage modern management. Whether approximate or exact, the building inventory figures are needed to establish a base line for judging space sufficiency, size, and condition.

As a planning method, the building inventory is then examined as to the consequences of four kinds of influences, factors, and circumstances. Box C lists typical programmatic factors that induce change, such as growth or decline in the campus population, new missions, administrative reorganization, and so on. Box D lists changes and adjustments that might occur in the space inventory because of comparisons between departments or groups, comparisons to peer institutions; or because of accreditation, or those space changes mandated or justified by internal and external space criteria, standards, laws, codes, and so on. Usually these statistical reckonings and projections straddle that which is imperative and that which is ideal.

Twos other sets of influences are also identifiable as discrete matters: Box E, Deferred Maintenance and Box F, Site and Environs Factors. As to site improvements, these may involve statistical reckonings (such as the number of parking spaces or campus acreage), or judgments based on the surveys and analysis of the site and environs, ranging from accessibility for handicapped, to the capacity of the infrastructure, to the quality of trees and landscape. As a list-making activity, specificity is desirable.

Designating demolition is likely to be a judgment call—not that physical conditions which support that conclusion will be marginal, but the unwillingness most institutions have to give up any space in the hope that it may have some possible use in the future. Further, unless it is vacant, the structure is assigned to some one. Occupancy and presence may be symbolically important when making these determinations. The empowerment that comes with having one's own turf is not to be underestimated as a campus planning factor.

The information is then sifted, confirmed, and evaluated to reach the list of items to be represented in the campus plan, Box G, Table 2. The list would include descriptions, dimensions, and probable costs for:

a. space continued
b. space reconstructed
c. space added, existing buildings
d. new space
e. major space reassigned

    f. space demolished

    g. reduction of deferred maintenance

    h. site improvements

As to dimensions, such as net and gross calculations, these can be approximate, at a scale suitable for the campus plan, that is, thousands, not hundreds of square feet. Costs should be expressed in current dollars and cover all project expenditures. An abbreviated version of the project budget summary illustrated on page 277 can be adapted for this purpose.

Having determined needs, it is useful then to arrange the items in order of priority, or logical phasing—Box J, Campus Plan Components, Priorities, and Sequence. Knowledge is power and shared governance is prized. Some institutions have found it useful to have different committees determine needs and priorities—believing that all items on the list are essential things, but not all things can be accomplished in the early phases of implementation. This approach spreads the responsibilities, increases participation, and helps mediate differences among competing interests.

For new campuses, the determination of needs follows a similar course: articulation of the institutional profile; descriptions of programs and special features; confirmation of number of faculty, students, and staff by department and group, or equivalent organizational unit; selection of space standards and criteria; calculation of needs by space taxonomies; determination of priorities and phasing.

The digest of needs and priorities (the campus plan agenda) is used in exam-

---

Table 3   Space Taxonomy

In 1973 the Western Interstate Commission on Higher Education established a space taxonomy system for the purposes of describing and quantifying space by function. By using the taxonomy, institutions can identify, compare, and evaluate the space available on their own campuses and compare their situation to other institutions, when such information is available in comparable formats. The functional categories and space identification numbers typically used are:

    100. Classroom facilities

    200. Laboratory facilities

    300. Office facilities

    400. Study facilities*

    500. Special use facilities**

    600. General use facilities***

    700. Supporting facilities****

    800. Health care facilities

    900. Residential facilities

    000. Unclassified

Each prime heading can be broken down into subcategories. Category 200, for example, can be designated into faculty offices, administrative offices, etc.

---

    *Such as library space.

    **Such as athletic and recreation.

    ***Such as assembly and dining facilities.

    ****Such as physical plant.

The University Of Connecticut
Residential Life Facilities Study
BUILDING SYSTEMS CONDITION

KEY
■ = System Replacement
● = Major Repairs
❖ = Minor Repairs
□ = Workable Situation
○ = New Subsystem

	Egress	Fire Alarm	Code Compliance	Ext. Disabled Acc.	Int. Disabled Acc.	Foundation	Superstructure	Roofing	Exterior Walls	Windows	Doors	Partitions	Wall Finishes	Floor Finishes	Ceiling	Elevators	HVAC Dist.	HVAC Equip.	HVAC Controls	Electrical Dist.	Electrical Equip.	Lighting	Plumbing Dist.	Plumbing Fixtures	Asbestos Present?
SECTOR A																									
Hartford																									
New Haven																									Y
New London																									Y
Fairfield																									Y
Windham																									Y
Litchfield																									Y
Middlesex																									Y
Tolland																									Y
Hurley																									Y
Baldwin																									Y
McConaughy																									Y
Hanks A,B																									Y
Goodyear A,B																									
Russell A,B,C,D																									Y
Batterson A,B,C,D																									Y
Terry A,B																									Y
Rogers A,B																									Y
Wright A,B																									Y
SECTOR B																									
Sherman, Tower 1																									Y
Webster, Tower 1																									Y
Colt, Tower 2																									Y
Jefferson, Tower 2																									Y
Sousa, Tower 3																									Y
Trumbull, Tower 3																									Y
Morgan, Tower 3																									Y
Lafayette, Tower 3																									Y
Wade, Tower 4																									Y
Fenwick, Tower 4																									Y
Hamilton, Tower 4																									Y
Keller, Tower 4																									Y
Beecher, Tower 5																									Y
Vinton, Tower 5																									Y
Allen, Tower 6																									Y
Kingston, Tower 6																									Y
SECTOR C																									
Holcomb																									Y
Whitney																									
Sprague																									Y
Hicks																									Y
Grange																									Y
SECTOR D																									
Shippee																									Y
Buckley																									Y

Dober, Lidsky, Craig and Associates, Inc.

Building condition index. University of Connecticut. (Dober, Lidsky, Craig and Associates, Inc.)

ining alternatives and synthesizing the eventual plan. The examination may clarify and modify the size and timing of each component, as the meaning and consequences are considered in greater detail, and the agenda for the campus plan revised. For example, a high priority building addition may not prove feasible in terms of site arrangements, and thus lead to a decision to incorporate the space in a new building, which in turn may change the project sequence.

IMPLEMENTATION

Few campus plans are implemented exactly as published. Changing assumptions, decreases or increases in funding, new priorities and initiatives which may arrive with new leadership, the unpredictable opportunities characteristic of a changing world, more precise reckonings or needs and responses as firm designs are provided for specific buildings and sites—any and all of these conditions will alter the original concept. A plan drawn too tightly will snap. Approximations and flexibility are desirable features. A well-formulated plan should be capable of incorporating adjustments and amendments. The slack will not diminish the contributions the plan and planning can make to institutional advancement: as a statement of faith in the future; as a catalyst for programmatic decision-making; as a device for clarifying organizational and management issues; as an influence on capital allocations; as an instrument for negotiating and effecting events in the campus environs; as a framework for coordinating large and small physical improvements; and as a jump-start for accelerating early action by communicating a convincing portrait of a sense of place and institutional image that deserves support for its vision and pragmatism.

Campus plans provide a general view of buildings and grounds as an ensemble. Specificity comes with implementation. A typical sequence of post-plan events is outlined in Table 4. To implement specific building proposals, seven kinds of information are required and decisions made accordingly. These are project purpose, project size, descriptions of the individual spaces (rooms) to be included in the building, their spatial proximity to each other, site location and area development objectives, institutional design standards or reference thereto, and project budget target. The latter includes construction costs and all other expenditures related to project execution. See typical project summary budget page 277.

The above routine is called facility programming. The result is a document that serves as a guide for launching, preparing, monitoring, reviewing, and agreeing to specific designs, plans, specifications, and costs as the proposal moves from a general proposition appearing in the campus plan to building occupancy. Sometimes the assumptions that defined the project in the campus plan have changed, and a substudy may be needed to test further and to define project feasibility and justification. The information is then incorporated in the facility program.

Those who will be using, operating, and managing the space should participate in the preparation of the facility program. In a typical sequence, their work is carried out through a committee structure, supported by professionals trained and experienced with facility programming. The committee may later be charged with the task of serving as a review committee during the design phases; though often that responsibility is assumed by a standing trustee committee, such as Buildings and Grounds. In that instance, the user group should be consulted as the designs

Table 4   Typical Implementation Sequence

Campus plan acceptance

Approval to proceed with first action*

Appointment of facility programming group

Briefing of facility programming group

Preparation of facility program

Reviews and approvals of facility program

Appointment of building review committee

Selection of architect/engineering team

Start and complete design cycle**

Reviews and approvals

Preparation bid and construct documents

Reviews, revisions, and approvals

Bidding and construction

Fitting out and occupancy

Postoccupancy evaluation

*Assumes a new building.
**Concepts, schematics, design development.

progress. Page 272–275 depict the Table of Contents from a typical facility program, a sample page of data and information, a site location diagram, and one technique for showing desired space proximities.

DESIGN CYCLE CONSIDERATIONS

As plans and designs proceed, the specific project characteristics, room sizes, relationships, site impact and project budget target should be reviewed and evaluated as to their conformance to the beginning assumptions. Page 279 provides a checklist for scrutinizing the designs methodically. The checklist can be used to help organize reviews and discussions, to record comments and suggestions, and to convey instructions to the design team.

Any significant variations from the objectives listed in the facility program should be fully explicated (especially cost targets) and adjustments made before proceeding to the next phase. Those seeking economies in project implementation will best find them in the facility programming stage where the amount of space, net to gross ratios, and a general determination of building quality is best settled. The design development phase is a particular decision-making threshold, which once crossed makes it difficult (if not imprudent) to achieve cost reductions without changing fundamental assumptions and criteria. If there is general agreement at this point on design and costs, favorable results can be anticipated in the remaining work and construction.

The above commentary has been wrapped around the development of a new building or major addition. Facility programming techniques can be (or should be) utilized for major reconstruction projects. The process and routines can also be

Facility program. Watson Center for Information Technology, Brown University.

COMPUTING BUILDING

TABLE OF CONTENTS

DOBER, LIDSKY, CRAIG AND ASSOCIATES, INC.
Campus and Facility Planning Consultants

Brown University, Computing Building Facility Prorgam. Table of contents. Sample page. Site diagram. Space adjacencies diagram. (Dober, Lidsky, Craig and Associates, Inc.)

```
Brown University                        SPACE NUMBER:    CS-50:51
COMPUTING BUILDING                      HEGIS CATEGORY:      310
DOBER, LIDSKY, CRAIG AND ASSOCIATES, INC.
Campus and Facility Planning Consultants


DEPARTMENT/USER GROUP:    Computer Science

NAME OF SPACE:            Software Manager

NUMBER OF SPACES:         2
NET SQUARE FEET:          170
TOTAL NET SQUARE FEET:    340

NUMBER OF STATIONS/USERS:  1


FUNCTION/INTENTION OF SPACE:

These Offices are in a group of offices for staff that supports
the Department's computer systems.  These offices will contain
various types of computer equipment, should foster the feeling
that these employees are part of a "support group" and must
provide a pleasant working environment.



KEY SPACE PLANNING REQUIREMENTS IF SPECIAL:

Should be located near Software Staff, CS-52:54, with easy access
to Machine Rooms, CS-166:167, and General Laboratories,
CS-155:158.
```

In addition to descriptions of size and function, facility program information typically includes such items as configuration ceiling heights, floor, wall and ceiling dimensions and treatments, lighting, acoustics and HVAC criteria, and a description of special conditions, as necessary to assist the client in communicating to the architect and engineering team project objectives, expectations, and limitations.

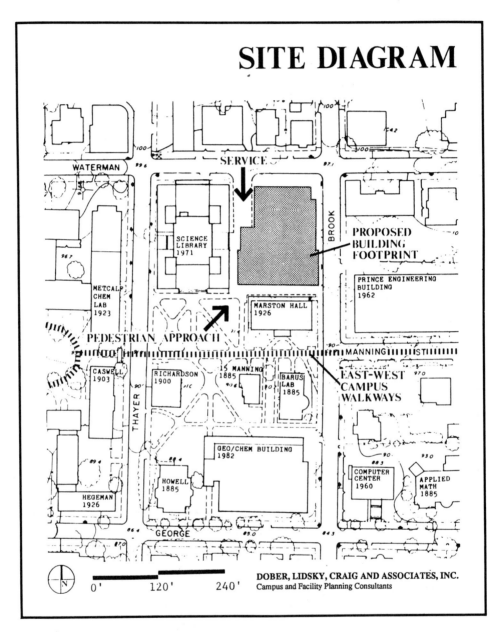

SITE DIAGRAM

WATERMAN

SERVICE

SCIENCE
LIBRARY
1971

METCALF
CHEM
LAB
1923

BROOK

PROPOSED
BUILDING
FOOTPRINT

PRINCE ENGINEERING
BUILDING
1962

MARSTON HALL
1926

PEDESTRIAN APPROACH

MANNING

CASWELL
1903

RICHARDSON
1900

15 MANNING
1885

BARUS
LAB
1885

EAST-WEST
CAMPUS
WALKWAYS

THAYER

GEO/CHEM BUILDING
1982

COMPUTER
CENTER
1960

APPLIED
MATH
1885

HOWELL
1885

HEGEMAN
1926

GEORGE

0'   120'   240'

DOBER, LIDSKY, CRAIG AND ASSOCIATES, INC.
Campus and Facility Planning Consultants

Brown University. A simple site diagram helps explain the project's physical relationship
to other buildings, as well as the client's assessment of the desirable location for service,
pedestrian circulation, entrances, and related considerations.

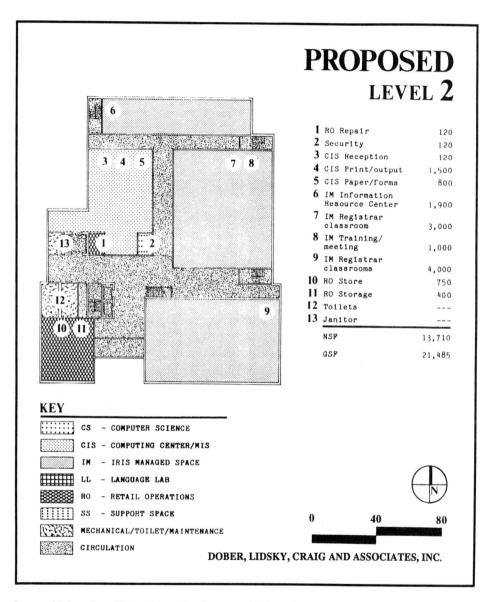

PROPOSED
LEVEL 2

1	RO Repair	120
2	Security	120
3	CIS Reception	120
4	CIS Print/output	1,500
5	CIS Paper/forms	800
6	IM Information Resource Center	1,900
7	IM Registrar classroom	3,000
8	IM Training/ meeting	1,000
9	IM Registrar classrooms	4,000
10	RO Store	750
11	RO Storage	400
12	Toilets	---
13	Janitor	---
	NSF	13,710
	GSF	21,485

KEY

	CS	- COMPUTER SCIENCE
	CIS	- COMPUTING CENTER/MIS
	IM	- IRIS MANAGED SPACE
	LL	- LANGUAGE LAB
	RO	- RETAIL OPERATIONS
	SS	- SUPPORT SPACE
		MECHANICAL/TOILET/MAINTENANCE
		CIRCULATION

0   40   80

DOBER, LIDSKY, CRAIG AND ASSOCIATES, INC.

Brown University. Client-determined space relationships can be shown through bubble diagrams or measured diagrams. At Brown University, the impact of a tight site and the requirements of a functionally intricate program was communicated by floor plan drawings that illustrated the adjacency criteria, while at the same time demonstrating project feasibility.

modified and applied for certain site improvements such as a campus arboretum, sculpture garden, or set of recreation fields.

The rational mind recommends a post-occupancy evaluation of the building area after it has been in operation long enough to measure its efficacy and the reactions and attitudes of users, visitors, managers. The procedure can help identify minor problems requiring remedy and establish objective criteria and insights for the facility programming and design of subsequent buildings.

COSTING

Facility programming is the opportune time to establish those design parameters and criteria which effect building quality and cost. One facet deserving early attention is the net to gross ratios and the dimensioning of interior public spaces and circulation spaces.

Net square feet is usable space; for example, the area inside a classroom from wall surface to wall surface. Gross square footage includes the net plus such items as hallways, elevator shafts, and thickness of walls. The net to square footage ratios will vary considerably among building types. Libraries and gymnasium will have a higher net to gross ratio than classroom and administrative office buildings. Variations will also occur within building types depending upon the efficiency of the layout and the degree of spaciousness desired in the overall design. The sense of being in a generously dimensioned proportioned building, or a comfortable space, or a tight space is a reflection of net to gross ratios, as well as the definition of ceiling heights, and the dimensions of corridors, stairwells and entrance areas. Minimal criteria are set by building codes; other dimensions are choices exercised by the client and designer.

Ratios and dimensions affect building cost targets. The adjective target is used because some reasonable cost objective should be set in the beginning so as to reach agreement on project feasibility and to discipline the design process. The target can be adjusted when there is reason to do so during the facility programming phase and design and construction cycle.

Building quality and cost is also determined by the selection and utilization of the subsystems which make up a completed building. Table 5 illustrates the range of cost variations in a typical classroom and library building. Similar qualitative and cost variations can be found in the design and execution of major renovations and site work. There is, however, no such thing as a low-cost institutional building. Higher maintenance and operating costs and repairs will soon gobble up any anticipated first-cost savings. Institutions are served best by aiming for middle-range cost targets, and moving upward on the cost component scale on the basis of achieving some predetermined objective, for example: a highly articulated facade, i.e. the signature of those advocating decorated sheds; custom-finished interiors; special furnishings; superior quality ventilation systems; a better than average site landscape.

As to the cost of regeneration, there are either questions concerning authenticity in historic restoration, aesthetic issues as to what looks right when budgets are tight, and the general cultural context that favors renewing rather than replacing. Each site and building has to be judged accordingly.

BROWN UNIVERSITY
Department of Planning and Construction

Project: Area (sq. ft.)

Description: Date:

Cost per SF: Revised Date:

UNIVERSITY BUDGET

Remarks: _____

1. Site	Boring & Site Preparation	_____	
	Survey	_____	
	Landscaping	_____	
			_____
2. Architectural Fees	Preliminary Planning	_____	
	Contract Documents	_____	
	Reimbursables	_____	
Engineering	Fees	_____	
Estimating	Fees	_____	
Consulting	Fees	_____	
			_____
3. Construction	General	_____	
	Plumbing	_____	
	HVAC	_____	
	Electrical	_____	
			_____
4. Change Orders			
to date thru C.O.	_____		
Changes pending	_____	_____	_____
5. Equipment	Fixed Equipment	_____	
	Furniture	_____	
	Supplies	_____	
	Moveable Equipment	_____	
			_____
6. Miscellaneous	Testing	_____	
	Moving	_____	
	Utilities	_____	
	Telephones	_____	
	Plant Charges	_____	
	Brunet (Computer)	_____	
	EMS (Energy System)	_____	
	Asbestos Removal	_____	
			_____
	SUBTOTAL	_____	
7. Contingency		_____	
8. Administrative Charges		_____	
	PROJECT TOTAL	_____	
	INCREASE IN ANNUAL O & M	_____	

Note: Financing and borrowing costs are not included.

Model Project Budget Summary. (Brown University)

PROJECT COST DIFFERENTIALS -- ACADEMIC BUILDING TYPES -- FALL 1990 -- BOSTON, MA. AREA

Classroom Buildings

Sub-System	Dollars/GSF Range			Dollars/GSF Difference Lower to Higher
	Lower	Middle	Higher	
1. Foundations & Floors on Grade	$3.20	$4.12	$5.04	$1.84
2. Superstructure	$12.96	$16.69	$20.41	$7.45
3. Roofing	$0.80	$1.03	$1.26	$0.46
4. Exterior Walls	$9.68	$12.46	$15.25	$5.57
5. Partitions	$6.64	$8.55	$10.46	$3.82
6. Interior Wall Finishes	$3.04	$3.91	$4.79	$1.75
7. Floor Finishes	$2.64	$3.40	$4.16	$1.52
8. Ceiling Finishes	$2.48	$3.19	$3.91	$1.43
9. Conveying Systems	$0.00	$0.00	$0.00	$0.00
10. Specialties	$3.92	$5.05	$6.17	$2.25
11. Fixed Equipment	$7.44	$9.58	$11.72	$4.28
12. HVAC	$12.08	$15.55	$19.02	$6.94
13. Plumbing	$6.00	$7.73	$9.45	$3.45
14. Electrical	$9.12	$11.74	$14.36	$5.24
TOTALS	$80.00	$103.00	$126.00	$46.00

Libraries

Sub-System	Dollars/GSF Range			Dollars/GSF Difference Lower to Higher
	Lower	Middle	Higher	
1. Foundations & Floors on Grade	$5.51	$6.50	$7.66	$2.15
2. Superstructure	$18.81	$22.18	$26.14	$7.33
3. Roofing	$2.57	$3.03	$3.57	$1.00
4. Exterior Walls	$8.64	$10.19	$12.01	$3.37
5. Partitions	$6.36	$7.50	$8.84	$2.48
6. Interior Wall Finishes	$3.99	$4.70	$5.54	$1.55
7. Floor Finishes	$2.85	$3.36	$3.96	$1.11
8. Ceiling Finishes	$3.04	$3.58	$4.22	$1.18
9. Conveying Systems	$1.33	$1.57	$1.85	$0.52
10. Specialties	$4.37	$5.15	$6.07	$1.70
11. Fixed Equipment	$9.50	$11.20	$13.20	$3.70
12. HVAC	$12.92	$15.23	$17.95	$5.03
13. Plumbing	$5.70	$6.72	$7.92	$2.22
14. Electrical	$9.41	$11.09	$13.07	$3.66
TOTALS	$95.00	$112.00	$132.00	$37.00

DLCA Database   Dober, Lidsky, Craig and Associates, Inc.

Academic and library buildings fall 1990 cost differential analysis. DLCA Data Base. (Dober, Lidsky, Craig and Associates, Inc.)

Project implementation, design checklist. ▷
(Dober, Lidsky, Craig and Associates, Inc.)

Design Checklist

The facility program provides the information used by the design team to generate plans and specifications for construction. The client reviews and approves the drawings and documents at three levels of specificity: concept design, schematic design, and design development.

Concept Phase

This is the initial design concept. Alternatives may be prepared for client discussion. The design(s) should be examined and checked against the program document in terms of net and gross square footage, site arrangements, interior space adjacencies, and project budget targets. Variances from the program should be rationalized and approved before proceeding.

Schematic Design

At this phase a firm plan is shown in measured terms. The design approach defined in the concept phase is fleshed out. The resulting plans and documents should be examined as to their congruence to the beginning (or revised) facility program. In addition, the following items should be reviewed and approved, or modified:

- structural systems
- floor loadings
- room size and configurations
- room adjacencies
- vertical and horizontal circulation
- ceiling heights
- roof type and configuration
- location and type of doors and windows
- facade design
- exterior cladding materials
- general building services provided
- site design
- building net and gross square footage
- project budget target.

Design Development

In this phase the same items reviewed in the schematic design, now elaborated, are reviewed and confirmed or modified; plus such program criteria as:

- acoustics
- illumination
- floor, wall, and ceiling finishes
- security and communications systems
- furnishing layouts
- planting plan and landscape details
- special factors and features

Summary

Campus design is a civic art that resonates with meaning and significance for our culture. The Greeks had their agora, the Romans their Forum, the Middle Ages their cathedral and town square, the Renaissance their palaces and enclaves for the privileged, and the 19th century their centers of commerce, transportation and government. The campus is uniquely our generation's contribution to communal placemaking and placemarking.

As discussed earlier, numbers alone would support this contention: about 3,500 campuses in the United States, with forty percent of the population having one or more years of direct experience, having been enrolled in formal, full-time programs.

My purpose in writing this book is to help all those who share the stewardship of a special art—the campus design. To suggest a single approach to this subject would be intellectually arrogant and demeaning to my main theme: each campus deserves to be a special place and to have a distinctive image that communicates, at the least, the institution's purpose, presence, domain, and values. There are certain methods for accomplishing this objective which I believe can be adapted to all campuses: placemaking and placemarking. These methods are well-rooted in traditional approaches to campus design as well as more recent routines which ensure that those effected by design outcomes can contribute to their formulation. For the novice, the book should help the reader to understand how a potentially complex and arcane undertaking (planning and designing a campus) can be simplified. For the experienced, the ideas and insights offered by history and the work of colleagues may serve as a reminder of what can be accomplished through disciplined efforts. For those seeking specific solutions on quotidian matters, I hope some answers will be found, or at least the inspiration to renew the search for new concepts and procedures which will advance the practice of campus design beyond the limits imposed by a book such as this. For those who have not found their favorite campus design in this particular compendium, mea culpa.

Stewards we are and stewards we should be; with the challenges and opportunities to create, protect and burnish this jewel called the campus design; so that on the outstretched finger of time, it will sparkle forever.

Sources and Acknowledgments

The principle sources for this book are: site visits, a collection of campus plans and reference works used in daily practice, regional and campus architectural guide books and brochures, and the typical gleanings that are gathered by one actively engaged in campus design over four decades. The gleanings include maps, memos, field notes, published and unpublished papers, news clips, articles, boxes of slides, photographs, letters, postcards, reports, documents, and other items—gathered because they once seemed interesting, stimulating, thought-provoking, relevant, and perhaps eventually useful.

From the fragments, the memorable stuff has been exhumed as citeable examples in support of the campus design methods and reasons outlined in the book. To bring certain ideas and concepts up to date, I have asked colleagues and professionals at various colleges and universities and their consultants, as well as members of the Society for College and University Planning, to supply me with current information about campus planning and campus design at some of the institutions included in this study and to provide illustrations. Their response was generous, valuable, and productive.

Accordingly, I am most grateful for the help provided by: David Alexander (Pomona College); Richard Arnett (Southern Methodist University); Calvert Audrain, SCUP (University of Chicago); David Basch (University of Connecticut); Margaret Bates (Duke University); Lynn Bender (University of Chicago); Carroll W. Brewster (Hobart and William Smith Colleges); C. William Brubaker, AIA, Perkins and Will (UMM Al Qura University); Norm Cable (Auraria Higher Education Center); Susan Carlisle (Tufts University); Keith A. Covey (Carleton College); Patricia Croneberger, Hoover, Berg, Desmond (Auraria Center for Higher Education); Anthony M. Cucchiara (Brooklyn College); Cynthia M. Dyer (Simpson College); Stewart O. Dawson, ASLA, Sasaki and Associates (University of Illinois and Vassar College); William R. Deno (University of Colorado); Donald H. Du Bay (University of California, Santa Barbara); Garrett Eckbo, ASLA, (University of California, Berkeley and University of New Mexico); Joyce Q. Erickson (St. Joseph's College); L. J. Evenden (Simon Fraser University); Harold Goyette (Harvard University); Robert M. Henry (Northwest Missouri State University); Lawrence H. Fauber (Oxford University); Ira Fink, AIA (University of California, Berkeley); Angela Giral (Avery Library, Columbia University); Henry Graupner (York University); Walter Graber (Simon Fraser University); William

Guerin (Auburn University); Clinton N. Hewitt (University of Minnesota); Richard Haag, ASLA (Central Washington University and University of Washington); Titus D. Hewryk (University of Pennsylvania); Judy Hershberg (The University of Vermont); Joseph Hibbard; ASLA, Sasaki and Associates (University of Illinois and Vassar College); Carol R. Johnson, ASLA (Harvard University); W. J. Karle (University of Manitoba); Wiliam E. King (Duke University), Robert Kronewitter (Auraria Higher Education Center); Florence B. Lathrop (Baker Library, Harvard Business School); Daniel O'Leary (Hamilton College); David A. Lieberman (University of Miami); Joseph Maybank, AIA, Architectural Resources, Inc. (Harvard University and Tufts University); Frederick W. Mayer (University of Michigan); Barry P. Maxwell (Bucknell University); Joe C. McKinney (University of New Mexico); Andrew Millard (The University of Manchester); Wendy R. McClure (University of Idaho); James A Paddock (Babson College); George E. Patton, ASLA (University of Pennsylvania and Temple University); Rafael Peruyera (University of Miami); Henry Ponder (Fisk University); Duane J. Reed (United States Air Force Academy); Persis C. Rickes (University of Connecticut); Richard Rigterink, ASLA, Johnson, Johnson & Roy (University of Michigan); Jack Robinson, SCUP, (University of Colorado); M. Richard Rose (Rochester Institute of Technology); Rodney Rose (University of California, Los Angeles); Lewis S. Roscoe (Cornell University); Dan Ryan (Illinois Institute of Technology); Robert A. Seal (University of Texas, El Paso); O. Robert Simha (Massachusetts Institute of Technology); Hinda Sklar, (Francis Loeb Library, Harvard University); James Steffy (Muhlenberg College); Pamela K. Stewart (University of Washington); Don F. Stout (Ohio University); Robert B. Stephens (University of California, Santa Cruz); Edward D. Stone, Jr, ASLA (Sinclair Community College); Daniel F. Sullivan (Allegheny College); William Van Arsdale (Gettysburg College); John L. Ullberg, ASLA (Cornell University); Robin Upton (Guelph University and Souel National University); Kirk R. White (Indiana University); Phillip C. Williams (Stanford University); Carol L. Wooten (Brown University); John L. Yeager (University of Pittsburgh); Peter Walker, ASLA (Foothills College, Harvard University, The University of Washington). As usual in an undertaking of this kind, they cannot be held responsible for the interpretations and evaluations I have made of the material and insights they kindly provided.

Apparently, in some quarters, it is not considered good form to thank those who helped the author in special ways. I do not share this view, obviously. During the manuscript preparation Dorothy A. Atwood, George Mathey, Sarah Russell, Karen Berchtold, Anne Krieg, Suha Khudairi, and Francis P. Thie assisted in compiling information, preparing illustrations, and commenting on drafts. Heather McFarlane sheparded the typescript through several reiterations with patience and timely suggestions. Charles Hutchinson and Everett Smethurst guided me through the shoals of publishing. Charles A. Craig and Arthur J. Lidsky supported this effort intellectually and logistically; without their friendship, creative contributions, and help the book would not have been realized.

And why do authors traditionally end their acknowledgments with thanks to their family? In my case, daughter, son, and wife were not only encouraging but were willing to make detours, take photographs, and collect information during their travels. With constant good cheer, they motivated the author to continue and complete a task which at times seemed formidable.

Bibliography

Bibliographically, in forming judgments and checking the gleanings, I found the following books and documents helpful:

Audrain, Calvert, Cannon, William B., and Wolff, Harold T. *A Review of Planning at the University of Chicago*. Chicago University Press, Chicago, 1978.

Batey, Mavis. *Oxford Gardens*. Humanities, Amersham, 1982.

Blake, Stephen. *The Compleat Gardeners Practice*. London, 1664.

Briggs, Martin S. *A Short History of the Building Crafts*. Oxford University Press, Oxford, 1925.

Broadbent, Geoffrey. *Signs, Symbols and Architecture*. Wiley; New York. 1980.

Brooke, Christopher, Highfield, Roger, and Swaan, Wim. *Oxford and Cambridge*. Cambridge University Press, 1988.

Brooks, Chris. *Signs for the Times; Symbolic Realism In the Mid-Victorian World*. London, 1985.

Brolin, Brent C. *Flight of Fancy, The Banishment and Return of Ornament*. St. Martin, London, 1985.

Brown, Mark M. *The Cathedral of Learning: Concept, Design, Construction*. Pittsburgh, 1987.

Bunting, Bainbridge. *Harvard, An Architectural History*. Cambridge, 1985.

Bunting, Bainbridge. *John Gaw Meem: Southwestern Architect*. University of New Mexico Press, Albuquerque, 1983.

Clifton-Taylor, Alec. *The Pattern of English Building*, 2 ed. Farber and Farber, London, 1972.

Collins, Peter. *Concrete. The Vision of the New Architecture*. London, 1959.

Crook, J. Mordaunt. *The Dilemma of Style*. London, 1987.

Cruikshank, Jeffrey L. *A Delicate Experiment, The Harvard Business School, 1908–1945*. Boston, 1987.

Davey, Norman. *A History of Building Materials*. London, 1961.

Dober, Richard P. *Campus Planning*. New York, 1963.

Dober, Richard P. *New Campus in Great Britain*. New York, 1964.

Downes, Kerry. Hawksmoor. London, 1979.

Encyclopedia of Architecture, Design, Engineering and Construction. Wiley, New York, 1990.

English Life Publications. Keble College; London, 1987.

French, John C. *A History of the Founding of John Hopkins University*. John Hopkins University Press, Baltimore, 1946.

Gombrich, E. H. *Style; Volume 15; International Encyclopedia of the Social Sciences*. New York, 1968.

Hamlin, Talbot. *Greek Revival Architecture in America*. Oxford University Press, Oxford, 1946.

Harvey, John. *Medieval Gardens*. London, 1981.

Hibbert, Christopher, and Hibbert, Edward. *The Encyclopedia of Oxford*. London, 1988.

Hobsbawn, Eric, and Ranger, Terence. *The Invention of Tradition*. Cambridge University Press, Cambridge, 1983.

Holden, Reuben A. *Yale, A Pictorial History*. Yale University Press, New Haven, 1967.

Jenks, Christopher. *The Language of Postmodern Architecture*. New York, 1977.

Klauder, Charles Z., and Wise, Herbert C. *Campus Architecture in America and Its Part in the Development of the Campus*. New York, 1926.

Lawfield, W. N. *Lawns and Sportsgreens*. London, 1959.

Le Corbusier. *Towards A New Architecture*. New York, 1931.

Lloyd, Nathaniel. *History of English Brickwork*. London, 1923.

Macmillian Encyclopedia of Architects; New York, 1972.

Morrison, Hugh. *Early American Architecture*. New York, 1952.

Newton, Norman T. *Design of the Land: The Development of Landscape Architecture*. Cambridge University Press, Cambridge, 1971.

Office of the University Architect, University of New Mexico, Hodgin Hall. Historic Structure Report, Albuquerque, 1979.

Onians, John. *Bearers of Meaning*. Princeton University Press, Princeton, 1988.

Parsons, Kermit C. *The Cornell Campus*. Cornell University Press, Ithaca, 1968.

Rashdall, H. *The Universities of Europe in the Middle Ages*. Oxford, 1936.

Roos, Frank J. Jr. *Bibliography of Early American Architecture*. Urbana, 1968.

Rudolph, Frederick. *The American College and University*. New York, 1962.

Schumann, Margaret E. *Stones, Bricks & Faces*. Durham, 1976.

Staff, United States Air Force Academy Library. *The Planning and Design of the Academy Grounds and Buildings. A Bibliography: 1954–1964*. Colorado Springs; 1966

Thomas, Mary Martha Hosford. *Southern Methodist University, Founding and Early Years*. SMU Press, Dallas, 1974.

Thompson, Paul. William Butterfield. London, 1971.

Tishler, William H., ed.; *American Landscape Architecture. Designers and Places*. Washington, 1989.

Turner, Paul Venable. *Campus, An American Planning Tradition*. MIT Press, Cambridge, 1984.

White, James F. *Architecture at SMU*. SMU Press, Dallas, 1966.

Zimmerschied, Gerd. *Brick as Design Element*. Berlin, 1961.

In addition, photocopies of two unpublished doctoral theses from Princeton University have time and again provided an intellectual framework, insights, delightful quotes, and directions to possible bibliographic sources on campus design issues and events as they are viewed by architectural historians:

Bush-Brown, Albert. "Image of a University: A Study of Architecture as an Expression of Eduction at Colleges and Universities," 1958.

Rhodes, William Bertolet. "The Colonial Revival," 1974.

Joseph Hudnut's seminal essay, "On Form in Universities" (*Architectural Forum*, November 1947) still serves, stirs, and stimulates after several readings. His manner of raising questions about an appropriate architectural style and image for colleges and universities remains fresh and provocative 40 years later.

As to current events and trends in campus development, the various publications of the Society for College and University Planning and the annual indices are rich sources. One hopes that a compendium of the leading articles and essays will be published in the near future. Campus architecture and landscape also receives good coverage in professional magazines and journals.

Index